Economies of the World

EDITED BY

NITA WATTS

D1784974

Japan

AN ECONOMIC SURVEY

1953-1973

BY

ANDREA BOLTHO

OXFORD UNIVERSITY PRESS

1975

Oxford University Press, Ely House, London W.1

GLASGOW NEW YORK TORONTO MELBOURNE WELLINGTON
CAPE TOWN IBADAN NAIROBI DAR ES SALAAM LUSAKA ADDIS ABABA
DELHI BOMBAY CALCUTTA MADRAS KARACHI LAHORE DACCA
KUALA LUMPUR SINGAPORE HONG KONG TOKYO

CASEBOUND ISBN 0 19 877036 7
PAPERBACK ISBN 0 19 877037 5

© OXFORD UNIVERSITY PRESS 1975

PRINTED IN GREAT BRITAIN
BY RICHARD CLAY (THE CHAUCER PRESS) LTD
BUNGAY, SUFFOLK

TO
FABRIZIO AND ALEXEI

EDITORIAL PREFACE

Economies of the World is designed as a series for readers in universities, business, and government, and provides brief reviews of economic developments during the last 20–25 years in each of a number of countries. The countries selected for study are either of obvious importance in the world economy or interesting because of particular features of their economic structure or recent history, or because their experience throws light on more widespread problems of economic development.

Each volume contains a summary description of the pace and pattern of economic growth in the period covered; and it outlines the main economic problems confronting government in the country, the objectives of economic policy, and the chosen means of economic management. But each author then focuses attention on those aspects of the country's development which he considers most deserving of more detailed examination. The volumes do not attempt to provide comprehensive descriptions and analyses, but they give enough statistical data to support the author's conclusions and a bibliography to suggest further reading.

The series is intended for those interested in problems of economic growth and development ouside the boundaries of the United Kingdom, and in the techniques of economic management available to governments. Some familiarity with the main arguments of economists concerned with such questions is assumed, but no more than can reasonably be expected of a university student.

N.W.

PREFACE

THIS book was written during a (far too brief) one-year stay in Tokyo while on leave of absence from the O.E.C.D.'s Economics Department. It was made possible by the Japan Foundation, which extended very generous financial support throughout my stay in Japan, and by the Economic Research Institute of the Economic Planning Agency which provided me with office space and research facilities. To these two institutions I am greatly indebted. Even if the final output does not live up to their expectations, they can at least be assured that the author and his family benefited from, and greatly enjoyed, their Japanese sojourn. A particular word of thanks I feel is due to Isamu Miyazaki, of the Economic Planning Agency, who was instrumental in arranging my invitation to Japan. Neither he, nor the E.P.A. nor, of course, the O.E.C.D. is in any way responsible for the views expressed in the following pages.

Perusing the prefaces of others who have stayed in, and written about, Japan, one is struck by a unanimous note—all felt that they had been treated with the utmost kindness and had been given all possible help. My experience is no exception to the general rule. Co-operation and friendliness were unstinted wherever I went. The list of those who, in one way or another, contributed to my 'intellectual output' is far too long to be mentioned in full. Among those who felt obliged to read my whole manuscript, Kazumasa Iwata, Masashi Katō, and Yoshihiro Kogane, all of the Economic Planning Agency, were particularly helpful. Interesting comments and constructive criticism also came from the Bank of Japan and notably from Hidegazu Eguchi. Back in Europe, Stephen Potter, among my O.E.C.D. colleagues, and Chris Allsopp and Nita Watts in Oxford, greatly improved my English and my economics. Stubbornness, laziness, or just incompetence meant that not all the suggestions received were taken into consideration, and imply that errors and insufficiencies, though seldom the better points of the arguments, are entirely my own responsibility.

The list of people to whom I am indebted is, in fact, a good deal longer. It includes all those who have written on the

Japanese economy in English. Unfortunately, my Japanese is barely elementary. This is a major, probably a fundamental, drawback for anyone who wants to do research on Japan's economy, even if such research is kept at a very macro-economic or statistical level. It means that the present book is based largely on secondary sources and draws heavily on other authors. While too late for me, I hope my warnings will be heeded by others. Whatever the number of translations, however theoretical one's approach, however much one relies on figures, one's understanding of this country is bound to be limited without the essential tool of its language.

Tokyo,
  Autumn 1974   A.B.

CONTENTS

PART ONE
A DESCRIPTION OF THE ECONOMY

PART TWO
FACTORS IN ECONOMIC GROWTH

LIST OF FIGURES

LIST OF TABLES

LIST OF ABBREVIATIONS

B.o.J.	Bank of Japan
B.S., O.P.M.	Bureau of Statistics, Office of the Prime Minister
DE	*The Developing Economies*
EDCC	*Economic Development and Cultural Change*
E.P.A.	Economic Planning Agency
ESJ	*Economic Survey of Japan*
FY	Fiscal Year
HJE	*Hitotsubashi Journal of Economics*
J.E.R.C.	Japan Economic Research Centre
M.I.T.I.	Ministry of International Trade and Industry
M.o.F.	Ministry of Finance
M.o.L.	Ministry of Labour
O.E.C.D.	Organization for Economic Co-operation and Development, Paris
RES	*Review of Economics and Statistics*
U.N.(E.C.E.)	United Nations (Economic Commission for Europe)

NOTES: Unless otherwise stated, references to years are always to calendar years. Billion = one thousand millions.

INTRODUCTION

To try to provide a full survey of an economy as complex as the Japanese one in less than 200 pages is a virtually impossible task. Inevitably, therefore, the contents of this book are selective rather than comprehensive and the following few paragraphs are intended to warn the reader of what is covered, of what was attempted and of what is omitted.

Part I tries to provide a summary picture of the economy's development, structure, and performance since the war. It starts with the growth record and cyclical fluctuations. It then describes some selected features of the country's industrial structure which have attracted attention either in Japan (economic dualism), or abroad (employment practices). It concludes with a tentative assessment of the weaknesses and strengths of the development process of the last twenty years.

Part II tries to isolate those factors which have, or are believed to have, contributed most to Japan's exceptional economic growth, and looks, if not very systematically, at how they may develop in the future. The discussion centres on capital formation and on labour supply, but some attention is also devoted to the rather elusive role of government policies and interventions. Two other aspects are treated which have a bearing on economic growth, though the cause–effect relationship need not be unequivocal—foreign trade (particularly exports) and income distribution; the former requires attention because it plays such a large role in foreign discussions on Japan, the latter because it brings out some interesting, if not always widely known, characteristics of the economy whose influence on growth may have been far from negligible. Some, but not all, the strains of the argument are taken up again in summary form in the concluding remarks, which also look at some, but not all, of the implications for the future.

The period covered stretches from 1953 to 1973. The first year was chosen for reasons explained in Chapter 1. The second date is partly a function of data availability. But in addition, 1973 may represent the closing of a certain pattern of Japanese economic growth. This is best shown by the stark contrast with the past provided by the 1974 pattern and by forecasts for 1975, which point to a number of developments unprecedented in the country's post-war economic history. Recent important events cannot be ignored and tentative judgements on them are offered in the text, but the analysis proper is generally limited to the twenty years to 1973.

While the attention is, of course, focused essentially on Japan, the Japanese economy is placed in an international context at the outset of most chapters, in order to see whether many of the peculiarities often ascribed to the country are really differences of kind or only of degree. Comparisons have been made before between Japan and some parts of the rest of the world, but their coverage has often been restricted to the United States and the United Kingdom, largely because of the Anglo-Saxon domination of most economics and the heavy United States bias of most studies on Japan—whether these come from American or from American-trained Japanese scholars. Yet it could well be argued that Japan has very little in common with the United States—the largest and one of the two most mature economies in the world—or even with Britain, and more in common with a number of other industrialized or partly industrialized countries. More telling comparisons might be made with countries whose levels of development are closer to Japan's and/or which are of similar size.* Hence, whenever possible, comparisons have been extended to cover not only the United Kingdom but also France, Germany, and Italy, a sample of countries which are similar to Japan in many aspects. At times the United States and the Soviet Union have also been brought into the picture, since parallels can be drawn with some elements in their economic structure or history. Other countries, developed or not, are mentioned only in passing, except in a few instances when Japanese trends look sufficiently special to warrant comparisons with a relatively large sample of other countries (e.g. in the field of saving propensities or income distribution).

Throughout, the approach is macro-economic and the analysis relies entirely on official statistics. This may qualify many of the conclusions reached, since the data may be deficient for some purposes—notably where international comparisons

---

* Size is not an indispensable characteristic, permitting valid comparisons, but it is bound to play a role in shaping an economy and not only in respect of foreign trade proportions.

are attempted. More importantly, the coverage of some official data may be considered too restrictive. This is, for instance, the case with the traditional national accounting magnitudes which have come under increasing criticism, particularly in Japan. A further important limitation (or omission), for a book published in 1975, is the virtual lack of econometric evidence. This may seem the more striking since Japan is a country in which econometrics is probably the single most important activity (or favourite pastime) of the economics profession. There are three main reasons for the exclusion of econometrics. First, I feel that there is nothing in economics which the English language, even when misused by a continental, cannot express as well as, or better than, any equation. Secondly, although econometrics may be useful for short-run forecasting purposes, its application to longer-run research is fraught with difficulties and ambiguities. Thirdly, and most important (perhaps the first two reasons are only excuses), is the author's basic ignorance of anything but the most elementary techniques of the art.

Though econometrics is, on the whole, missing from this study, Japan's experience is sometimes subjected to a theoretical interpretation, even if no claim is made to a consistent theoretical framework. To apply such a framework in Japan's case might, indeed, be rather difficult. For one thing, over the last twenty years the economy has moved from a stage of relative underdevelopment to one in which it faces some of the problems of an advanced industrial society. For another, few theoretical approaches seem to have been devised with the idea of a 10 per cent annual growth rate of output in mind. Neo-classical tools may sometimes seem very attractive. After all, Japan's wage determination process can be explained by 'Phillips-curve' type mechanisms; factor intensities among firms vary according to factor prices; changes in monetary policies have a strong impact on investment propensities; and many product markets are extremely competitive. But on the other hand, neo-classical economics is basically an economics of equilibrium in which disturbances are marginal and changes small. It seems ill-fitted to cope with the macro-economic problems of a country which has undergone the most rapid growth and transformation witnessed in modern economic history. The same may also be true of some of the approaches of Keynesian or neo-Keynesian economics, far too preoccupied with problems of unemployment or of the 'creeping' growth of economies like Britain. As for fully fledged growth theory, its assumptions 'emasculate history' (Joan Robinson), and its results resemble 'cathedrals of the mind' (Peter Wiles). Hence the approach in the following pages is fairly eclectic. It uses tools from the economics of underdevelopment as well as from Marxist, neo-classical and Keynesian economics, without at any stage pretending to provide a clear and comprehensive theoretical explanation.

A final, and crucial, omission concerns non-economic factors. This is not because 'what is not measurable does not exist'. On the contrary, it is clear that sociological factors (broadly defined) play a very important role in any explanation of Japanese economic growth, especially when comparisons are made with other countries. It is rather because the introduction of sociology into economics introduces a new dimension, requires a different approach and necessitates a linguistic and cultural knowledge well beyond the present author's competence. It was felt preferable to pursue purely economic arguments rather than put forward ill-digested non-economic explanations. These are mentioned at times, more as questions than as answers, whenever they seem plausible or have been recognized as important in other, more authoritative, works. To those who feel that Chicago economics and a computer are able to explain everything, even this may seem unacceptable. To others who think that only sociology can provide the *real* key to an understanding of Japanese growth, the present approach may seem too restrictive. This book is really meant for the 'practical' applied economist who can make a reasonable guess at how much (or little) confidence he can have in the data and who knows how relevant (or irrelevant) most economic theory is to an understanding of the real world.

PART ONE

A DESCRIPTION OF THE ECONOMY

CHAPTER 1

A SUMMARY OF POST-WAR TRENDS

THE broad outlines of Japan's post-war economic growth are, by now, a fairly familiar story. Knowledge of things Japanese may still be fairly limited in the West, especially in Europe, but few are unaware that Japan's growth rate of gross national product (GNP) overshadows that of practically any country (developed or not) which has at one time or another been blessed with an 'economic miracle'. This chapter will therefore provide only a very brief sketch of Japan's post-war economic performance, with the emphasis on the growth of output and inputs by broad sectors, and on cyclical developments.

Growth

Any discussion of growth rates depends crucially on the time period chosen, especially for countries whose economies were affected by post-World War II reconstruction efforts. Japan's growth in the late 1940s and early 1950s was extremely rapid, but represented no more than a catching up with previously attained levels of GNP. If one's interest lies in the autonomous forces which have propelled the economy, the incorporation of this period in the analysis would clearly be misleading. Equally misleading, however, would be to argue (as has been done by some)[1] that Japan's return to post-war normality was achieved only in the early 1960s, as the economy reached a point on a trend line of output growth extrapolated from the beginning of the century. This argument ignores the very sharp differences between the pre-war and post-war economies in almost all fields (growth tempo, size and speed of structural shifts, price movements, foreign trade performance, government policy, external environment, etc.). World War II was too much of a watershed for the economy. A return to an earlier long-run trend determined by completely different forces from those operating in the post-war world was highly unlikely. Indeed, nothing can illustrate this better than the evidence of the economy having shot through the theoretical 'growth' ceiling in the early 1960s and having continued to grow at consistently faster rates over the following decade.

More realistically, post-war reconstruction may be said to have been broadly completed by 1953. In that year *per capita* real income was again equal to the average attained in the last 'normal' pre-war years, 1934–6, while aggregate output and labour force participation rates had returned to their 1938 levels. In addition, some of the abnormal factors associated with the war or its immediate aftermath were also disappearing at that time. 1952–3 saw the end of the occupation, a gradual relaxation of the widespread controls which had previously been imposed on the economy, the disappearance of excess capacity, and a sharp drop in a hitherto runaway rate of inflation. Despite the inevitable simplifications involved in choosing a demarcation line,[2] 1953 would seem to be a reasonably satisfactory starting point for a description of post-war economic growth.

Over the twenty years or so between 1953 and 1973, Japan's economic growth was of the order of 10 per cent per annum, with hardly any deceleration over the period as a whole. 1971 witnessed a slight recession, but growth in 1972–3 was back to the trend rate. This 10 per cent rate of growth is well above what other developed economies have achieved; Table 1.1 shows the lower growth rates of output in several countries which, with the exception of the United States, are roughly comparable with Japan in size and/or level of development. But Japan's post-war growth performance outstrips also that of practically any other economy, developed or developing. Though some countries have mustered GNP or NMP (net material product) growth rates in double figures for some year, or even a few years, none seems to have been able to do so consistently over as long a time-span as Japan.*

Table 1.1 also provides figures on output growth by three broad sectors. In line with the experience of other countries, growth in Japan has been most rapid in industry and slowest in agriculture,

* Japan's position seems not to have been unique in the pre-war period. Figures presented in S. Kuznets, *Economic Growth of Nations*, Harvard University Press 1971, pp. 30–1 and 38–40, suggest that in the forty years or so up to 1925–29, growth in the United States was probably as rapid as in Japan (and even more rapid in Argentina over a slightly shorter period). Inclusion of the 1930s, or allowance for population growth, would enhance Japan's performance in relation to these two countries, but on a *per capita* basis Sweden's record would come very close to that of Japan. Among the post-war 'success stories' of the developing world, the most rapid growth rates over the last two decades seem to have been, at most, of the order of 8 to 8½ per cent per annum (recorded by Taiwan's GNP and Rumania's NMP). Figures closer to those of Japan have been achieved over shorter periods (for instance the 1960s and early 1970s) by South Korea, Iran and, again, Taiwan.

TABLE I.I

Growth rates of output, employment, and productivity—1953 to 1972

(trend rates of growth)

	TOTAL	AGRICULTURE	INDUSTRY[1]	SERVICES
I. Output[2]				
Japan	9·7	2·5	12·5	9·6
France	5·5	2·0	6·4	4·8
Germany	5·2	1·7	6·0	4·7
Italy	5·3	2·4	6·8	4·9
United Kingdom	2·6	2·5	2·9	2·4
United States	3·7	1·9	3·6	4·1
Soviet Union[3]	7·6	3·8	10·3	6·9
II. Employment				
Japan	1·4	−3·6	3·7	3·0
France	0·5	−3·7	1·0	2·2
Germany	0·5	−4·4	1·0	1·6
Italy	−0·3	−5·0	1·8	1·5
United Kingdom	0·4	−2·9	0	1·1
United States	1·6	−3·8	0·9	2·6
Soviet Union[3]	2·0	−0·9	3·2	4·3
III. Productivity[4]				
Japan	8·3	6·1	8·9	6·5
France	4·9	5·7	5·4	2·6
Germany	4·7	6·1	5·0	3·1
Italy	5·6	7·4	5·0	3·3
United Kingdom	2·2	5·4	3·0	1·4
United States	2·2	5·7	2·7	1·5
Soviet Union[3]	5·5	4·7	6·9	2·5

Note: The growth rates shown are based on the equation $\log Y = \log a + bt$ (where Y stands for output, or employment, t for time and b is the growth rate), so as to minimize distortions resulting from initial or terminal years belonging to different cyclical phases.

1. Mining, manufacturing, construction and public utilities.

2. G.D.P. at constant prices; detail may not add because total includes residual errors.

3. 1950–2 to 1967–9; average annual growth rate.

4. Output per worker employed.

Sources: Japan: E.P.A., *National Income Statistics*, unpublished estimates on output by sectors at constant prices, and O.E.C.D., *Labour Force Statistics*; Soviet Union: U.N.(E.C.E.), *Economic Survey of Europe in 1971*, Pt. I; Other countries: O.E.C.D., *National Accounts of O.E.C.D. Countries* and *Labour Force Statistics* (formerly *Manpower Statistics*).

with output in the services sector rising at roughly average speed. To some extent these differences reflect varying growth rates of labour force. The expansion of total employment has been somewhat faster in Japan than in most of the other countries shown in the table, with both industry and services benefiting from rapidly rising labour inputs.* In contrast with developments elsewhere, however, employment growth was somewhat slower in the tertiary sector than in industry, reflecting the already very high proportion of workers in service activities at the beginning of the period.

Part III of Table 1.1 brings together the data on growth of output and of employment, to show the growth of output per worker between 1953 and 1972. No attempt was made to estimate productivity per man-hour, figures on hours worked seldom being available for all the main sectors of the economy. In Japan, average hours worked, which were still rising in the 1950s, declined by only 0·3 per cent per annum over the period as a whole; and this seems to be less than in other major economies, with the possible exception of France. Japan's productivity growth is, therefore, somewhat overstated compared with most other countries, but the distortion is unlikely to be very large. As might be expected, Japan's over-all performance is well above average, with growth in industrial value-added per worker of the order of 9 per cent per annum and very rapid expansion of productivity in the tertiary sector also. The growth of real output per worker in services is a difficult concept to define at the best of times, and statistical comparisons are often influenced by countries' different conventions in compiling their national accounts, notably in the field of government services. Nevertheless, Japan's figure is sufficiently above that of the other countries to suggest that genuine, and very rapid, real growth in some tertiary industries (notably in trade and financial services) played a significant role in the over-all economic expansion. Labour productivity in agriculture, on the other hand, seems to have lagged behind the other two sectors, in contrast with the other market economies shown, in which the agricultural sector ranks first in this respect. This is the more surprising, as disguised unemployment on the land is likely to have been very large in Japan at the outset of the period.

The differences in productivity growth from country to country can, to a large extent, be traced to differing capital inputs, for which data are shown in Table 1.2. It should be noted that these

* It should be noted that two labour force series are available for Japan—an annual one, based on a Ministry of Labour survey (used here), and a quinquennial one, derived from census data. The latter shows a somewhat faster growth rate of total employment (1·9 per cent per annum between 1955 and 1970, as against 1·5 per cent for the M.o.L. data).

figures are far from perfectly comparable and are shown only to provide some very rough orders of magnitude of inter-country differences.* As such, they point to an extremely rapid growth of

TABLE 1.2

Growth rates of gross capital stock

(average annual percentage changes; selected periods)

	TOTAL	AGRICULTURE	INDUSTRY	SERVICES
Japan[1] (1954 to 1971)[2]	10·1	5·6	12·5	9·6
France[3] (1953 to 1970)	5·3	4·3	5·8	4·7
Germany[1] (1952 to 1971)[2]	6·4	3·4	6·9	
Italy[3] (1953 to 1971)	5·8	4·6	6·6	6·2
United Kingdom[4] (1954 to 1972)[2]	3·8	2·7	4·2	3·6
United States[5] (1953 to 1970)[2]	3·6	1·9	3·3	3·9
Soviet Union[6] (1950–2 to 1967–9)	8·8	7·4	10·8	8·3

Note: Figures are not strictly comparable. For further detail see text.

1. Private, excluding dwellings.
2. End-year to end-year.
3. Excluding public administration and dwellings.
4. Total, excluding dwellings; industry excludes textiles which are incorporated in services.
5. Private, excluding dwellings; industry covers manufacturing only.
6. Excluding dwellings.

Sources: Japan: E.P.A., 'Gross Fixed Capital Stock of Private Enterprises', mimeo, 1973; France: J. Mairesse, *L'Évolution du capital fixe productif*, Collections de l'INSEE, Série C, 1972; Italy: G. Esposito, 'Il capitale fisso in Italia per settori di attività economica nel periodo 1951–71', *Annali di Statistica*, vol. 27, ISTAT 1973; Germany: *Wirtschaft und Statistik*, Oct. 1971 and Nov. 1972; United Kingdom: *National Income and Expenditure, 1964* and *1973*; United States: *Survey of Current Business*, March 1974; Soviet Union: U.N.(E.C.E.), *Economic Survey of Europe in 1971*, Pt. I.

capital inputs in all the three main sectors of the Japanese economy and provide the major explanation for the exceptional productivity growth mentioned above. Japan's capital stock seems to have risen two to three times faster than that of most other market economies and faster also than the (possibly over-

* As is well known, estimates of capital stock in constant prices are subject to a great number of difficulties, both theoretical and practical, to which no really satisfactory solution has been found. Estimation methods and coverage vary widely between countries, notably in their treatment of the public sector.

estimated) increase shown for the Soviet Union. Particularly striking is the expansion of the industrial capital stock, propelled by the manufacturing sector; in seventeen years the fixed capital of manufacturing industry increased eightfold (or by some 13 per cent per annum).

Ideally, the growth of capital productivity should be measured by relating capital stock and output data, but the rather uncertain figures in Table 1.2 could not stand the strain of such manipulation. An alternative concept of capital productivity can be measured by means of the incremental capital–output ratio, using more reliable, and more internationally comparable, national accounts data for output and investment. Ratios for six countries are shown in Table 1.3, and in many ways they parallel the story

TABLE 1.3

Incremental gross capital–output ratios

(based on data at constant prices; selected periods)

	TOTAL	AGRICULTURE	INDUSTRY	SERVICES
Japan (1954 to 1972)[1]	2·8	7·0	2·0	3·4
France (1955 to 1973)	3·8	7·7	2·4	6·4
Germany (1955 to 1969)	4·6	15·7	2·5	7·5
Italy (1954 to 1973)	3·5	5·4	2·5	5·3
United Kingdom (1956 to 1973)	6·1	6·5	4·9	9·0
United States (1956 to 1973)	4·4	..	..	..

Note: The incremental capital–output ratio is here defined as the ratio of the percentage share of investment in output (over the period 1 to t-1), to the average annual percentage change in output (between periods 1 and t). The time periods differ slightly from country to country since they have been adjusted as necessary to ensure that they begin and end for each country with years of similar levels of capacity utilization. This was done by using O.E.C.D. estimates of gaps between actual and potential output (see O.E.C.D., 'The Measurement of Domestic Cyclical Fluctuations', *Economic Outlook—Occasional Studies*, July 1973).

1 Japanese investment data in constant prices by sectors are not available. These figures were obtained by using a constant price series for the private sector estimated by the E.P.A. (on a calendar year basis) and applying the implicit private sector deflators to government investment data for fiscal years in current values. They are therefore a hybrid of fiscal and calendar year figures, but over so long a period this is unlikely to distort results significantly.

Sources: Japan: E.P.A., 'Gross Fixed Capital Stock of Private Enterprises', mimeo, 1973, unpublished data on output by sector at constant prices, and author's estimates. Other countries: O.E.C.D., *National Accounts of O.E.C.D. Countries*.

of the earlier comparisons of growth of labour productivity. The growth of over-all capital productivity, as well as that in industry and in the tertiary sectors, has been much higher in Japan than in all the other countries shown.* But agriculture is again an exception, with Japanese performance much closer to that of the other countries.

The agricultural picture is, in fact, complicated by both geographical and institutional characteristics. Average land holdings are very small in Japan, partly because of the relatively small size of the cultivable area and partly as a result of redistribution under the post-war land reform. In addition, the very large share of rice growing in total farming output (nearly 40 per cent in 1970), limits the application of highly mechanized techniques. Thus, neither labour productivity (despite rapidly growing capital inputs) nor capital productivity could increase much faster than in other countries and their absolute levels are probably well below those recorded in the advanced Western economies. Estimates of land productivity, on the other hand, show Japan's output per hectare of agricultural land as much higher than that of countries such as Denmark or the Netherlands,[3] even if such figures are to some extent distorted by Japan's protection of agriculture and the resulting high relative prices of many farm products.

Having presented growth rates of both output and inputs, it would now be possible, following a well-known approach,[4] to 'explain' Japan's economic expansion by measuring the respective contributions of the two factors of production to output growth, making an allowance for the effects of structural shifts, etc., and coming up with some residual meant to reflect 'disembodied technological progress' or 'unexplainable factors in growth'. But such a procedure has not been followed here. For one thing, there is already a relative abundance of studies of this nature on the Japanese economy.[5] For another, this type of exercise can often become a search for progressively more refined (and/or arbitrary) assumptions on the nature of technical progress, 'quality' improvements, effects of trade liberalization or economies of scale, and so on, designed to produce the lowest possible values for

---

* Data for the Soviet Union have not been included since the much lower relative price of investment goods in that country artificially depresses the value of the incremental capital–output ratios.

residuals.* More fundamentally, the approach requires the heroic assumptions that perfect competition prevails and that productive factors are 'rewarded' according to their marginal productivities. In any case, even if the assumptions were realistic and all the adjustments made were plausible, such a 'growth accounting' analysis would still be unable to shed much light on why rates of accumulation were what they were or on the dynamic inter-actions which make economic growth possible. As Kindleberger once wrote: 'An economy is a system not an aggregation.'

An examination of Tables 1.1 to 1.3 will give the reader a sufficient inkling, without need for more 'sophisticated' analysis, of the basic difference between Japan's and other countries' economic performance over this period—namely a much more rapid rate of capital accumulation in Japan. This does not mean that the expansion in labour supply had no impact on Japanese growth. On the contrary, the possibility of drawing on a large reservoir of workers in agriculture and services must have greatly facilitated the investment effort. But it was the latter which led growth, while labour played a largely permissive role.

Cycles

Japan's rapid growth rate was far from even over this period, and it would have been surprising if it had been. But until 1974 cyclical fluctuations, not unlike those in Europe, took the form of variations in annual growth rates that were always positive, with GNP never declining from one year to the next or even, after 1954, from half year to half year. Up to 1952–3, the economy was still recovering from war losses. Growth rates were consequently

* The studies referred to above show widely differing results, the percentage of growth accounted for by increasing factor inputs stretching from 40 per cent (Kanamori, 1955 to 1968), to roughly two-thirds (Ohkawa–Rosovsky, 1955 to 1964).

FIG. 1. *Selected business cycle indicators*

Note: The cumulated diffusion index in panel A is a simple summary measure combining 25 economic indicators. It shows the number of series which are increasing minus the number of series decreasing as a percentage of the total number of series cumulated from the beginning of the period.

Sources: E.P.A., *Business Cycle Indicators, Japanese Economic Indicators* and *Nationa Income Statistics*; O.E.C.D., 'The Measurement of Domestic Cyclical Fluctuations', *Economic Outlook—Occasional Studies*, July 1973.

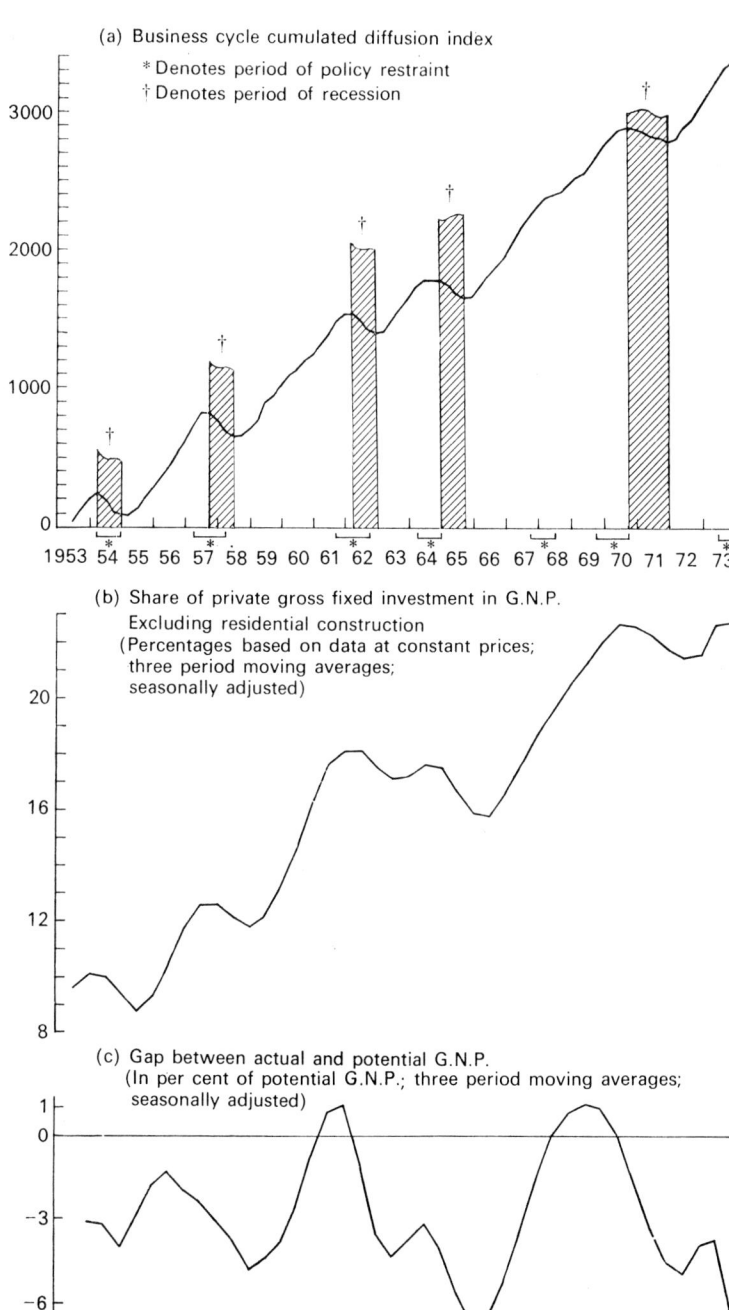

(a) Business cycle cumulated diffusion index

* Denotes period of policy restraint
† Denotes period of recession

(b) Share of private gross fixed investment in G.N.P.

Excluding residential construction
(Percentages based on data at constant prices;
three period moving averages;
seasonally adjusted)

(c) Gap between actual and potential G.N.P.
(In per cent of potential G.N.P.; three period moving averages;
seasonally adjusted)

high, and cyclical movements limited to a short-lived slowdown in 1949–50 induced by stringent anti-inflationary policies, but soon reversed by the Korean-war boom. The process of recovery took longer than elsewhere, and was also steeper since the material damages inflicted by the war were extremely large. Roughly 30 per cent of the country's capital stock had been destroyed,[6] and GNP in 1946 had fallen back to a level already attained in 1917–19.*

As the factors associated with post-war recovery and the Korean-war boom receded, the economy's momentum decelerated to what was regarded at the time as a more normal pace—GNP growth rates of 6–7 per cent per annum, against the 10·5 per cent trend rate of 1946–52. But the apparent slowdown was short-lived and, stimulated by new factors, vigorous, if uneven, growth was resumed. It is from this time (1952–3) that a fairly typical business-cycle pattern took shape, to be repeated for the next twenty years—rapid, and frequently accelerating, growth for three to five years followed by a brief (one year) period of recession, giving way to a renewed spurt. According to the E.P.A.'s business cycle indicators, shown in Fig. 1, there were four or five such phases between 1953 and 1973, lasting on average some four years. But even during 'recessions' the growth of GNP from one calendar year to the next never fell below 4 per cent until 1974.

The common characteristic of the three long upswings (1955–7, 1958–61, and 1966–70) was buoyant business fixed-investment; and downswings were similarly related to declining investment propensities. Turning points seem to have been closely associated with the imposition and removal of restrictive policies, especially in the first half of the twenty-year period. The normal cyclical pattern thus began with very rapid investment growth, first in stocks and later in plant and equipment. The spreading and strengthening of this expansion did not, on the whole, bring about any marked acceleration of price inflation, at least until very recently; but it usually entailed a worsening trade balance as accelerating growth sucked in more imports without necessarily generating an equivalent volume of exports. Given a relatively low level of foreign exchange reserves and a commitment to a

---

* Japan's economy was probably affected by the war more than that of any other country. In 1947 GNP stood at 56 per cent of its 1938 level as against some 90 per cent in France, Italy, or the Soviet Union. Estimates of West Germany's GNP in 1947 show losses roughly similar to those of Japan, but Germany's industrial output seems to have declined less than Japan's.

fixed exchange rate, restrictive measures then became inevitable. These, taken mainly in the monetary field, acted with great effectiveness first on stock building and then on fixed investment. Falls in investment and relatively swift improvements in the foreign balance allowed policy relaxations soon after which were, in turn, fairly effective in reviving investment demand.

This very simplified picture of Japanese cycles suggests that turning points were determined by policy intervention rather than by the economy hitting the physical ceilings and floors of traditional trade-cycle theory. This is somewhat surprising in view of the momentum of investment growth. In some years business fixed-investment rose by 30–40 per cent in real terms, with manufacturing investment and capacity increasing by up to 60 per cent and 20 per cent, respectively.

Such tempos could have been expected to generate either bottlenecks and accelerating inflation (as in the post-war European experience), or alternatively periodic bouts of excess capacity and crises of overproduction. But both these dangers were largely avoided, thanks to the availability of some unemployed or under-employed resources at the outset of each boom, brief gestation periods for fixed investment,[7] and a high marginal propensity to save. 'Leakages' to saving and to imports and a relatively elastic supply could therefore accommodate the 'within period' multiplier effects of an investment spurt without inflationary consequences; and in succeeding periods past investment had created sufficient capacity to meet the demand generated by both past and present investment spending. In other words, investment itself was continuously lifting the ceiling. Over-capacity was nevertheless usually avoided, thanks to the dynamic growth of demand for investment, spurred by optimistic expectations, and thanks to the steady growth of consumption. In the brief spells of recession in the growth of domestic demand a further outlet could be, and was, found in foreign markets. Under these circumstances, the only effective ceiling on expansion was imposed by the balance of payments.

This, again, is of course a very simplified picture. It fits reasonably well the experience up to 1962–3, if with some important qualifications, but becomes progressively less applicable through the late 1960s and early 1970s. In the first half of the period some physical bottlenecks were present at upper turning points, as is best shown by the sharp increases in imports of semi-manufactures and machinery in the later stages of upswings, when domestic capacity was unable to keep pace with accelerating demand.[8] From 1964–5 onwards, it is the opposite phenomenon which is more in evidence. Enough capacity had been created to relieve most sectoral bottlenecks, and demand for manufactures seldom spilled over on to imports. But the creation of capacity could go too far, as witnessed by the sluggishness with which investment reacted to the 1965 monetary relaxation, or by the autonomous deceleration in private investment recorded in 1970–1. The relative brevity of these partly endogenous recessions shows, however, that even such excess capacity crises were fairly mild.

Paralleling the rising importance of autonomous investment cycles is a gradual decline in the effectiveness of monetary policy in controlling the cycle. Little impact was obtained by restrictive action in 1967 and 1969, and both the 1966 and 1972 recoveries owed more to vigorous fiscal intervention than to monetary relaxation. But admittedly, the degree of restraint in 1967 was only moderate while the 1969 restrictions were taken, for the first time, for purely domestic reasons. In the absence of the 'overriding balance of payments constraint which imposed an unavoidable, and generally accepted, line of action'[9] reactions and expectations could have been expected to differ from those in earlier periods of restraint.

It is apparent from the middle panel of Fig. 1 that the four- to five-year cycles just described can also be seen as segments of investment cycles of somewhat longer duration (e.g. from 1954 to 1965 or from 1961 to 1970), cycles which have, on the whole, been absent from the post-war experience of other market economies. On this basis, it has been argued that Japan's fluctuations have in fact been largely autonomous Juglar-type investment cycles rather than the shorter 'investment spurt *cum* policy intervention' cycles sketched above.* But this thesis would seem to be backed by little more than the purely statistical evidence shown in the diagram. Autonomous forces were clearly propelling investment throughout the period, but it is unlikely that these forces were characterized by periodic waves of similar duration. It is more plausible to

* This thesis has frequently been put forward by M. Shinohara, who has also provided evidence showing that similar cycles took place in the pre-war period and in the 1945–55 years; cf. *Growth and Cycles in the Japanese Economy*, Tokyo 1962, Ch. 6; 'Causes and Patterns in the Postwar Growth', *DE*, December 1970 and 'Kuznets and Juglar Cycles during the Industrialization of 1874–1940', in Ohkawa and Hayami (eds.), *Economic Growth*.

assume instead that investment propensities were consistently strong over these years and were curbed, at irregular intervals, by policy restraint or temporary phases of excess capacity.

Fluctuations have clearly been wide. Panel C of Fig. 1, showing deviations of actual output from a short-run measure of potential output, indicates that, if anything, fluctuations increased over time, with boom periods lengthening, at least until 1970, and slowdowns becoming progressively more severe. Japan has recorded fluctuations a good deal more pronounced than those in other developed market economies. Taking as a reasonably comparable measure of the amplitude of fluctuations the standard deviation of gaps between actual and potential output over the 1955–72 period, as estimated by the O.E.C.D.,[10] Japan's figure is more than twice as large as France's and roughly one and a half times those of Germany, Italy, or Britain.

While this seems to throw an unfavourable light on Japanese performance, it still has to be remembered that Japan never experienced actual declines in GNP over this period, unlike most other countries, and also grew a good deal faster. It can also be argued quite plausibly that Japan's sharp cycles were actually growth promoting. The expectations of further growth created by the breakneck speed at which the economy developed whenever the balance of payments allowed it might never have been attained had expansion been more even and balanced, and the momentum over the long period might well have been less. The following statement by Kaldor seems to fit Japan's experience admirably:

'. . . far from the trend rate of growth determining the strength or duration of booms, it is the strength and duration of booms which shapes the trend rate of growth. It is the economy in which businessmen are reckless and speculative, where expectations are highly volatile, but with an underlying bias towards optimism, where high and growing profits are projected into the future and lead to the hasty adoption of "unsound" projects involving over-expansion, which is likely to show a high rate of progress over long periods.'[11]

A bird's-eye-view

The foregoing discussion has highlighted the fact that Japan's experience has been unique because of its growth rate. Despite relatively wide cyclical fluctuations, Japan's economic growth has, for over two decades, been consistently faster, and by a wide margin, than that of any other country. At a more disaggregated level, this has been particularly true of industry, but the output of the service sector has also risen extremely rapidly when seen in an international context. The largest single contributing factor to this performance seems to have been a massive growth of a highly

Elasticities of sectoral output growth rates in market and centrally planned economies

(based on data at constant prices; selected periods)

	AGRICULTURE	INDUSTRY	SERVICES
Japan (1953 to 1972)	0·25	1·29	0·98
O.E.C.D. Europe[1] (1955 to 1968)	0·36	1·17	0·98
United States (1953 to 1972)	0·51	0·96	1·09
Eastern Europe[2] (1950–2 to 1967–9)	0·25	1·47	0·92
Soviet Union (1950–2 to 1967–9)	0·50	1·36	0·91

Note: Elasticities are with respect to the growth of total output; based on trend growth rates except for non-market economies, for which they are annual averages.

   1. Unweighted average of 11 industrialized countries.
   2. Excludes Soviet Union; unweighted average of 6 countries.

Sources: Japan and United States: Table 1.1; Western Europe: O.E.C.D., *The Growth of Output, 1960–1980*; Socialist countries: U.N.(E.C.E.), *Economic Survey of Europe in 1971*, Part I.

productive capital stock. But, given Japan's high growth rate, differences in the rates of development of various sectors have not been particularly striking. Indeed, the pattern of growth (roughly measured by elasticities of sectoral to total output growth rates) seems to have been broadly in between the patterns recorded by the developed market and non-market economies. The expansion of industry has been proportionately more rapid than in the West; but the official emphasis and encouragement given to this sector has probably been less pronounced than in Eastern Europe. Conversely, the output of the service sector has lagged, in relative terms, behind that of the other capitalist economies, but has outstripped that of the socialist ones. On this very broad level, therefore, it could be argued that Japanese economic growth, despite wide cycles and a very fast tempo, was relatively 'balanced'.

NOTES

1. S. Tsuru, 'Growth and Stability of the Postwar Japanese Economy', *American Economic Review*, May 1961, p. 407; L. R. Klein, 'A Model of Japanese Economic Growth, 1878–1937', *Econometrica*, July 1961, pp. 291–2.

2. Discussed in greater detail in K. Ohkawa and H. Rosovsky, *Japanese Economic Growth*, Stanford University Press 1973, pp. 23–4.

3. E.P.A., *ESJ (1966–1967)*, p. 58, and *ESJ (1969–1970)*, p. 90.

4. For the best-known example see E. Denison, *Why Growth Rates Differ*, The Brookings Institution 1967.

5. Some relatively recent contributions are: H. Kanamori, 'What Accounts for Japan's High Rate of Growth', *Review of Income and Wealth*, June 1972; M. Ezaki and D. W. Jorgenson, 'Measurement of Macroeconomic Performance in Japan, 1951–1968', and R. Yoshihara, 'Productivity Changes in the Manufacturing Sector, 1906–1965', both in K. Ohkawa and Y. Hayami (eds.), *Economic Growth—The Japanese Experience since the Meiji Era*, J.E.R.C. Tokyo 1973; a very complete and balanced study is to be found in Ohkawa and Rosovsky, *Japanese Economic Growth*.

6. A tentative estimate based on sectoral figures and 1953 weights as shown in Ohkawa and Rosovsky, *Japanese Economic Growth*, p. 62.

7. The average gestation period for manufacturing investment (for 1952–63), was estimated at $2\frac{1}{2}$ quarters (K. Sato, 'A Model of Investment Behaviour: Fixed Investment and Capacity in Japanese Manufacturing, 1952–1963', *Riron Keizai Gaku*, (*The Economic Studies Quarterly*), June 1966, p. 10. The multiplier for (government) investment implicit in the E.P.A.'s 'Econometric Master Model' reaches its highest value three quarters after the initial investment outlay.

8. H. T. Patrick, 'Cyclical Instability and Fiscal-Monetary Policy in Postwar Japan', in W. W. Lockwood (ed.), *The State and Economic Enterprise in Japan*, Princeton 1969.

9. O.E.C.D., *ESJ, 1971*, p. 14.

10. O.E.C.D., 'The Measurement of Domestic Cyclical Fluctuations'.

11. N. Kaldor, 'The Relation of Economic Growth and Cyclical Fluctuations', *Economic Journal*, March 1954, pp. 68–9.

CHAPTER 2

SOME STRUCTURAL FEATURES

EXTREMELY rapid growth inevitably entailed large and drastic changes in the economy's structure, highlighted, as elsewhere, by a dwindling role for agriculture and the rising weight of industry. In the mid-1950s nearly 50 per cent of the labour force was still primarily occupied on the land; by the early 1970s the proportion had shrunk to barely 15 per cent. Conversely, there was rapid growth in industrial employment and, even more strikingly, in this sector's share in total output which rose from just over one quarter to 45 per cent of GNP (at constant 1965 prices). These sharp changes, accomplished in barely twenty years,* were of course accompanied by large population movements away from the countryside, further urbanization in an already highly urbanized society, intra-sectoral shifts from relatively labour-intensive to relatively capital-intensive activities, changes in consumption patterns, etc.

Japan's economy in 1953 could well be described as being at a '... mid position in the scale of economic development'.[1] Agriculture loomed large, manufacturing productivity was estimated at barely 15 per cent of the United States level,[2] the high share of the labour force in tertiary activities was a reflection of chronic underemployment rather than of economic maturity, and the balance of payments was being propped up by large United States miliary expenditures. Twenty years later, following a more than sixfold increase in total output, and two revaluations of the currency, Japan's economic structure broadly matched those of the small group of highly industrialized nations. The shares of the three main sectors in output and employment suggest that, in terms of these broad aggregates, some differences from very mature economies like Britain and the United States still remain. But comparisons with, for instance, France or Italy, indicate a number of similarities (see Table 2,1);[3] and on the basis of the frequently used, if not very reliable, statistics, of *per*

* Both Britain and Germany took some forty to fifty years to raise the share of industrial output in GNP by a similar percentage and Italy one hundred years to move from 20 per cent to 40 per cent.

TABLE 2.1

The structure of output and employment by broad sectors, 1969–71

(percentages of total)

		AGRICULTURE	INDUSTRY	SERVICES	MEASURE OF INEQUALITY[1]
Japan	O[2]	6·8	45·3	47·9	21·2
	N[3]	17·4	35·6	47·0	
France	O	6·0	49·0	45·0	20·6
	N	14·1	38·7	47·2	
Germany	O	3·2	53·6	43·2	11·6
	N	9·0	50·0	41·0	
Italy	O	10·3	39·4	50·3	28·4
	N	20·2	43·7	36·1	
United	O	3·0	43·9	52·7	4·6
Kingdom	N	2·8	46·4	50·8	
United	O	3·0	34·4	63·2	3·5
States	N	4·4	32·3	63·2	
Soviet	O	14·4	47·5	38·1	36·2
Union[4]	N	29·0	29·4	41·6	

Note: Detail may not add because of residual errors in national accounts figures.

1. Measured as the sum of absolute differences (irrespective of sign), between output and employment shares; see S. Kuznets, *Economic Growth of Nations,* Harvard University Press 1971, pp. 290–2.
2. O = GDP at current prices.
3. N = Employment.
4. 1967–69. Output shares are derived from data at constant 1963 prices.

Sources: E.P.A., *National Income Statistics;* O.E.C.D., *National Accounts of O.E.C.D. Countries* and *Labour Force Statistics;* U.N.(E.C.E.), *Economic Survey of Europe in 1971,* Pt. I.

capita national income, Japan had, by 1972, reached a level comparable with those of the United Kingdom, Austria or Finland.

Nevertheless, Japan's economy is often regarded as radically different from most other Western economies. Foreign observers frequently refer to so-called 'feudal' characteristics which apparently impregnate the employment and wage practices of enterprises. Japanese observers, on the other hand, stress the country's 'dual economic structure', which would also seem to relegate Japan to a somewhat earlier stage of development.

A 'dual economy'

'Dualism' is not a very precise concept. At its broadest, it means the division of a country into two separate economic (as

well as social and cultural) spheres with limited mutual interactions. Usually associated with the developing world, the notion
has been applied to countries in which an export-oriented
monoculture or, more frequently, a small industrialized and
urbanized enclave, has existed side by side with a vast agricultural
hinterland barely touched by the modern sector's market
economy.* Other characteristic features (e.g. differences in
income- or wage-levels between the two sectors, differing factor
intensities and productivity levels) have frequently been added
to this picture and, most notably, a regional dimension whose
relevance has not been limited to the developing world.

The discussions on Japanese dualism have focused on both
the basic agriculture-versus-industry dichotomy and the problems
of regional disparities. The former is prominent in the literature
on economic growth before World War II, and Japan's experience has become for some an almost textbook case of the
development of a dual economy.[4] Regional dualism, or at least
sizeable and persistent income differences between regions, has
also attracted some attention, though more perhaps in economic
planning documents than in academic discussion. Throughout
the 1950s regional problems were in fact neglected as priority
was given to over-all growth; but the inevitable worsening of
regional differentials led to a reappraisal of this strategy. From
the early 1960s increasing importance has been given, at least in
plan formulation if not always in practice, to the need for a
regionally more balanced growth pattern, culminating in the
1972 proposals of the then M.I.T.I. Minister K. Tanaka, for a
'remodelling of the Japanese archipelago'.[5]

But most of the discussion of 'dualism' has not in fact been
concerned with regional disparities. To a foreign observer this
may seem surprising since, seen in an international context,
regional disparity would appear to be as serious a problem in
Japan as in several industrialized Western economies where a
good deal of attention is devoted to the issue. The table below
provides a very rough measure of regional economic dispersion—
the (normalized and weighted) standard deviations of regional
per capita incomes. This indicator is clearly imperfect and can be

* This is clearly a great simplification. Some contacts between the two sectors
are part and parcel of dualistic theories of development, if only because the
traditional economy performs the crucial role of providing the investible surplus
and the reservoir of labour which permit the modern sector to grow. But
otherwise, interactions are limited.

sensitive to the geographical breakdown adopted; but the orders of magnitude suggest that Japan's disparities are fairly large by the standards of those developed countries which are commonly thought to suffer from regional inequalities. This conclusion is broadly confirmed by a more detailed breakdown attempted for Italy and Japan, based on 93 and 46 regions respectively. The 1969 Japanese coefficient of variation of regional *per capita* incomes (0·27) remains close to the Italian one (0·32). It is true that a north–south dichotomy is absent from Japan, but an equally

Comparative regional per capita *income disparities*

	YEAR	NUMBER OF REGIONS	STANDARD DEVIATION[1]
Japan	FY 1970	14	0·23
France	1968	11	0·19
Germany	1970	11	0·14
Italy	1969	18	0·27
United Kingdom	1970	11	0·12

Note: Figures are not strictly comparable since income concepts vary and the regional breakdowns tend to correspond to administrative rather than to economic criteria. Income is represented by national income (Japan), gross household income (France), GDP at market prices (Germany) and at factor cost (United Kingdom), or NDP at factor cost (Italy). Figures for the United States or the Soviet Union are not shown, the size of these countries precluding a meaningful comparison.

1. Average *per capita* income having been made equal to 100, the results can also be considered as coefficients of variation. Deviations between national and regional incomes were weighted by each region's population.

Sources: Japan: B.S., O.P.M., *Japan Statistical Yearbook*; France: INSEE, *Statistiques et indicateurs des régions françaises*, Collections de l'INSEE, Série R, 1973; Germany: *Statistisches Jahrbuch*; Italy: G. Tagliacarne, 'I conti provinciali e regionali', *Moneta e Credito*, 4 1970; United Kingdom: *Economic Trends*, November 1973.

serious geographical problem exists, with an over-developed belt along the central Pacific coast standing in sharp contrast to the poorer outlying regions (the southern part of Kyūshū and the northern part of Honshū). As elsewhere, inequalities reflect differing industrial structures, as well as the more general problem of external diseconomies, with the country's less developed regions characterized by above average shares of agriculture, a limited and relatively small-scale manufacturing sector, unemployment, and emigration.[6]

But, as already mentioned, the problem of 'dualism' has usually

TABLE 2.2

Scale of manufacturing establishments

YEAR	% OF ESTABLISHMENTS WITH				% OF EMPLOYEES IN ESTABLISHMENTS WITH			
	1–9	10–99 EMPLOYEES	100–999	1,000+	1–9	10–99 EMPLOYEES	100–999	1,000+
Japan 1970	73·4	24·2	2·3	0·1	16·4	35·2	20·9	17·5
France 1966	81·8	15·4	2·6	0·1	10·4	30·0	44·4	15·2
Germany 1970	78·1	18·5	3·1	0·3	10·6	22·9	36·4	30·0
Italy 1971	88·9	10·0	1·0	0·1	23·3	31·2	29·8	15·7
United Kingdom 1968	37·9[1]	45·3[2]	15·4	1·4	2·1[1]	16·7[2]	46·1	35·2
United States 1967	51·3	37·8	10·1	0·8	2·5	20·9	43·9	32·8

1. 1–10 employees.
2. 11–99 employees.

Sources: Japan and United States: *Censuses of Manufactures*; France, Germany, Italy, and United Kingdom: *Statistical Yearbooks*.

been seen in a different light; and the economy has usually been regarded as 'dual' because of the simultaneous presence of a modern, efficient, large-scale, high-wage sector, and of a host of small, labour-intensive, low-wage firms, both sets of enterprises coexisting not only within the same regions but also within the same industrial branches.[7] However, the lack of direct contact between the modern corporation and the self-employed peasant or artisan, implicit in the more usual definitions of dualism, seems to be absent in Japan. On the contrary, stress has been laid upon the interactions between the two sectors in such fields as competition and sub-contracting, absorption and transmission of cyclical fluctuations or behaviour of capital and labour markets.

But at this level, Japan's economic structure is not in fact as unusual as it is often made out to be. Small firms, sub-contracting, or differences in capital–labour ratios according to scale, exist practically everywhere without the economies concerned being necessarily dubbed 'dual'. Some elements which may help in comparing Japan's industrial structure with the structures of a few other countries are shown in Table 2.2. While Japanese statistics provide a wealth of figures on almost any economic variable distinguished by size of firm, the same is not true for many other countries. This analysis is, therefore, limited to the manufacturing sector, which is both the most comparable internationally and best covered statistically. In any case, either very large or very small units predominate in many tertiary activities in most economies (e.g. retailing and personal services on the one hand or banking and social services on the other), while the scale of agricultural establishments is dependent on a number of institutional and geographical conditions which preclude meaningful comparisons.

It can be seen that the size distribution of Japanese manufacturing establishments does not differ very markedly from that of some of the major European economies. Very large firms clearly account for a higher percentage of employment in the United States, Britain and Germany than they do in Japan, but this is not the case in either France or Italy. The relative importance of very small establishments is not dissimilar in the last four countries.[8] At most, it could be claimed that the weight of medium-sized firms (100–999 employees) is somewhat smaller in Japan, but even here the differences are not striking.

A more relevant dimension has, however, often been added to the distribution-by-size argument for 'dualism'—the existence of relatively wide inter-firm wage differentials dependent on scale. Though international comparisons in this field are not easy, the evidence presented in Table 2.3 suggests that the

TABLE 2.3

Wage differentials by scale in manufacturing

(wages in establishments with more than 1,000 employees = 100)

SCALE (NUMBER OF EMPLOYEES)	JAPAN (1970)	FRANCE (1966)	GERMANY (1966)	ITALY (1966)	UNITED KINGDOM (1954)	UNITED STATES (1967)
10– 19	60·3	83·5	87·0	67·5	79·3[1]	75·5
20– 49	66·6	81·7	86·1	70·8	80·3[2]	73·7
50– 99	66·9	79·1	87·0	74·2	80·9	73·4
100–199	70·5	80·0	87·0	79·2	82·0	74·3[3]
200–499	78·4	83·5	89·8	82·5	85·0	76·3[4]
500–999	84·9	91·3	92·6	88·3	89·3	81·7
Degree of differential[5]	7·5 (7·6)	3·3 (2·7)	2·5 (3·9)	6·3 (11·4)	3·8 (4·7)	4·3 (2·7)

Notes: Gross annual earnings of employees for Japan, the United Kingdom, and the United States; gross hourly earnings of workers for France, Germany, and Italy.

1. 10–24 employees.
2. 25–49 employees.
3. 100–249 employees.
4. 250–499 employees.
5. Measured by the value of the slope (or the coefficient b) in equations of the form $y = a + b \log x$, where y stands for the wage indices here shown and x for scale (mid-points of the intervals). Figures in brackets are t-ratios.

Sources: Japan and the United States: *Censuses of Manufactures*; France, Germany, and Italy: C.E.E., *Structure et répartition des salaires, 1966*, Série spéciale 8, 1970; United Kingdom: M. Shinohara, *Structural Changes in Japan's Economic Development*, Tokyo 1970.

differences between Japan and other countries are sufficiently large for them to reflect more than purely statistical problems; and a comparison made for the mid-1950s showed that Japanese wage differentials by size were then as large as, or even larger than, those recorded in several underdeveloped countries.[9]

Three arguments reinforce the conclusion suggested by the statistics. It has been shown that Japanese wage differentials by scale are, at least in part, genuine and do not merely reflect differences in the skills, occupation, industry distribution, age or sex of the firms' employees.[10] In other words, workers in very small establishments may receive wages which are only a fraction of those received in larger enterprises for no good reason other than that they are employed in smaller firms. It is not known whether this is the case elsewhere, but following wage theory it could be argued that inter-firm wage differentials due solely to size are not as likely as age-, sex- or skill-related disparities. Secondly, some of the figures shown in the table are based on hourly earnings, while Japan's data are for annual earnings. An adjustment for hours worked would increase Japanese differentials yet further—for example, in the 1970s, increasing the differential between establishments with 10–99 workers and those with more than 1,000 workers by $7\frac{1}{2}$ per cent. Finally, it is well known that in Japan firms grant a number of indirect welfare benefits to their workers, notably in the fields of health insurance, pensions, housing and holidays, and generosity in this respect decreases as companies get smaller.[11] Though indirect benefits provided by the company are not unknown in the West, the existence of national, or otherwise comprehensive, health and pension schemes makes such benefits far less significant in relation to wages than in Japan.

Wage differences between the 'modern' and the 'traditional' sectors play a crucial role in dualistic theories of economic development, since it is largely through their existence that different factor intensities and productivity levels are made possible. Following this criterion, Japan's economy can be defined as 'dual', or at least more dual than those of other highly industrialized countries. A more appropriate definition might, however, be 'differential' rather than 'dual',[12] since it is not so much wage differences between two sectors which characterize Japan, but rather a continuous spread of earnings from the largest to the smallest firm. Very similar spreads exist for *per capita* value added and capital intensity (Fig. 2).

The explanation of the existence of such a dual or differential structure, as typified by the presence of differentials, related to size of establishment, has been the object of a vast literature which has stressed the particular path of economic growth followed by Japan in the first half of the twentieth century, and notably the development of heavy industry in the 1920s.[13]

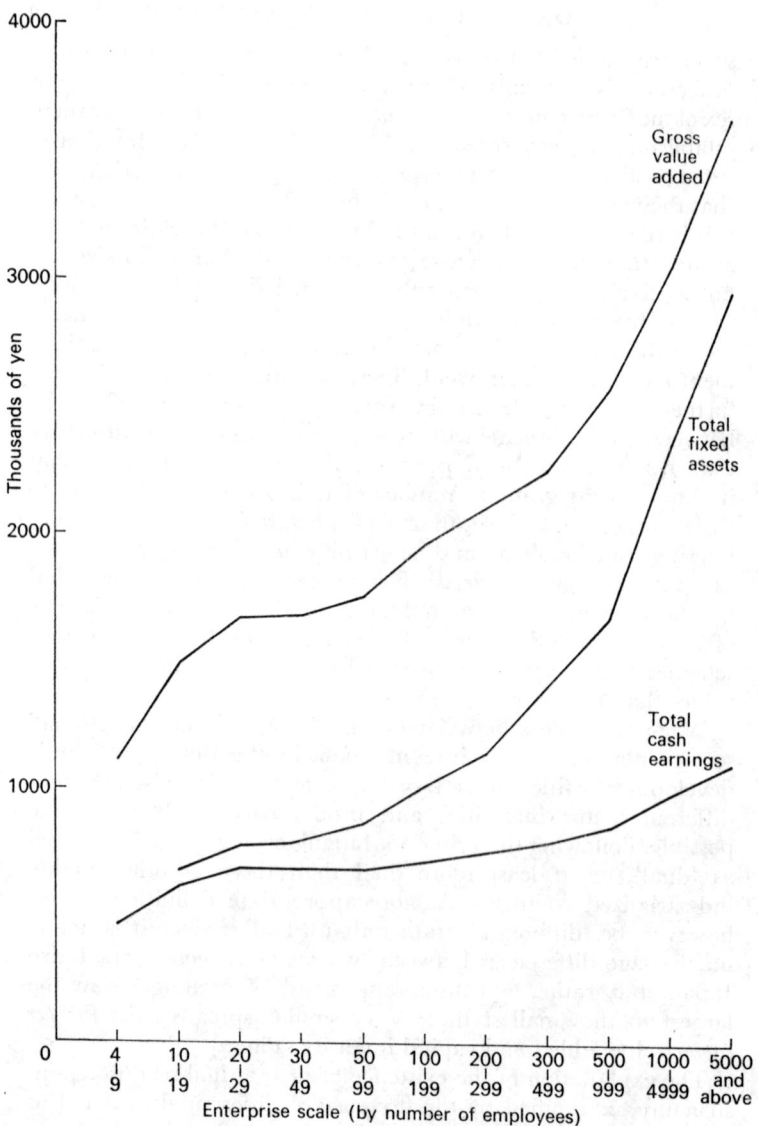

FIG. 2. *Capital, output, and wages per employee in manufacturing by enterprise scale,
1970*

Source: M.I.T.I., *Census of Manufactures.*

Be this as it may, the more usual explanations provided for the persistence of this phenomenon, throughout the post-war period, emphasize interactions between a relatively abundant supply of labour and a relatively tight supply of capital, with the labour market open to all firms on equal terms but access to the capital market restricted in various ways.[14]

The capital market hypothesis has been particularly stressed by Shinohara.[15] According to him, Japan's major commercial banks (the so-called City banks) and most of the private and public long-term credit institutions have consistently favoured larger firms in terms of both cost and availability of credit. Supply of funds to smaller firms has been either a residual, dependent on conditions in the money market, or has come from specialized financial institutions for medium and small businesses. The latter, however, have frequently been short of funds and/or have charged higher interest rates.* For the small firms, a restricted supply of relatively expensive funds meant a slower growth of investment and hence of productivity; this in turn compressed profits and the wage bill. For the larger firms, on the other hand, easy availability of funds allowed, *ceteris paribus*, massive investment expansion, rapid productivity growth, and high profits, and made it *possible* to grant high wages.

But capital market imperfections and differing terms for loans are not peculiar to Japan. Credit-worthiness varies between firms everywhere and one of the crucial variables in its assessment is very likely to be size. Three factors may, however, have intensified the importance of this phenomenon in Japan. First, the heavier reliance of Japanese firms, both big and small, on external financing (on which more in Chapter 6 below), meant that discrimination in this field had a proportionately larger impact on smaller firms' investment financing possibilities than it would have had elsewhere. Secondly, the government's active encouragement of large-scale production (notably in the 1950s), meant that preferential loans were extended mainly to large firms. Thirdly, public help was paralleled by a similar preferential treatment extended by the City banks to the companies with

---

* The E.P.A. showed that in the late 1960s nominal rates on loans to smaller firms were some 2 per cent higher than to large firms; and the effective interest rate gap was nearly 4 per cent, since the percentage of loans traditionally retained in the form of a semi-compulsory deposit by banks is larger, the smaller the firm; E.P.A., *ESJ* (*1969–1970*), pp. 197–8.

which they were financially associated. In the early 1960s, for instance, it has been estimated that up to 30 per cent of the finance supplied to the major constituent enterprises of each of the very large Japanese conglomerates (or *zaibatsus*) came from the financial institutions of the group itself.[16]

The main reasons for the translation of these capital market imperfections into actual, as opposed to just potential, wage differentials involve a number of institutional and economic factors. The traditional explanation for the seemingly irrational granting of high wages by large enterprises in a situation of labour abundance has been in terms of employers' self-interest interacting with economic forces within the firm. High wages, combined with the practice of 'life employment',* ensure the availability of a skilled and stable labour force which, in turn, because of the training acquired, can command a high level of earnings.[17] This argument, while undoubtedly plausible in explaining the appearance of wage differentials in the 1920s, when the supply of skilled labour was very limited, loses much of its force in the post-war situation in which most of the work force has been highly educated.[18]

This change is confirmed by the present near-uniformity of wages of young entrants into the labour force; sizeable wage differentials apply only to older workers. The value of acquired training may play a role here, but the pressure of labour supply and the likely obsolescence of many skills in a period of rapid technological progress could easily offset this factor. The special characteristics of Japanese trade unions are likely to be a good deal more important.[19]

As is well known, Japanese unions are essentially company unions and their influence, on the whole, is restricted to larger firms.† Within these, they are virtual monopolists and could, at the limit, obtain concessions '. . . to the extent that the profit of each enterprise was reduced to a level just sufficient to keep it from going out of business.'[20] Though they obviously do not do

---

* By which is meant a strong insurance against dismissal combined with regular increases in earnings based on age rather than on qualifications. For more detail, see below.

† In 1969 (or 1972), nearly three-quarters of workers in manufacturing firms with more than 500 employees were unionized but this proportion fell to less than 40 per cent for firms with 100 to 499 workers and to 10 and 1½ per cent only for firms with 30 to 99 and with less than 30 workers respectively.

this, they are able, like all monopolists to obtain a price above what a competitive market would provide. This is clearly not the case for the non-unionized workers in smaller firms and for the 'temporary' workers in larger establishments. Indeed, the existence of such workers confirms the importance of trade unions, relative to other factors, in explaining wage differentials. Many of these workers are, for all practical purposes, 'permanent temporary' employees, by virtue of continuous contract renewals,[21] and presumably benefit from on-the-job training and acquisition of skill. Despite this, however, their employment conditions are far inferior to those of the regular workers.

In the past, wage gaps reflected the relative abundance of labour in an economy characterized by a large outflow from agriculture and rapid natural growth of the labour force, combined with the differential impact of trade unions *and* the near absence of a minimum wage legislation. At present, and given a roughly uniform starting wage for everybody, it can be argued that two different markets for labour have evolved—a competitive market for young entrants and for small firms' workers and a closed-shop market for those who have found employment in larger firms. In the latter, mobility is relatively restricted, wage bills are strongly influenced by trade union pressures, and pay scales by management which has perpetuated a seniority wage system. In the former, mobility is much greater, monopolistic forces are weaker, and the individual's wage rises but little through his career.

Thus, the main differences between conditions in Japan and in the West seem to lie in two institutional factors—the particular trade union structure and the existence of a seniority wage system in larger, but not in smaller, firms. In addition, in the 1950s and early 1960s, the absence of government intervention in the wage field was also significant. Elsewhere the existence of a legal minimum wage and/or of some powerful national trade union federation has typically provided a floor to earnings. To be sure, such floors have been undermined in conditions of large-scale unemployment, but the effects have usually been marginal. In Japan, by contrast, unions have not been egalitarian and their membership has been restricted to a (relative) élite, while government policy, apart from fostering big business, has not otherwise been willing to interfere with market forces. These factors have clearly contributed to the appearance of wide wage differentials by scale of establishment.[22] At present, a floor to earnings is provided by market demand and supply for younger workers, but differentials are still assured by different wage-setting mechanisms within enterprises. These differentials, in turn, by allowing persisting differences in capital-intensity and productivity, which seem larger than those in the West, have created an industrial structure which can, loosely, be called more 'dual' or 'differential' than those of most other highly industrialized countries.

Employment practices

Japanese observers may have been struck by their country's dual economic structure. Foreign observers have more usually been impressed by a number of employment practices which seem peculiar to Japan. The best known among these are, of course, the loosely defined 'life employment' and 'seniority wage' systems which were briefly mentioned above. 'Life employment' implies that once a worker has been engaged he is, more or less, assured of a permanent job until retirement age. And 'wages by seniority' imply that the same worker will, in principle, obtain regular annual increases in his salary based more on age than on qualifications or performance. Such institutional practices clearly look somewhat different from those prevailing in the West; yet the differences can be exaggerated, since neither of the two systems is as widespread in Japan as is often claimed, nor are similar characteristics totally absent from wage systems in other countries.

Data on the extent of life employment practices are not easily forthcoming. But it is generally agreed that the system applies only in large firms and in the public sector. Smaller enterprises, be it because their mortality rates are much higher or because they employ a larger number of women or for other reasons, very seldom give life commitments to their employees. And even in the large firms, it is only the regular work force which benefits from the system. The relatively large numbers of temporary or casual workers are completely excluded. These are officially estimated at some 10 per cent of the total number of employees in the 1960s. Some observers have argued that the published data grossly underestimate their numbers, and that in the early 1960s their share in the labour force could have been almost double the official estimate.[23]

Taking into account the likelihood that most temporary and casual workers are concentrated in large firms, which account for roughly one quarter of total employment, it can be seen that life employment practices are restricted to a rather small segment of the labour force. A very rough estimate for the early 1970s would include in their number the four million or so public employees, the declared number of regular employees in firms with more than 1,000 dependents, or some eight million workers, and perhaps another million workers, or half the labour force employed in the 500–999 scale firms. Together, these three categories would amount to perhaps 40 per cent of all employees, but only one quarter of the labour force. And even these figures may overestimate the extent of life employment since they do not allow for the likelihood that female employees benefit to a much lesser extent from the system than do men.

It is true, however, that even if life employment is not quite as all pervading as it is made out to be, employment is still somewhat more permanent in Japan than elsewhere, as is shown by the low over-all mobility of the labour force. Comparisons between the United States and Japan indicate that average monthly separation rates are a good deal higher in the USA, even when temporary workers are included in the Japanese figures. Between 1960 and 1970, the rate oscillates between 2 and $2\frac{1}{2}$ in Japanese manufacturing and between 4 and $4\frac{1}{2}$ in manufacturing industry in the United States. The United States is, of course, a particularly mobile society. Comparisons with Western Europe show that differences are less marked. In British manufacturing, the 1960–70 average rate was 2·7 (as against Japan's 2·3) and tentative O.E.C.D. estimates for the 1950s or early 1960s for France and Germany show figures of $3\frac{1}{2}$ and $2\frac{1}{2}$ respectively.[24] Similarly, the number of (manual) workers who remain for more than 10 years within the same firm is virtually no higher in Japan's manufacturing sector (27 per cent of the labour force) than in French, German, or Italian industry (where the share in 1966 varied between 24 and 28 per cent).

Limited mobility is in any case not so much due to life commitment on the part of the firm, as to the loss of earnings which moves usually imply. A relatively old survey showed that workers who changed establishments had a 60 per cent chance of receiving a lower wage.[25] Things have clearly changed from the late 1950s, but broadly it is still true that moves are usually associated with more risks than benefits. In fact, mobility seems largely restricted to two categories of workers—the temporary and the young. Temporary workers move from large to small firms and vice versa, depending on cyclical fluctuations; young workers who do not yet forfeit much by trying to find alternative employment usually attempt to move upwards from small to large-scale firms.

Lack of mobility thus seems to be much more a function of the seniority wage system than of permanent employment practices. Here again, one is in the presence of a system which as mentioned earlier, is not universal (even if it is more widespread than life commitment). Regular wage increases as a function of age are a prerogative of government and large firms' employees. Lower down the scale, age-differentials exist, notably for men, but they become progressively less significant. An estimate made for 1960 suggested that perhaps 8 million workers benefited from the system.[26] Applying the same simple hypotheses made in that estimate to the early 1970s, would give a figure of perhaps 16–17 million workers, or roughly one-third of the total labour force (and about half of the wage-earning population). For these workers, earnings do indeed differ according to seniority, with peak wages at the age of 55 being up to three or four times the entrants' wages. In smaller firms, on the other hand, the peak wage is reached much earlier. Wages go up quite steeply until the age of 30 to 35 years, by which time they are double the wages of young entrants, but then remain flat.

It is difficult to know to what extent such a system differs in practical effect from those elsewhere. Comparisons with the United States are, as usual, most developed, but may reveal only the most extreme national differences. On the basis of figures as comparable as possible, they show that the maximum age–wage spread in the United States is up to 2·3 times the entrants' wage (i.e. a spread of 1 to 2·3) in the case of college graduates who become managers, but the spreads are more usually of the order of 1 to 1·5. In Japan, by contrast, they can be from 1 to 4 or 5, depending on initial education levels.[27] The evidence available for Europe is less directly comparable. Figures for manual workers suggest that the differences are quite pronounced, at least for male workers (Table 2.4). But if data were available for all employees they might qualify this impression since British figures

TABLE 2.4

Extent of wage differentials by age

(manual workers)

	TOTAL		MALES		FEMALES	
	AGE	AGE^2	AGE	AGE^2	AGE	AGE^2
Japan[1] (1970)	9·46	−0·11	10·63	−0·13	(2·35)	−0·03
large scale enterprises[2]	12·85	−0·15	11·78	−0·14	6·79	−0·09
small scale enterprises[3]	6·61	−0·08	8·67	−0·10	(1·39)	(−0·02)
France (1966)	5·37	(−0·06)	4·92	−0·06	3·79	−0·04
Germany (1966)	4·65	(−0·05)	4·63	−0·05	3·28	−0·04
Italy (1966)	4·02	−0·04	3·90	−0·04	3·09	−0·03
United Kingdom (1968)	..	..	5·96	0·07	1·36	−0·18

Note: The figures shown are the coefficients obtained for the age and age^2 terms in equations of the form $W = a + bA + cA^2$, where W is an index (average wage = 100) of wages by age classes. Results are not strictly comparable because the age breakdown differs slightly across countries. Wages are measured by annual or weekly earnings for Japan and Britain and gross hourly earnings for the other countries. Figures in brackets are statistically not significant at the 5 per cent confidence level.

　1. Manufacturing only.
　2. With more than 1,000 employees.
　3. With 10 to 99 employees.

Sources: Japan: M.o.L., *Yearbook of Labour Statistics*; France, Germany, and Italy: same as Table 2.3; United Kingdom: *Employment and Productivity Gazette*, May 1969.

suggest that age–wage hierarchies may in fact be quite pronounced in Europe.*

The relative efficiency or inefficiency of these two facets of Japanese labour relations have evoked heated discussions. Without repeating these it perhaps suffices to say that life employment and regular wage increases with age, even if their scope is less wide than commonly thought must facilitate the acceptance of technological progress by workers (since there is no reason to fear redundancy), reinforce the consensus and the cohesion of a group, as well as provide an inbuilt advantage to rapidly expanding firms, which benefit from a higher share of relatively low-paid young workers in their labour force. It is any case difficult to see

* For Britain, coefficients similar to those shown in Table 2.4 for all employees are (for the age term) 8·37 for male and 5.25 for females. The comparable Japanese figures are 11·22 and 4·41.

how employment relations closer to Western patterns, which have been tried in isolated and not always successful cases, could have enhanced Japan's actual economic performance.

But a further alleged economic consequence of the system is to make firms' cost structures highly inflexible since labour inputs can hardly be changed. If one adds to this the relatively large interest rate burden shouldered by Japanese firms, given the very high ratio of borrowed funds to total capital, the whole structure of production costs becomes very inflexible. Through the cycle, the only variable elements would then seem to be material inputs and the rather small amount of dividends.

To some extent these arguments are correct. Interest payments represent a larger fixed burden for all Japanese firms (large and small) than they do in the West. But labour costs are only partly fixed. For one thing, the scope of life employment is, of course, restricted to larger firms. For another, the presence of temporary workers ensures some degree of flexibility. And additional flexibility is provided by changes in overtime work and in one very important component of the wage bill—bonus payments. The latter represent by now roughly one quarter of total wage earnings, and more in larger firms. Since such payments are partly a function of enterprise profits, they can be quite volatile. In the twenty years to 1973 the standard deviation of annual percentage changes in bonuses was nearly twice the size of that of regular wage rises. Thus these various loopholes allow even those firms which work under a life employment system to vary their labour costs to some extent.

But it nevertheless seems that Japanese labour costs are somewhat less flexible than those of other major economies. Fluctuations in unit labour costs in manufacturing (defined as percentage changes in total employee compensation over percentage changes in value added at constant prices) seem to be a good deal more marked in Japan than they are elsewhere; and this suggests that wage bills respond relatively little to output fluctuations.* When the interest rate payments mentioned above are added, it would appear that Japanese firms have to cope with a greater share of fixed items in their total costs than do those of other market

* Over the 1954–72 period, Japan's standard deviation of annual percentage changes in manufacturing unit labour costs is more than double those of France and the United States, one third larger than those of Germany and Britain, and roughly similar to that of Italy (whose figure, is, however, distorted by the two exceptional 1970–1 observations).

economies. Some more direct confirmation for this is provided by a United States–Japanese comparison for nylon production which shows that the fixed element in total costs is 70 per cent in the Japanese case and just over 50 per cent in the American one.[28]

Yet there is still a further practice which provides a supplementary degree of flexibility to Japanese large enterprises— namely sub-contracting. This system combines features of the dualism mentioned earlier with what many consider to be some more permanent characteristics of Japanese labour and social relations. It has, for instance, been argued that the links between parent companies and sub-contractors are but the outcome of '. . . a highly complex and hierarchical social structure within industrial production', which reflects the very special links between master and student or boss and worker in the field of personal relations.[29] Be this as it may, it seems that sub-contracting practices are indeed widespread in Japan and probably more so than elsewhere.* It is true that a comparative study of the British and Japanese automobile industries concluded that in both countries sub-contracting was widely used, with differences largely a matter of degree;[30] but it can be argued that motor-car firms are almost everywhere known for their high reliance on purchased components.

More general indirect evidence, linked to the economy's dualism, suggests that sub-contracting is likely to loom large in Japan. First there is the simultaneous presence of both large and small units within the same industrial branch. It is true that within each industry sets of firms may have their own fields, with smaller enterprises specializing in limited product lines or catering for particular tastes, local markets or exports.[31] Outright competition between large oligopolies and small companies may also be possible in some instances. But there is a strong presumption that vertical relations must also exist; and it is reinforced when wage differentials by scale and life-employment practices in bigger firms are also brought into the picture. Given relatively high internal labour costs, large enterprises clearly have a strong

* In the early 1960s, the E.P.A. put reliance of parent firms on sub-contractors (measured in terms of working hours) at some 50 per cent in the automobile and machinery sectors (*ESJ* (*1960–1961*), pp. 278–9), while a 1966 survey showed that nearly 55 per cent of all small enterprises sub-contracted to larger corporations, with ratios of up to 80 per cent in textiles, metal processing and machinery (cited in N. Tatsumi, 'Small–Medium Enterprises and Big Corporations', in Yamanaka (ed.), *Small Business*, p. 83).

incentive to commission work outside, so as to benefit from the much lower wage levels of smaller firms; and given a policy of ensuring virtually permanent employment to the regular labour force, whatever the conditions of the market, it is almost indispensable for the larger concerns to have a safety valve, in the form of sub-contractors to whom the impact of cyclical fluctuations can be at least partially transferred. The existence of a whole range of differentials spreads the phenomenon, creating an intricate network of parent firms at the top, followed by major sub-contractors who sub-contract to smaller firms who, in their turn, sub-contract further down the scale, until 'putting out' forms of work reach one- or two-man establishments.[32]

The resilience of differentials

Several of the features of Japan's labour market which have just been discussed seem to reflect particular characteristics of the country's economy and society which may not change very rapidly. But this need not be generally true of 'dualism' which is normally associated with a particular phase of economic development, namely the transition from an overwhelmingly agrarian to a largely industrial structure.

It is usually expected that, with the spread of the 'modern' sector and of commercial relations, capital and labour markets will be unified and sectoral productivity and income levels will tend towards greater equality.[33] The best evidence for the transitory nature of dualism is to be found in the general progress and present-day structure of the more developed Western European economies for which even very broad definitions of dualism no longer seem appropriate. But determining the 'turning point' after which economic growth begins to erode rather than reinforce dualism is no easy matter. It is generally agreed that in Japan the 1920s saw the appearance of sizeable differentials as heavy industry and modern technology were imported from abroad. It might, conversely, have been expected that the consolidation of the industrial structure, combined with extremely rapid growth and the achievement of the third highest GNP in the world, would gradually have eliminated dualism in the post-war period.

To some extent this seems to have happened. The Japan of the early 1970s may seem fairly 'dual' by the standards of other developed countries; the Japan of the early 1950s was even more so. But the changes between these two dates seem relatively small when compared with the momentum of economic growth. For a part of the period (the 1950s) dualism was actually reinforced. Differences in capital–labour ratios, productivity and wages between large and small firms, as well as regional income differentials, increased. Indeed, in the 1950s wage differentials may have reached an all-time peak. They were certainly greater than those recorded in 1909, 1914, and 1932, the only pre-war years for which data are available.[34] And regional differentials were apparently no smaller than in the earlier part of the century.[35] It was in the 1950s that smaller enterprises, and notably sub-contractors, were made to bear the heaviest impact of cyclical fluctuations, being starved of funds during monetary squeezes and being forced to accept price cuts, delayed payments, and reduced orders from parent companies in recessions.

To some extent these developments stemmed from the strategies which were being followed, as well as from the speed of growth itself. Since the government had given priority to heavy industry and to export competitiveness, the 'traditional' sector was neglected and could survive only thanks to below-average labour costs. A similar mechanism was at work at the regional level, with very rapid expansion in already industrialized areas enhancing external economies and increasing the attraction of the richer regions.

Simulations made on an econometric model of Japan's dual structure confirm that rapid growth may have reinforced differentials. The threshold values obtained for a period going from the mid-1950s to the mid-1960s show that regional income disparities could worsen when GNP grew by more than $7\frac{1}{2}$ per cent per annum while wage differentials related to size of firm widened with growth rates above 13 per cent per annum.[36] Even allowing for the simplifying assumptions inevitable in such models, the results suggest that, in the absence of corrective policy action, market forces could not be trusted to reduce Japan's dualism in a situation of labour abundance and very buoyant growth.

Reductions of differentials had to wait for the 1960s. It was in that decade that a number of the features that had been responsible for the existence and reinforcement of the dual structure in the 1950s—notably the role of the government, restricted access to the capital market, and, of course, a very elastic labour supply—lost some of their force. The labour market tightened progressively with demand for labour, fuelled by output growth, increasing

very rapidly but labour supply to industry showing no acceleration. By 1967, the number of vacancies had outstripped that of job
seekers. At the same time as the labour market was tightening, the
capital market open to smaller firms expanded.* The attitude of
'City banks' changed, with the proportion of intra-*zaibatsu* loans
falling and that of the more lucrative loans to smaller firms
rising.[37] Even the traditional curtailment of finance to smaller
enterprises in periods of policy restraint was actually reversed
during the 1969–70 monetary tightening. And some narrowing of
the interest rate gap, mentioned above, also occurred.[38]

The institutional framework which had, in many ways, helped
to perpetuate dualism in the 1950s also gradually changed. The
government's earlier emphasis on large-scale operations gave way
to a recognition that discrimination against small business (which
accounted for over 50 per cent of total exports throughout the
1950s and still for roughly one-fifth in 1970) could not continue
for ever. New policies and laws led to an expansion of government
financing of small firms and improved access for them to the
capital market. While trade unions remained essentially restricted
to large firms, the position of workers in smaller establishments
was reinforced by the slow, but none the less noticeable, development of national wage offensives in which the country-wide
labour federations began to play a gradually more important role.

The combined effects of a dwindling labour surplus, of diminishing capital market imperfections and government discrimination, and of a more uniform trade union push might have been
expected to produce some reduction in the number of small
businesses, a general increase in the scale of operations, and a
closing of the various gaps between firms. Indeed, a good deal of
the Japanese literature on dualism hailed the early 1960s as the
turning point in Japan's economic development, after which
labour supply would no longer be unlimited and dualism would
gradually disappear.[39]

To some extent these predictions were realized. Throughout
the 1960s the financial position of smaller firms improved and
they were able to survive cyclical fluctuations much better than
in the previous decade. Easier access to funds also meant that

* Thus, the proportion of loans and discounts extended by all banks to
smaller firms, which had been falling from some 36 per cent in 1953–5 to 26 per
cent ten years later, rose again, by roughly 5 per cent in the period 1965–73
(changes in the coverage of small firms between 1964 and 1965 and, again, in
October 1973, impair the direct comparability of the data).

investment could be stepped up and, especially in the later 1960s, the differential between capital–labour ratios lessened sharply. Regional differentials declined from their peak of the early 1960s to a level in 1969–70 not far above that recorded in the mid-1950s. But in other respects the differential structure proved to be very resilient. Both the proportion of workers employed in, and the share of (current price) output produced by, smaller manufacturing enterprises (10 to 99 employees), declined by only 5 per cent in the 15 or 20 years after 1955, though in real terms the share of shipments accounted for by small business declined to a greater extent, as price increases were much more rapid among smaller than among larger firms. Even more surprisingly, in view of a tightening labour market and the increased capital-intensity of production in smaller firms, neither wage nor productivity differentials disappeared. The former have shown some convergence since the 1958 recession but remain, as was seen earlier, very large by international standards. The latter continued to diverge in real terms, though at a slower rate than in the second half of the 1950s.*

The movement of wage differentials is particularly difficult to understand. They closed very rapidly in the years immediately following their 1958 peak and were at their lowest in the next cyclically comparable year of 1965, in contrast to previous experience when recessions had usually seen widenings (Fig. 3). The closing was not confined to differentials by scale, but was paralleled by similar movements in age, sex, and industrial differentials.[40] But the movement came to a stop in 1965. By 1972, again a year cyclically comparable with 1958 and 1965, wage differentials by scale were no smaller than seven years earlier, and on an hourly basis were a good deal wider—somehow as if the differentials of 1965 had been the narrowest which the economy could have borne.

Changes in the composition of the labour force of different sized establishments are unable to shed much light on this. It is true that, relative to large firms (with more than 1,000 employees), small enterprises (with 10 to 99 employees) shifted their employment structure towards less qualified workers, as well as towards

* Estimates of price deflators by scale of establishment suggest that while the nominal productivity gap (between establishments with 10 to 299 and with more than 300 workers) closed by over 20 per cent between 1956 and 1970, it opened by nearly the same amount in real terms; E.P.A., *ESJ* (*1969–1970*), p. 181.

more women and older workers.* But the effect of these structural changes was small. A rough calculation (a standardization of wages on the basis of the 1965 employment structure) suggests that they can account for the small widening of the differential between these two sets of firms from 1965 to 1972. Without them this differential would simply have remained stable; it would not have narrowed.

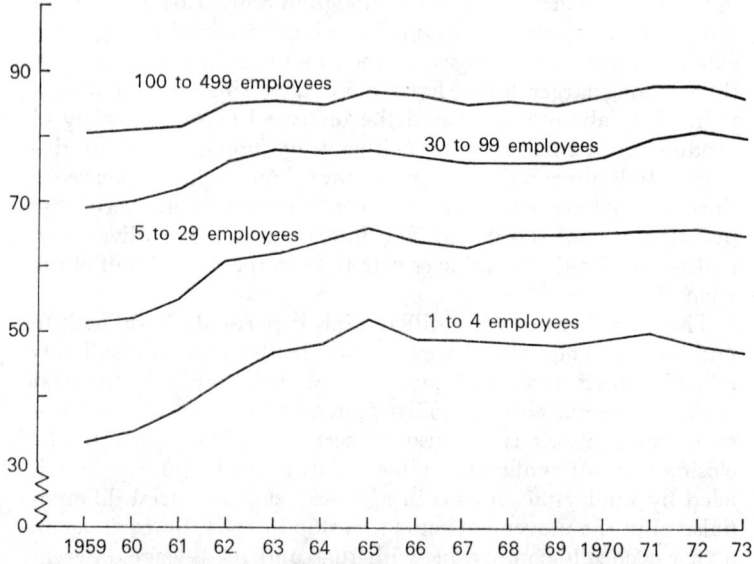

FIG. 3. *Wage differentials by size of establishment* (Total cash earnings per regular employee; indices, establishments with more than 500 employees = 100)

Source: M.o.L., *Yearbook of Labour Statistics.*

The narrowing of wage differentials which had taken place until 1965 had been largely confined to younger workers and it is for them that differentials widened again in the subsequent years. For older workers, some movement towards wage equalization was taking place all the time, but at a very slow pace. The virtual equalization of young entrants' wages in the mid-1960s made

---

* A growing share of both older and less qualified workers in the labour force may well explain the continuing increase in productivity gaps noted above, despite the rising capital intensity of small firms.

economic sense. Given the prevalence of a much stronger wage-by-seniority system in larger firms, it was only through equally high, if not higher, initial payments that younger workers could have been enticed into smaller enterprises in a market in which their supply was relatively scarce. But the same is as true, if not more so, of the latter half of the 1960s. Demand for younger workers, whether recent school-leavers or not, was three to four times higher than supply in 1972 (and even more in 1969 or 1970), well above the 1965 demand–supply imbalance.

It is, indeed, difficult to find a plausible explanation for the behaviour of young workers' wage differentials over the 1960s. It could be argued that, in a system in which wages are broadly a function of age, demand for younger (and therefore cheaper) workers was particularly strong, but that this strong demand could not be translated into very large wage increases without either leading to a breakdown of within-firm wage differentials— with the ensuing dangers of dissatisfaction among established workers, trade union action, etc.—or entailing similar wage rises for all and a disproportionate increase in the wage bill. Smaller firms, for a time, were able to erode the absolute advantage of larger firms in recruiting young workers, but they achieved this by compressing their internal wage hierarchy. Larger firms, faced in the mid-1960s with a sudden weakening in their power to employ new entrants, stepped up their recruitment effort by following a similar policy. It is possible that smaller enterprises were then unable to continue reducing their wage–age differentials at the same speed and could not pass through to all their workers the wage rises which large enterprises had been able to grant.

Some indirect evidence of this is the speed of compression of wage differentials by age (as measured by the coefficient of variation) for firms of different size. In the 10–99 employees category, the coefficient of variation declined very rapidly (from 31 per cent to 19 per cent) between 1958 and 1965, but only relatively slowly (to 14 per cent) in the next seven years. For larger firms (more than 1,000 employees), the pattern was exactly opposite—a small decline from 1958 to 1965 (46 to 43 per cent), but a more rapid one between 1965 and 1972 (43 to 31 per cent). No firmer quantifiable evidence can be provided for this very tentative explanation; and if the explanation is correct, there still remains the questions why a particular category of firms should at some point

find further compression of age–wage differentials impossible, and
for how long such an inhibition remains in force.

A summary

Though not as exceptional as it has seemed to many observers,
Japan's economic structure presents some paradoxes. On the one
hand, the country in the early 1970s could boast of the third
largest GNP in the world, one of the highest ratios of industrial to
total output, and within that industrial output, a very high share
for heavy industry, and some of the most efficient and productive
plants, in particular lines of activity to be found anywhere (shipbuilding, cars, some electronic products). But, on the other hand,
it also presented a picture of a somewhat greater share of its
industrial labour force in very small establishments than in most
other industrialized countries, of larger wage and productivity
gaps between firms of different sizes, of a higher share of self-
employed and unpaid family workers in the non-agricultural
labour force, and of a stronger seniority wage system than in
practically any other comparable developed market economy.

Japan's large firms, the only ones which have attracted attention abroad, present some rather special features. They are probably among the earliest examples of conglomeration in the world,
their competitive spirit, on which more in Chapter 4 below, has
few parallels in the West, and their employment and wage practices seem to be unique. For the industrial relations specialist they
must be a fascinating field of study. For the economist it is arguable that the persistence of wage and productivity differentials
between these large concerns and the scores of smaller firms raises
more interesting questions. The presence of small firms is not, *per
se*, difficult to explain. Many good reasons can be advanced for
their continuing existence in all developed countries, despite the
growing weight of oligopolies or monopolies. But what is surprising about Japan's experience is that, despite exceptionally rapid
growth, differentials between small and large firms remained
substantial.

The economic and institutional characteristics looked at above
throw a good deal of light on Japan's experience, but some broader
considerations may also be helpful. The generally accepted argument that dualism is but a transitory stage in a country's economic
development reflects the historical record of today's mature economies. In these economies, past rates of capital accumulation,

usually combined with forms of technical progress suited to the country's factor endowments, were sufficiently rapid in the modern sector to provide employment opportunities rising at least in line with the growth of the labour force. But the continuation, or indeed aggravation, of dualism in many of today's semi-developed economies (Italy, Yugoslavia, or Ireland may be examples in the European context), despite large government efforts to overcome the problem, suggests that such a path may not be so easy to find nowadays. The more frequent presence of oligopolies or monopolies, combined with imported and labour-saving technical progress, implies that job-creation in the modern sector may be insufficient to make inroads in the reserve army of the un- or under-employed. At the same time, 'demonstration effects' in consumption patterns lower the income elasticity of demand for the products of the traditional sector, even below what it might otherwise have been. As a consequence, the developed sector continues to grow in terms of output, but not to anything like the same extent in terms of employment, while the backward sector stagnates. If anything, differentials widen.[41]

Japan's experience does not seem to fit either of the two models. Dualism did not disappear, despite rapid industrialization; but neither was it reinforced, despite the existence of powerful oligopolies, the widespread use of foreign techniques, the adoption of many foreign consumption habits, and even the active encouragement to big business provided by the government. Both sectors in fact managed to grow at remarkable and roughly similar speeds. The modern sector's oligopolies turned out to be highly dynamic and competitive and, despite labour-saving technical progress, their investment and output grew rapidly enough for employment also to rise quite fast. Among smaller firms, the widespread use of second-hand machinery and the availability of cheap and abundant labour ensured a fairly high degree of efficiency. This is confirmed by econometric estimates of technical progress among smaller firms which show that the latter were technical innovators in their own right.[42] Combined with very swift adaptability to changes in demand ('A plant which had been producing toys yesterday, starts to manufacture automobile parts today'[43]), this meant that smaller firms were able to expand roughly *pari passu* with the large-scale enterprises.

More generally, the buoyant growth of Japan's 'traditional' sector may owe something to two characteristics on the demand side of its market not always shared by today's developing economies—the widespread existence of sub-contracting and some particular features of consumer behaviour. The close contacts between large and small enterprises and the obvious self-interest which the former had in keeping the latter alive over the longer run meant that growth in the modern sector was transmitted fairly rapidly to the backward one. Mortality rates among smaller firms may have been high during recessions, but recessions were short-lived and during the long prosperity phases sub-contractors were 'pulled along' by their parent companies.[44] For those firms which produced more for traditional needs and were less touched by the growth of the modern sector, demand was still forthcoming, partly because of the speed of income growth, and partly because social and cultural patterns allowed only a partial adoption of Western consumption habits.[45] Neither declining demand nor the introduction of mass production techniques wiped out traditional handicrafts, services, or small-scale industries.

Small business thus managed to prosper, contrary perhaps to expectations. And indeed, if large differentials characterize many facets of the activity of big, medium, and small enterprises, this is hardly so in the field of profitability. Estimates of the rate of return on total fixed assets show that profit rates are fairly similar for most types of firms, with little change in the small differentials over time and, if anything, an inverse relation to scale.[46] To some extent such findings are influenced by the accounting procedures of small unincorporated firms, in which returns to capital and to labour are grouped together as profits. But to a much greater extent they are, of course, a function of wage differentials. Without these, many of Japan's smaller firms would long since have disappeared.

As argued earlier, the scope for small business should gradually diminish as growth continues. Some of the factors making for changes in the 'differential' structure have already been outlined. The yen's revaluation is likely to be one further important influence reducing the weight of small-scale and relatively labour-intensive production. But more generally it could be argued that the present state of Japanese dualism, as typified by the stabilization of over-all wage differentials by size of firm for a number of years, reflects the country's trade union set-up, business structure, and labour market conditions. The eventual disappearance of 'dualism' can be expected, but only when outflows of labour from agriculture (as well as the potential outflow from several over-manned, and frequently low-pay, service branches) are reduced to a trickle and/or trade unionism spreads to the whole industrial labour force. In other words, some narrowing of wage differentials came as Japan passed the (loosely defined) stage of unlimited supplies of labour—perhaps in the early 1960s. The eventual closing of the gap will come only when the present stage of 'limited', but not yet 'fixed', supplies comes to an end.

NOTES

1. W. W. Lockwood, *The Economic Development of Japan*, Princeton 1968, p. 81; Lockwood uses this definition to describe 1937 Japan but it can be applied equally aptly to the 1953 economy which in many ways (e.g. output and employment structure or level of GNP), was very similar to that of 1937.

2. Economic Planning Board, *ESJ (1954–1955)*, p. 69.

3. Comparative figures for several countries for 1954–5 and 1968–9 are shown in O.E.C.D., *ESJ, 1972*, pp. 54–5.

4. For some interpretations see J. C. H. Fei and G. Ranis, *Development of the Labor Surplus Economy: Theory and Policy*, Homewood, Ill. 1964; D. W. Jorgenson, 'Testing Alternative Theories of the Development of a Dual Economy', in I. Adelman and E. Thorbecke (eds.), *The Theory and Design of Economic Development*, Baltimore 1966, and R. Minami, *The Turning Point in Economic Development: Japan's Experience*, Tokyo 1973.

5. For a survey of regional policies see A. Shimokobe and N. Nishifuji, 'The Planning and Policies of Regional Development—The Methodology in Japan', in *Economic Planning and Macro Economic Policy* (Proceedings of a Conference held by the J.E.R.C.), Tokyo 1970.

6. M. Shinohara, *Structural Changes in Japan's Economic Development*, Tokyo 1970, pp. 436–7.

7. For a comprehensive survey of Japanese writings on the problems of smaller enterprises see M. Shinohara, 'A Survey of the Japanese Literature on Small Industry', in B. F. Hoselitz (ed.), *The Role of Small Industry in the Process of Economic Growth*, The Hague 1968.

8. A similar conclusion is reached in a much fuller investigation of this issue, based on data for the early 1960s, by J. P. Nioche, *Taille des établissements industriels dans sept pays développés*, Collections de l'INSEE, Série E, 1969.

9. K. Taira, 'Wage Differentials in Developing Countries: A Survey of Findings', *International Labour Review*, March 1966, p. 285.

10. T. Blumenthal, 'The Effect of Socio-Economic Factors on Wage Differentials in Japanese Manufacturing Industries', *Riron Keizai Gaku (The Economic Studies Quarterly)*, September 1966; K. Odaka, 'On Employment and Wage-differential Structure in Japan: A Survey', *HJE*, June 1967. For a very complete survey of the issue of wage differentials in Japan see Suzanne H. Paine, 'Wage Differentials in the Japanese Manufacturing Sector', *Oxford Economic Papers*, July 1971.

11. Shinohara, 'A Survey of the Japanese Literature', p. 41; T. Mizuno,

'Japan's Small Business and Labor', in T. Yamanaka (ed.), *Small Business in Japan's Economic Progress*, Tokyo 1971, pp. 60–2.

12. K. Ohkawa, *Differential Structure and Agriculture: Essays on Dualistic Growth*, Tokyo 1972, p. 61.

13. K. Taira, *Economic Development and the Labor Market in Japan*, New York 1970.

14. K. Miyazawa, 'The Dual Structure of the Japanese Economy and its Growth Pattern', *DE*, June 1964, pp. 150–1.

15. Shinohara, *Structural Changes*, pp. 321–39.

16. H. Kawaguchi, 'The "Dual Structure" of Finance in Post-war Japan', *DE*, June 1967, p. 328.

17. Odaka, 'On Employment and Wage-differential Structure', p. 61.

18. T. Watanabe ('Improvements of Labor Quality and Economic Growth—Japan's Postwar Experience', *EDCC*, October 1972, p. 37) gives figures showing that the average number of years of schooling in Japan in 1960 was second only to that of the United States.

19. For a complete survey of Japanese trade unions, see S. B. Levine, 'Labor Markets and Collective Bargaining in Japan', in Lockwood (ed.), *The State and Economic Enterprise*.

20. Taira, *Economic Development*, p. 168.

21. K. Kobayashi, 'The Employment and Wage System in Postwar Japan', *DE*, June 1969, pp. 190–3.

22. The importance of trade unions (and of the lack of a legal minimum wage) in establishing and perpetuating wage differentials has been stressed by T. Watanabe, 'Economic Aspects of Dualism in the Industrial Development of Japan', *EDCC*, April 1965, pp. 305–6, and by Taira, *Economic Development*, Ch. 7.

23. Taira, *Economic Development*, p. 181.

24. O.E.C.D., *Wages and Labour Mobility*, 1965, pp. 50–1.

25. E.P.A., *ESJ (1959–1960)*, p. 295.

26. Levine, 'Labor Markets and Collective Bargaining', p. 661.

27. R. M. Marsh and H. Mannari, 'A New look at "Lifetime Commitment" in Japanese Industry', *EDCC*, July 1972, pp. 614–15.

28. J. C. Abegglen and W. V. Rapp, 'Japanese Managerial Behaviour and "Excessive Competition"', *DE*, December 1970, p. 431. This article assumes that all Japanese labour costs are fixed. The Bank of Japan estimates, on the other hand, that only some 50 per cent of wage costs represent a fixed element. But even if this were the case, the share of fixed costs would still be higher in Japan in the particular example chosen.

29. B. F. Hoselitz, 'Small Industry in Underdeveloped Countries', *Journal of Economic History*, December 1959, pp. 606–7.

30. M. Toike, 'Recent Changes in the Subcontracting System of the Japanese Motor Industry: A Comparison with the British Model', *HJE*, February 1967, pp. 59–60.

31. Shinohara, 'A Survey of the Japanese Literature', pp. 65–6; Tatsumi, 'Small-Medium Enterprises', pp. 74–8.

32. This is vividly described in S. Broadbridge, *Industrial Dualism in Japan*, London 1966, Ch. 4.

33. This has been confirmed by an intercountry analysis of regional dualism: '. . . increasing regional inequality is generated during the early

development stages, while mature growth has produced regional convergence or a reduction in differentials.' (J. G. Williamson, 'Regional Inequality and the Process of National Development: A Description of the Pattern', *EDCC*, July 1965, p. 44.)

34. Taira, *Economic Development*, pp. 175–6.

35. Shinohara, *Structural Changes*, pp. 433–5.

36. T. Fukuchi and M. Nobokuni, 'An Econometric Analysis of National Growth and Regional Income Inequality', *International Economic Review*, February 1970, pp. 99–100; T. Fukuchi and N. Oguchi, 'The Trend of the Dual Structure and the Backwash Effect in Japan', *Riron Keizai Gaku (The Economic Studies Quarterly)*, August 1972, p. 68.

37. E.P.A., *ESJ (1969–1970)*, p. 197.

38. E.P.A., *ESJ (1968–1969)*, p. 184.

39. See, for instance, Shinohara, *Structural Changes*, Ch. 8; Ohkawa, *Differential Structure*, Parts I and II; Minami, *The Turning Point*.

40. T. Blumenthal, 'Scarcity of Labor and Wage Differentials in the Japanese Economy, 1958–64', *EDCC*, October 1968, pp. 22–4.

41. These points are developed more fully in L. Spaventa, 'Dualism in Economic Growth', *Banca Nazionale del Lavoro Quarterly Review*, December 1959.

42. M. A. Abe, 'The Growth Path of Firms and the Development Process of the Economy: The Case of Japan', *DE*, June 1972, pp. 202–3.

43. E.P.A., *ESJ (1960–1961)*, p. 39.

44. This thesis is also developed by C. Sautter, *Japon—le prix de la puissance*, Paris 1973, p. 106.

45. This point is taken up in Chapter 4 below.

46. See, for instance, Shinohara, 'A Survey of the Japanese Literature', pp. 48–9; Y. Kobayashi, 'Analyses of Small Business Management', in Yamanaka (ed.), *Small Business*, pp. 112–14; E.P.A., *ESJ (1969–1970)*, p. 31.

CHAPTER 3

PERFORMANCE

THE two preceding chapters have given a brief summary of post-war growth and structural change. The present section attempts to provide a preliminary assessment of the economy's performance over the last twenty years. Any such assessment is, of necessity, highly subjective, as is the choice of criteria by which 'performance' can be evaluated. Judgements based on theoretical models of 'perfect' resource allocation (whatever this may mean), are impossible and would be irrelevant. Use of Marxian rather than neo-classical standards would clearly be more appropriate, but is unlikely to be very illuminating. Japan has been a highly capitalist economy throughout the period; its goals have been determined by a small élite in which the business world has played a preponderant role; the economic surplus created by labour was privately appropriated, and social justice or redistribution of income and power, let alone the creation of a less alienated society, have hardly figured among the policy targets of successive Japanese governments. From the standpoint of an economic theory assuming Marxian policy goals, there is probably little that can be learned from Japan's experience. Yet if judged by the standards of contemporary market economies, that experience provides an interesting story of both successes and failures. The set of (usually partially incompatible) aims which most capitalist economies have set for themselves throughout the post-war period will, therefore, be adopted here as a 'standard of reference'.

Briefly stated, these aims are rapid and stable growth, full employment, balance of payments equilibrium and price stability. Naturally, such aims can only be understood in relative terms, depending on a country's economic structure and past history. Thus 'balance of payments equilibrium' should not mean the same thing for a mature, advanced economy and for the less developed Japan of the 1950s, while the price stability (or, rather, 'moderate' inflation) target can only be quantified in relation to past trends. The list of aims is not exhaustive, and the less growth-minded world of the 1970s may well want to add income redistribution or protection of the environment to the traditional goals; but for the 1950s and 1960s, the latter seem to correspond fairly closely to the wishes and recommendations expressed in most industrial countries by policy-makers and advisers alike.[1]

On a superficial reading, Japan has been remarkably successful in fulfilling these various aims in the twenty years or so to 1973. The economy grew very rapidly and enjoyed almost continuous full employment of labour, the yen became one of the strongest currencies in the world and the rate of price inflation, when looked at in conjunction with the speed of real growth, was hardly alarming. A more careful analysis, however, might show a less rosy picture, especially if the more recent, and less favourable, developments of inflation, growth and external payments are seen not merely as the results of some special exogenous factors but also as partial consequences of some of the imbalances and disequilibria created in the two preceding decades. *Stable* growth, one of the five aims set out above, was hardly achieved in Japan, and a number of the country's present-day difficulties could well be traced to an 'unbalanced' process of economic development over the last twenty years.

The 'success stories'

As regards rapid growth, full employment, and balance of payments equilibrium, Japan's past record is clearly one of unmitigated success with few, if any, parallels elsewhere. The first chapter has already briefly looked at Japan's unparallelled growth performance. Growth is not, of course, usually considered an aim *per se*[2] and can only be properly assessed in terms of its effects on people's living standards. It is not the intention to provide here a detailed survey of the changes and improvements in Japanese consumption patterns over the last twenty years. But looking only at broad macro-economic variables, the country's achievements in raising consumption standards seems as remarkable as its overall growth.

Between 1953 and 1972, *per capita* total output increased by $8\frac{1}{2}$ per cent a year and, despite a massive and rising investment effort, private consumption per head (probably the most appropriate national accounting indicator of living standards), rose fivefold, or by nearly $7\frac{1}{2}$ per cent per annum. Recently, preliminary estimates have become available of Japan's Net National

Welfare (NNW), obtained by adjusting conventional GNP data for pollution and urbanization costs, benefits from social overhead capital, leisure or non-market activities, etc.[3] Between FYs 1955 and 1970, NNW rose more slowly than GNP but the 6 per cent *per capita* annual growth rate, tentatively estimated, remains an impressive figure.

Equally remarkable, perhaps, is the apparent record of virtual full employment achieved throughout most of the period. In the 1950s, unemployment was of the order of 2 per cent of the labour force. In the 1960s and early 1970s, this rate fell to barely 1–1·5 per cent and seemed little affected by cyclical fluctuations of output. As mentioned earlier, Japan's unemployment rate is influenced by both statistical and economic factors which may somewhat exaggerate the extent and stability of 'full employment'. Thus the definition of the unemployed may seem excessively restrictive, since one hour's work a week is sufficient for a person to be considered employed. Yet attempts made by the U.S. Department of Labor to standardize various countries' unemployment rates to United States concepts (which are themselves very close to standardized international definitions), show that Japan's figures need hardly any net adjustment. For the 1960s as a whole, Japan's average unemployment rate is 1·3 per cent whether one follows national or United States definitions. Standardized unemployment rates on the latter basis for other major countries over the same period are: 1·5 per cent for France, 1·0 per cent for Germany, 3·4 per cent for Italy, 1·9 per cent for the United Kingdom, 4·8 per cent for the United States and, according to a tentative estimate, 1·3 per cent (in 1962–3) for the Soviet Union.[4]

More important are the economic problems of defining unemployment in a country in which small unincorporated enterprises and agriculture still account for a relatively large percentage of the labour force. It is clear that the apparent inelasticity of unemployment in relation to cyclical fluctuations in output reflects the labour absorption/release role played by these sectors during downswings and upswings. This is confirmed by the anti-cyclical movements in the number of self-employed and unpaid family workers and in employment in agriculture and commerce; all tend to rise in recessions, while female participation rates follow the opposite course.[5] But such phenomena are not unknown in other countries in which, in addition, a migrant foreign labour force has at times played a similar cushioning role; and though they qualify, to some extent, any direct international comparison, it does not seem that they can fundamentally detract from the economy's performance. Underemployment in a relatively low-paid branch or firm is clearly less preferable than full employment in, say, manufacturing; but it is, surely, a good deal more desirable than the waste of resources combined with the social stigma and psychological stresses inherent in open unemployment.

Assessments of Japan's balance of payments record are apt to focus on post-1971 developments. In fact, the picture is more mixed. In the first half of the 1950s, Japan was still heavily dependent on United States help in balancing its foreign accounts; throughout the period under review it relied on a number of controls, regulations and trade-promotion measures to protect the yen; until the mid-1960s at least, its gold and foreign exchange reserves were low in relation both to imports and to levels of reserves in other countries. On a few occasions (1957, 1961, 1963–4), severely restrictive policies and subsequent recessions were made inevitable by the appearance of large current-account deficits. More generally, the frequent occurrence of the term 'balance of payments ceiling' in the literature on Japanese economic history and policy suggests that the country was facing continuous difficulties in this field.

And yet, looking at the period as a whole, equally striking features are the rapid falls in the weight of United States military expenditure through the 1950s,* the progress in liberalization of trade and capital movements† and the noticeable strengthening of the trade and current balances (Table 3.1). More fundamentally, and barring the three or four crisis years mentioned above, both the current and the basic balances were in rough equilibrium between 1954 and 1965. Though growth may have been slowed down in a few years because of the balance of payments situation, the 'ceiling' was at most times a fairly high one, or Japan would not have been able to achieve the longer-run

* 'Special procurement expenditure' (mainly payments for goods and services provided to American forces stationed in Japan) fell, as a percentage of total current receipts, from a 37 per cent peak in 1952–3 to 11 per cent in 1959–60.

† The liberalizaation of capital controls applied mainly to outward movements. Inward flows, despite strong pressures from United States business, are still (rightly and understandably) subject to a number of restrictions. Japan has been a good deal more successful than Western Europe in protecting itself from the onslaughts of multinational corporations.

growth record that it did. Then in the late 1960s the country's external position strengthened spectacularly. Substantial surpluses were recorded on the trade, current, and basic balances; short- and long-term foreign assets were accumulated and the trend towards improvement actually accelerated until the two successive revaluations of 1971 and 1973.

TABLE 3.1

Balance of payments trends—1950 to 1973

(annual averages; U.S. $ millions)

	1950–3	1954–7	1958–61	1962–4	1965–70	1971–3
Trade balance	−362	−253	110	204	2,588	6,815
Invisibles, net	568	133	−164	−640	−1,469	−2,720
Current balance	206	−120	−54	−436	1,119	4,095
Long-term capital, net	−68	16	−46	249	−670	−5,106
Basic balance	138	−104	−99	−188	519	−1,011
Change in official reserves	..	−75	241	171	400	2,616

Note: The choice of initial and terminal years ensures that each period roughly covers a full cycle (as shown in Fig. 1 above) from trough to peak.

Sources: M.o.F., *Zaiseniū Tōkei Geppō* (*Monthly Report on Financial Statistics*), June 1973 (for pre-1965 data); B.o.J., *Balance of Payments Monthly*.

In the early 1950s Japan's balance of payments seemed destined to be in permanent deficit; by the early 1970s it had swung full circle and was, for a period, in 'fundamental disequilibrium', i.e. ready for a parity change to correct a surplus. But it can be argued that between these two dates, and ignoring some of the sudden year-to-year changes, the development of the balance of payments kept pace with that of the economy as a whole. The Japan of the mid-1950s was still, as seen earlier, an economy in a transition phase for which balance or small deficits on current account were probably the most suitable accompaniment. The Japan of the early 1970s had joined the small group of highly industrialized economies for which current account surpluses and net transfers of resources abroad were clearly appropriate. The country's regional balance of payments reflects these changes fairly faithfully with surpluses *vis-à-vis* the developing world growing through time and the current account with developed countries passing from deficit in the 1950s to surplus in the late 1960s.[6] Evidence for the relative stability of Japan's balance of payments is also provided by the resilience of the 1 U.S. $= 360 yen exchange rate, which until 1970 witnessed no major crisis. In other words, Japan's balance of payments position between 1955 and 1970 could be broadly defined as one of 'fundamental equilibrium'—in keeping with the country's degree of development as well as with its growth aim.[7]

Inflation

Success in stabilizing prices may seem somewhat less obvious than that in achieving longer-run growth or balance of payments equilibrium. The twenty years or so to the end of 1972 witnessed wholesale-price stability but fairly rapid rises in consumer prices (see Table 3.2). And in 1973–4, inflation has been almost

TABLE 3.2

Price trends—1953 to 1972

(average annual percentage changes)

	GDP DEFLATOR	WHOLESALE PRICES (W.P.)[1]	CONSUMER PRICES (C.P.)	1972 C.P./W.P (INDEX, 1953 = 100)
Japan	4·5	0·2	4·3	212·0
France	4·7	3·0	4·3	127·7
Germany	3·4	1·0[2]	2·6	134·3
Italy	3·9	1·5	3·4	141·3
United Kingdom	4·2	2·8	4·0	124·9
United States	2·7	1·7	2·5	112·9

1. Industrial (or manufactured) commodities.
2. Producers' prices; roughly adjusted for the end-1967 changes in indirect taxation.

Sources: E.P.A., *National Income Statistics;* O.E.C.D., *National Accounts of O.E.C.D. Countries;* B.o.J., *Wholesale Price Indices Annual* and *Economic Statistics Annual;* various national statistical yearbooks and statistical bulletins.

explosive, with annual price increases of 20 or 30 per cent—well above those being recorded in other developed economies. Yet, looking at earlier trends, and ignoring for the moment the recent upsurge in prices, Japan's inflationary record seems hardly disquieting by either pre-war or present-day standards. Between the end of the last century and of World War II, consumer and wholesale prices more than doubled, with annual price rises averaging 2–2½ per cent.

More importantly, Japan's performance is quite impressive when seen in an international perspective, especially once it is remembered that the growth of real output was so much more rapid than elsewhere. Consumer price increases of the order of 4–4·5 per cent per annum were not much out of step with inflation rates in other major countries, while the almost complete stability of wholesale prices over a period of twenty years is not only remarkable, but probably unparalleled in post-war market economies. Equally striking are the very divergent movements displayed by these two price indices over time. Elsewhere too, the rise in wholesale prices has tended to lag behind that of consumer prices, but nowhere has the gap been as conspicuous as in Japan.

This divergence largely reflects the already mentioned 'dual' characteristics of the economy. Commodities which enter the wholesale price index are overwhelmingly produced in large-scale enterprises in which productivity growth has been extremely rapid. Conversely, changes in the cost of living reflect the relatively slow productivity growth recorded by small-scale firms (in industry and agriculture), which cater to a much larger extent for the consumer market.* In addition, they are also influenced, as elsewhere, by developments in the services sector where prices follow money wages much more closely.

Macro-economic explanations of past inflationary pressures in terms of cost-push and demand-pull have been put forward in the literature. It has been argued, for instance, that profit- and wage-push have kept wholesale prices from falling while demand-pull, in the face of labour shortages, has led to rising consumer prices.[8] More broadly, wage and price determination in the economy as a whole have been explained by labour market imbalances, and fairly good fits have been obtained for traditional 'Phillips curves'—better, in fact, that in many comparable attempts made for European economies.[9]

Yet most of these attempts at explanation tend to miss the more 'structural' elements in Japan's price experience. A much better understanding of price movements, at least until the late

---

* Enterprises whose capital assets were valued at 50 million yen or more produced in 1970 63 per cent of the commodities entering the wholesale price index but only 23 per cent of the items entering the consumer price index. A rough reconciliation between data on size of firms by capital assets (provided by the M.o.F.), and by employment (published by the M.I.T.I.) suggests that the corresponding employment scale would be 200 employees or more.

1960s, is provided by a model which explicitly allows for the economy's 'dual' structure and for the existence of wage differentials by scale of firms. In this model, as in reality, wage increases are first determined in the large enterprise sector as a function of (exogeneously determined) productivity changes. They are then transmitted, more or less proportionately, to small-scale firms. The extent of the transmission, which will depend on the state of the labour market, will lead to either a closing or an opening of wage differentials. Assuming unchanged profit margins, prices will remain roughly stable in the advanced sector, since productivity increases will be sufficiently large to satisfy even very ambitious wage claims. Prices in the backward sector will be a function of large-scale firms' wage increases, labour market disequilibria, and exogeneously given (and relatively slow) productivity growth.

The model can be set up (as is done by Ohkawa[10]) in the following three equations in which W stands for wages, P for prices, Y for productivity, U for an indicator of labour market tightness, the subscripts 1 and 2 for the advanced and backward sectors respectively and all variables, except U, are expressed in terms of percentage changes:

$$W_1 = a + bY_1 \qquad (1)$$
$$W_2 - W_1 = c + dU \qquad (2)$$
$$(\text{let } c + dU = e)$$
$$P_2 = f + g(W_1 + e - Y_2) \qquad (3)$$

with (usually) $b = 1$ (and therefore $P_1 = 0$), and $W_1 > Y_2$ (and therefore variations in the longer-run trend of P_2 depending on $e \gtreqless 0$.

This model is, of course, a simplified description and could not provide answers to all questions. It ignores, for instance, the possibility of feedbacks from P_2 to W_1. Nor does it explore all the links between productivity growth and inflation. As it stands it would suggest that the faster Y_1 is, the more rapid P_2 will be— *prima facie* a somewhat unexpected result.*

* It may be noted that this model has similarities with a set of models developed for some of the very open and fully employed smaller economies of Northern Europe in which changes in world prices and in productivity in the export sector determine the (uniform) rate of wage changes for both the 'exposed' and the 'sheltered' sectors of the economy and, therefore, also the rate of inflation for commodities which are not traded internationally and for which productivity changes are slower; see, for instance: E. Lundberg, 'Productivity and Structural Change—A Policy Issue in Sweden', *Economic*

Nevertheless, the model is useful in explaining the behaviour of Japanese prices, particularly between 1953 and the mid-1960s. This period can be divided into two phases. The first, roughly the years up to 1959–60, witnessed stability in both wholesale and consumer prices, or P_1 and P_2 (Fig. 4). In this period, as will be remembered, wage differentials actually increased (e was negative) and wage increases in small firms were kept close to the rate of growth of productivity. The rapid narrowing of wage differentials between 1959–60 and 1965, consequent upon a tightening labour market, made price increases inevitable among small firms, despite some acceleration of productivity growth. From 1966 to 1972 is a new phase again in which, together with continuous rises in consumer prices, wholesale prices also begin to increase, if at a slow pace. This is the period in which, contrary to expectations, wage differentials fail to close. But the mechanism for consumer price increases (now that e = 0), works through $b > 1$,* and therefore through a greater gap between W_1 and Y_2. The main reason for the larger values of b is to be found, presumably, in the already mentioned scarcity of younger workers which in large firms drove up not only their wages but also, indirectly, the whole wage bill. In addition, competitive forces may have been less strong in this period. The tendency for the yen to be undervalued allowed wage increases to be passed through to prices without endangering international competitiveness; and the intensity of domestic competition, as measured by the degree of concentration of production among each industry's top three or ten companies, which had declined from 1956 to 1964, rose thereafter.[11]

The issue of competition is, of course, crucial to a deeper understanding of Japan's price (and not only price) performance. Views on this issue differ widely; some observers argue that fierce competition, of a kind unparalleled in Europe, prevails in the economy, while others maintain that oligopolistic practices are

---

Journal, March 1972 (Supplement). There are, however, three main differences with the present model: (i) in Japan the growth of value productivity has depended but little on the growth of world prices; (ii) domestic and not foreign competition has prevented prices from rising in the advanced sector; and (iii) the transmission to the low productivity sector has not been automatic but has taken into account the existence of wide wage differentials.

* Recorded values of b show that it was below 1 in the 1950s, equal to 1 in the first half of the 1960s and above 1 in the latter half (0·68, 0·99, and 1·13 for 1956–60, 1960–4, and 1964–70 respectively).

common among larger enterprises. It is difficult to substantiate either claim, let alone to try to compare the degree of competition in Japan with that in other countries. Very broadly, it appears that competitive forces are strong among smaller firms, as price theory would lead one to expect. This also fits with what was said earlier on the relative importance of sub-contracting in Japan, which provides larger enterprises with a strong weapon to enforce price and quality competition on their smaller dependants. On competition among large-scale producers, the evidence is more mixed. International comparisons suggest that Japan's 'modern' sector has '. . . an appreciably more monopolistic structure than American or British industry'.[12] Similarly, the traditional emphasis on Japan's huge trusts (*zaibatsu*), reflecting memories of the latters' great powers in pre-war years, has led many to believe that a few large conglomerates operating in many spheres of activity have been able to control most markets. This impression is often reinforced by the knowledge that the government (notably the M.I.T.I.) has tended to favour large-scale firms, has done little to combat monopolistic tendencies, and has actually encouraged cartel formation whenever the economy has started to slide into recession.

Yet all this evidence does not provide a complete picture and could even be considered more misleading than useful. For one thing, true monopolies have been almost absent from Japan; and highly concentrated sectors, in which two or three enterprises share more than 70 per cent of the market, accounted for only some 5 per cent of the items covered by the wholesale price index in the late 1950s, a proportion which is unlikely to have changed very significantly since then.[13] Secondly, the post-war *zaibatsu* have been much less prominent than the pre-war ones. To some extent this was due to the anti-monopoly policies followed by the United States occupation authorities who, in the late 1940s, tried to dismantle the large trusts. It is true that these policies were quickly reversed once the Japanese government regained independence. But the reconstituted post-war *zaibatsu* (and notably the three major groups Mitsubishi, Mitsui, and Sumitomo) never regained the cohesion and power of their pre-war ancestors.[14] The stage had been set (relatively) free for the growth of other firms in the early 1950s, and in a rapidly expanding economy opportunities were found to be enormous. Studies made of the top three or ten corporations in each of a number of

industrial branches in the post-war period show that in many of
them rank and composition changed from one year to the next,
suggesting that no single firm was able to enjoy monopoly power
for very long.[15] Even if the *zaibatsus* had been as all-pervading
and powerful as they had been before the war, they might well
have found it difficult to monopolize more than a few branches,
given the very rapid expansion of the market. As it was, by the
time they had managed to put together the bits and pieces
broken earlier, competitive conditions had changed, aggressive
newcomers had established themselves in many fields, and completely new products and markets had been created.

More importantly, even in the cases in which only a few firms,
possibly belonging to one *zaibatsu* or another, came to dominate
the market, their behaviour sometimes differed from that of most,
more cautious, Western oligopolies. An example of this difference
is the frequent price cuts made in the export business by Japanese
firms openly competing with each other for market shares. At
home, price cuts were less frequent—strikingly so if seen in the
light of productivity developments—but price competition was
not entirely absent, especially in fast growing sectors. And even
when high profits were being achieved, it can be argued that
they made for longer-run price stability, or for quality improvements, since they were invariably ploughed back in the almost
permanent investment drives (on which more in Chapter 4
below) which best show the strength of Japanese competition.

The relatively favourable price picture sketched so far depended
on one further crucial condition, shared by the whole developed
world, namely stable import prices. In the earlier period (1953
to 1959–60), import prices actually fell by some 20 per cent; and
they were roughly stable, in yen terms, throughout the 1960s
and until 1972. The near-explosion of import prices in 1973–4
(an increase of roughly 100 per cent over the two years) is clearly
the main factor explaining the difference between Japan's
recent and earlier price experience.

This is not to say, however, that the country's present-day

FIG. 4. *Price trends* (Indices 1960 = 100; log scale)

Sources: B.S., O.P.M., *Annual Report on the Consumer Price Index*; B.o.J., *Wholesale
Price Indices Annual, Economic Statistics Annual* and *Economic Statistics Monthly;*
E.P.A., *ESJ (1972–1973)* (Japanese version) for pre-1965 wholesale prices by
firms' scale.

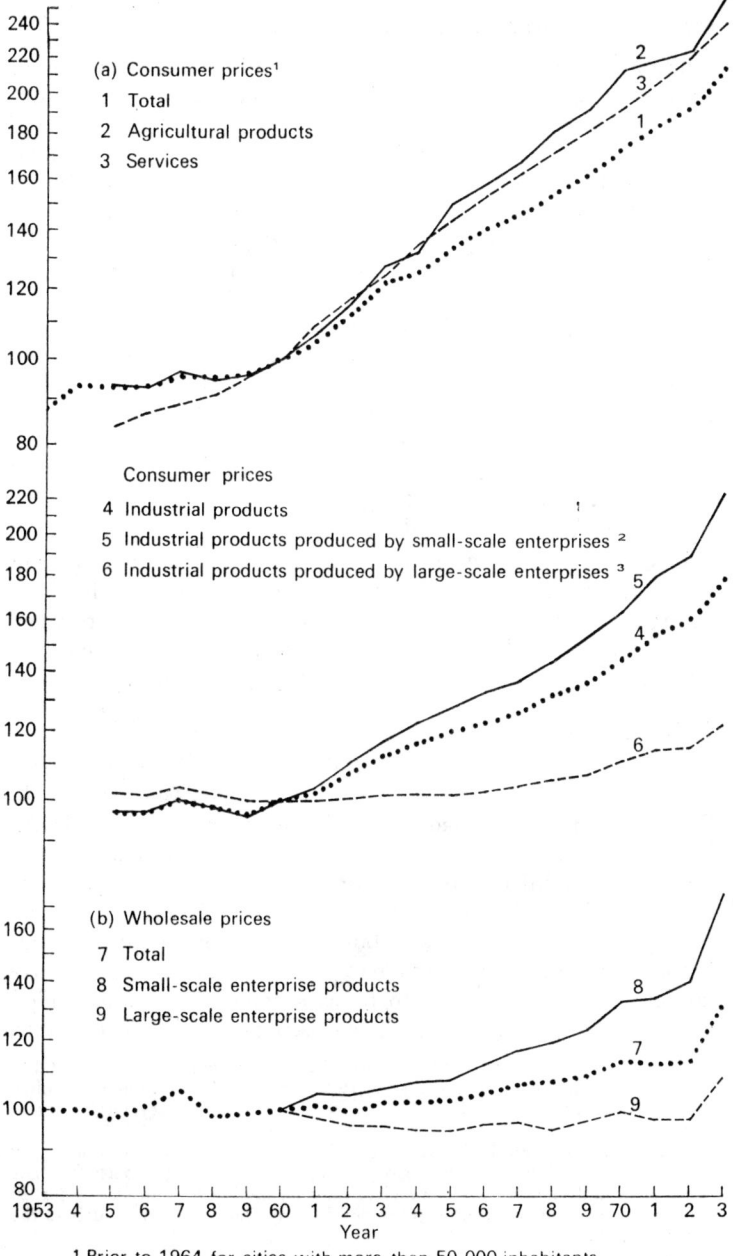

(a) Consumer prices[1]
1 Total
2 Agricultural products
3 Services

Consumer prices
4 Industrial products
5 Industrial products produced by small-scale enterprises [2]
6 Industrial products produced by large-scale enterprises [3]

(b) Wholesale prices
7 Total
8 Small-scale enterprise products
9 Large-scale enterprise products

Year

[1] Prior to 1964 for cities with more than 50 000 inhabitants
[2] Until 1969 including all durable goods
[3] Until 1969 including all textile goods

inflation is entirely exogenous or would disappear should commodity prices slump again. The sharp increases in commodity prices in 1973 were influenced by the very rapid expansion of Japanese demand following the 1971 recession. By the early 1970s Japan had become the world's largest single importer of primary products and its price-setting function in world commodity markets may have been reinforced by the speculative hoarding of raw materials carried out by many of the country's trading firms.* In addition, very strong internal demand in 1972–3 drove up the prices of domestic products, notably in the construction sector in which supply bottlenecks appeared soon after the government increased its public works programme. And many of the cartels created during the 1971 recession were kept in being until late 1972 despite the obvious improvement in the business climate.[16] By the time (late 1973) the government reversed its economic policies in order to reduce demand pressures, inflationary expectations, fuelled also by the rise in oil prices, had become extremely strong. Labour costs per worker in manufacturing, which had not risen by more than productivity in 1973, accelerated sharply after the 1974 Spring wage renegotiations, and by the close of the year Japan was faced with powerful and only slowly abating cost-push pressures.

Unbalanced growth

It was suggested above that the major failure in Japan's economic performance was an 'unbalanced' growth path. 'Unbalanced growth', like 'dualism', has never been defined with any precision. Traditionally, the concept has been applied to developing countries and has, broadly, described a process of expansion in which sectoral growth rates diverge sufficiently widely to create tensions and bottlenecks in production. In this sense, however, as mentioned earlier, Japan's growth was relatively 'balanced', as was to be expected of a large, diversified and already relatively 'developed' economy.† Statistical tests,

* Such activities were made possible by the large amount of liquidity pumped into the economy during the 1971–2 phase of easy monetary policy and were encouraged by a government embarrassed by very large current account surpluses.

† Indeed, it is arguable that unbalanced growth in this sense can only apply to countries at much earlier stages of development, in which imports (for lack of reserves and/or absorptive capacity) may be unable to compensate for all shortages, or to fairly autarkic (and rapidly growing) economies such as the Soviet Union.

made on the basis of restrictive assumptions, have produced contrasting answers,[17] but a superficial examination of Japan's post-war growth suggests that real bottlenecks have been few and short lived. Except during 1955–61, a period which witnessed some pronounced differences in sectoral growth rates,* expansion was relatively uniform, and at least in line with the likely values of income elasticities of demand. Supply–demand imbalances were on the whole limited to specific food products and to some industrial commodities for which, at the top of booms, needs could outstrip domestic availabilities. But such shortages were usually short-lived, with most bottlenecks quickly alleviated by rapid capacity expansion and/or recourse to imports.

Alternative interpretations of unbalanced growth might stress the occurrence of wide cyclical fluctuations, differing growth rates for major sectors of national expenditure, or the worsening of regional and sectoral income differentials. On these scores, Japanese growth may, with somewhat more justification, be called unbalanced. Very rapid growth was achieved by a relative neglect of consumption in favour of investment and by a further concentration of activity and income, at least until recently, in the country's richer regions. Little was done, as has been seen above, to diminish the dual nature of the industrial structure, and business cycle fluctuations were clearly wide by international standards. But it could also be argued that cyclical fluctuations were largely confined to investment and left private consumption and employment relatively unaffected; that the failure of differentials to disappear, or to narrow decisively, may reflect some more basic tendencies inherent in the growth path of most contemporary economies; and that the relative neglect of consumption in favour of investment probably allowed a faster growth of consumption over the long period than would otherwise have taken place.

More generally, these various imbalances may well have reflected important elements stimulating over-all economic growth. Without the external economies reaped through regional concentration, the low wages made possible by 'dualism', and the momentum created by phases of breakneck expansion, the economy might never have been able to achieve rapid growth

* In this period, machinery output rose by more than 30 per cent per annum, while chemical production went up by only 14 per cent (and textiles by 8 per cent).

for so long. Nor were all the imbalances created irreversible. Recessions had relatively limited welfare effects and were rapidly overcome, dualism should continue its gradual, if slow, decline, and market forces, as well as public efforts, are now stimulating a somewhat more balanced regional development.

The same cannot be said, however, for another field in which lags and neglect, whatever their effect in the past, may by now have become a positive hindrance to further growth. This is the field of, very broadly defined, social goods. The real imbalance of the Japanese economy was between the huge direct and indirect claims on resources made by the private sector and the residual which was left over to satisfy the demand for social goods and most forms of public consumption. This neglect was not only the result of autonomous economic forces, but also stemmed from a conscious policy pursued consistently until the late 1960s. There were many aspects of this neglect—the most important of which were the abdication of responsibility for many social services and the concentration of public effort on reinforcing the country's industrial power.[18]

Thus, parts of Japan's health insurance system and a good deal of its higher education are run and financed by the private sector. Larger corporations may provide fairly satisfactory medical facilities and some of the private universities are on a par with the country's prestigious national universities, but for the bulk of the population health insurance standards are far from uniform and higher education either financially unattainable or of mediocre quality. Moreover, in a country in which the traditional family system is rapidly breaking up, and the normal retirement age is between 55 and 60, there is virtually no national pension scheme—or, more precisely, a scheme exists to which most of the population subscribes but from which benefits are, as yet, extended to only a small percentage of the old. In the meantime, the large sums accumulated by this fund have been used to finance public investment.[19] More broadly, in the fields of public consumption (excluding defence) and transfers to the private sector, Japan holds the unenviable record of having the lowest share in GNP, as well as the lowest elasticity with respect to GNP, among O.E.C.D. countries.*

* With the possible exceptions of Portugal and Turkey: cf. O.E.C.D., *ESJ*, *1972*, p. 50 and *Expenditure Trends in O.E.C.D. Countries, 1960–1980*, 1972, pp. 66–8. Within the limited total of social expenditures in Japan children's

A similar international comparison of government investment would show Japan in a much more favourable light. But such a comparison would be highly misleading. The resources the government obtained through taxation (or pension contributions) were overwhelmingly devoted to creating an infrastructure not of a social nature but for the benefit of private business. It has been estimated by the E.P.A. that between FYs 1959 and 1968, from 70 to 80 per cent of total government investment outlays '. . . were devoted to expenditures closely linked to, and indeed fostering, the development of the business sector—e.g. roads, harbours, railways, the preparation of industrial sites—while less than one quarter was spent on investment in fields such as health, welfare, or education'.[20] More broadly, the ratio of social infrastructure to the economy's private capital stock declined more or less steadily throughout the 1955–70 period;[21] a development which followed an earlier period of neglect going back to the mid-1930s. Thus for some thirty-five years first the requirements of a war economy or of reconstruction and later a number of 'constraints' (the need to dampen demand in boom periods, the lack of financial resources during slowdowns, the inflationary impact of public construction, the Ministry of Finance's absurd view of 'sound fiscal policy', etc.) as well as the drive to encourage the private sector, stifled the growth of social overhead capital, and this in a period of rapid urbanization and structural change. The following statement, taken from an official publication, epitomizes Japan's growth strategy: 'It is impossible to produce 3,000 tons of pig iron in a blast furnace capable of producing only 1,000 tons, but it is possible to crowd in three times the passenger capacity in an electric train, a phenomenon which is being witnessed on the Yamate Loop Line in Tokyo.'[22]

The neglect of social needs was not confined to those fields in which the government could intervene directly, but spread pervasively throughout the economy, as witnessed by the problems posed by housing. These would have been difficult to tackle in an overcrowded and highly urbanized country even given the best of intentions and wide powers to intervene in price formation. As it was, residential construction was left almost

---

allowances, as well as pensions, have been kept to a minimum, as if only the able-bodied members of the population—those, in other words, who contributed to production—were considered to deserve social security (Jinushi, 'Social Security System in Transition', pp. 500–1).

entirely to private interests. Partly as a consequence, housing standards are among the lowest in the developed world,* but urban land prices are probably the highest (and have risen 23-fold in the 18 years to 1973, as against a less than sevenfold increase in wages).

Finally, the indiscriminate growth of the private economy has created pollution and natural resource problems whose magnitude may well be unparalleled. Much has been written by now on the seriousness of the environment issue within Japan. The recent commodity price explosion and oil crisis have shown how much the country absorbs in terms of the world's resources, as well as its high degree of dependence on outside raw materials.

But criticism of Japan's performance based on its 'failure' in these two fields is perhaps unfair. The whole developed world has come through the last twenty years assuming that natural resources would always be cheap and oblivious of the probability that the favourable terms of trade it enjoyed could not last. (Over the longer run, the more rapid growth of productivity in manufacturing than in other sectors and declining colonial and imperialist influences should worsen the terms of trade of the industrialized world.) Similarly, the universal stress on measurable growth meant that pollution and environmental issues were hardly ever an important consideration in the minds of policy-makers. But the particularly acute nature of these problems in Japan can be linked to the general growth strategy pursued by the country—a strategy which almost blindly concentrated all resources and efforts into one single pursuit.

A tentative assessment

The aim pursued was, of course, growth maximization. Japan may have paid lip service to all the four or five aims mentioned above. But in fact it established a very clear order of preference among them and, to be fair, any assessment of the country's performance should take into account its avowed priorities. Over-all growth was the primary aim as it had been, if not always

---

* The exiguity of Japanese homes may be difficult to visualize for the Western observer. As an example, the total housing space per person in urban areas has been estimated at 4·9 *tatamis* in 1968, or 8 m². An average-sized dwelling for a family of four would thus measure some 30–35 m², and less in Tokyo (E.P.A., *ESJ* (*1970–1971*) p. 133). These crude figures tend, however, to exaggerate the contrast with Western standards since they do not take into account a different style of life and different social conventions.

for the same reasons, from the days of the Meiji restoration. Balance of payments equilibrium was seen less as an aim *per se* than as a means to achieve the primary target; and much of Japan's economic policy until the late 1960s was concerned with the difficult, but not impossible, task of reconciling growth maximization with the least possible disturbance on the external front. As for full employment, it was felt, with good reason, that growth maximization would tend to absorb disguised unemployment while open unemployment never represented a real problem.

Price stability or a more balanced growth path did not figure very prominently in Japan's 'social welfare function'. Price stability became a policy aim only in the mid-1960s.[23] Indeed, until then, consumer price increases had been almost welcomed, ostensibly because they meant that wage differentials were closing and standards of living rising.* To some extent this was true and the divergence between wholesale and consumer price trends reflected changing factor scarcities. But it also meant, if to a limited extent, a transfer of resources from the household to the business sector and thereby furthered growth. It was only when wholesale prices began to rise, and it was (in the event wrongly) feared that this would impair the country's competitiveness, that policies were applied specifically to curb price increases.

Social overhead capital or welfare arrangements were the least of the policy-makers' worries, until very recently. In the 1950s it was actually felt that social overhead capital formation implied a waste of resources.[24] By the early or mid-1960s some recognition began to be given to the importance of this issue and pious wishes, but not much more, proliferated in planning documents. Some partial translation into reality came only in 1971–2 when, for the first time, a prolonged recession allowed the government to embark on a massive investment programme (a 40 per cent rise between 1970 and 1972). But even this effort was short-lived; and the FY 1974 budget, to combat inflation, decided on a zero growth rate, in money terms, for public works expenditure.

Pollution control measures came somewhat earlier and the effects have not been negligible. In the last few years more than

* This is a very summary version of the arguments developed to justify a moderate degree of inflation at the retail level (and stability, but not falls, of wholesale prices), by O. Shimomura, the most influential government economic adviser in the early 1960s; see his 'Consumer Price Problems', *The Oriental Economist*, November and December 1963.

10 per cent of manufacturing investment expenditures have been on anti-pollution equipment.

For twenty full years or more, until 1972, Japan's economic strategy was highly successful by its own standards. Yet seen with hindsight, and in a broader perspective, one cannot fail to be struck by some of its limitations. Rapid growth achieved many aims; but twenty years of neglect of some basic issues have created problems which are difficult to solve in the framework of a market economy. Pollution is one example; yet despite its present seriousness, this problem is not intractable. It is basically a technical one and on the technical level Japan can confidently be expected to find efficient solutions. But the same is much less true for the broader issues of land utilization and social infra-structure. It is too late to change the profile of the Tokyo–Ōsaka coast line—an almost uninterrupted industrial belt—and it is extremely difficult to reverse an established order of priorities in the field of social versus private goods in a basically capitalist economic structure.

The present inflationary trends may, in no small part, be a direct and indirect consequence of past growth patterns. One example is provided by the public investment effort of 1971–2. Although only a timid inroad into some of the problems, it led to bottlenecks and fuelled inflation of prices of land and construction materials. Rather than experiencing bottlenecks and disequilibria between sectors at an earlier stage of development and balanced growth later, Japan seems almost to have followed the opposite course! More fundamentally, Japan's present inflation seems to owe a lot to the disappearance of two of the major conditions which until recently made relative price stability in the modern sector possible: wage rises less than those of productivity and practical price stability for raw material inputs. It can be argued that the changes in both trends reflect in varying degrees past imbalances—imbalances in the growth of Japan's industrial economy *vis-à-vis* the world as a whole, which made Japan a major economic power but also the largest absorber of the world's exported natural resources and thus a prime target for the impact of fairer world trading conditions; imbalances between the expansion of the business sector and the increase of the population's welfare which, albeit slowly, are bringing about a growing feeling that enjoyment of some of the fruits of economic growth is being too long delayed. Both these imbalances have already manifested themselves in rising monetary claims—higher commodity prices and larger wage increases; and over the longer run they will increasingly call in question the strategy and priorities of the past.

Until recently, '. . . the Japanese have basked in the warmth of international admiration'.[25] An assessment made at present would probably be more mixed or even possibly negative, though all such conclusions are inevitably coloured by the contemporary situation and standards. Some achievements were remarkable, but over-all they may have been essentially short-run successes; and they have created problems whose solution may be difficult and require painful adjustments. An apparently successful growth strategy was pursued for too long; the inevitable lags in policy reactions to new problems, common to all countries, seem to have been particularly protracted; in fact, even as late as 1974, strategies and policies still seem geared to traditional aims and targets rather than to resolving some of the contradictions of present-day Japan.

NOTES

1. As enshrined, for instance, in countless resolutions passed by international organizations, Economic Reports to the President (U.S.A.), the 1959 Radcliffe Report (U.K.), the 1967 German Stabilization Law etc.

2. Though the '. . . cornucopia of burgeoning indices' so decried by the anti-growth school (cf. E. J. Mishan, *The Costs of Economic Growth*, London 1967, p. 4) may have provided the Japanese people with a positive, welfare-enhancing pleasure, at least until recently.

3. Economic Council of Japan, *Measuring Net National Welfare of Japan*, Tokyo 1973.

4. U.S. Department of Labor, *Monthly Labor Review*, September 1970 and P. J. D. Wiles, 'A Note on Soviet Unemployment on U.S. Definitions', *Soviet Studies*, April 1972, p. 626.

5. M. Umemura, 'An Analysis of Employment Structure in Japan', *HJE*, March 1962, pp. 23–8.

6. Figures on longer-run trends in Japan's regional balance of payments can be found in O.E.C.D., *ESJ, 1972*, pp. 39–44.

7. A similar conclusion is reached by Ohkawa and Rosovsky, *Japanese Economic Growth*, p. 187.

8. See, for instance, H. Niida, 'Price Problems', in R. Komiya (ed.), *Postwar Economic Growth in Japan*, University of California Press 1966, pp. 65–7.

9. See, for instance, T. Watanabe, 'Price Changes and the Rate of Change of Money Wage Earnings in Japan, 1955–1962', *Quarterly Journal of Economics*, February 1966; T. Toyoda, 'Price Expectations and the Short-run and Long-run Phillips Curves in Japan, 1956–1968', *RES*, August 1972: R. Minami, 'Transformation of the Labour Market in Postwar Japan' *HJE*, June 1972 and 'Wage Adjustment in Postwar Japan: An Alternative Approach to the Phillips–Lipsey Curve', *HJE*, June 1973.

10. Ohkawa, *Differential Structure*, pp. 77–93.

11. E.P.A., *ESJ* (*1964–1965*), pp. 74–6 and *ESJ* (*1972–1973*), pp. 134–5.

12. J. S. Bain, *International Differences in Industrial Structure*, New Haven 1966, p. 90.

13. E.P.A., *ESJ* (*1961–1962*), pp. 297–8.

14. Very good descriptions of the changed role and importance of post-war *zaibatsu* can be found in G. C. Allen, *Japan's Economic Expansion*, London 1965, Ch. 10 and K. Yamamura, *Economic Policy in Postwar Japan*, Berkeley and Los Angeles 1967, Ch. 7.

15. E.P.A., *ESJ* (*1964–1965*), pp. 75–8.

16. E.P.A., *ESJ* (*1972–1973*), p. 134.

17. For the 1950s one test shows that Japan's growth may have been one of the most unbalanced in a sample of some 40 countries (D. S. Swamy, 'Statistical Evidence of Balanced and Unbalanced Growth', *RES*, August 1967). But a similar and statistically somewhat more sophisticated approach produces almost the opposite conclusion (P. A. Yotopoulos and L. J. Lau, 'A Test for Balanced and Unbalanced Growth', *RES*, November 1970).

18. Recent years have seen a proliferation of writings on Japan's social infrastructure, social services and environmental problems. For some surveys and international comparisons, all of which point to Japan's relative backwardness in these fields, see the more recent E.P.A.'s *ESJ*s (notably *1968–1969*, *1970–1971*, and *1971–1972*), the December 1972 issue of *The Developing Economies*, or the O.E.C.D.'s 1972 *ESJ*.

19. S. Jinushi, 'Social Security System in Transition', *DE*, December 1972, p. 501.

20. O.E.C.D., *ESJ*, *1972*, p. 47.

21. *Basic Economic and Social Plan, 1973–1977*, Tokyo 1973, p. 159.

22. E.P.A., *ESJ* (*1962–1963*), p. 35.

23. A wholesale prices target appeared for the first time in the Fourth Plan (FYs 1964–8) and a consumer prices target in the Fifth Plan (FYs 1966–71); Y. Kogane, 'The Objectives and their Attainment in Long-term Planning in Japan', mimeo, 1973.

24. This seems to have been implicit in Shimomura's thinking; see K. Kurihara, *The Growth Potential of the Japanese Economy*, The Johns Hopkins Press 1971, pp. 46–7.

25. K. Ohkawa and H. Rosovsky, 'A Century of Japanese Economic Growth', in Lockwood (ed.), *The State and Economic Enterprise*, p. 83.

PART TWO

FACTORS IN ECONOMIC GROWTH

CHAPTER 4

CAPITAL

THAT capital accumulation is the mainspring of economic growth has long been one of the basic truisms of economic theory; and nowhere is it truer than in Japan. The expansion of the labour force was also an important contributory factor, but abundant labour would have remained largely inoperative without capital formation. It is the latter which provided rising employment opportunities, embodied new techniques, enlarged scales of operation, and raised labour productivity, while at the same time increasing income and demand. Of the alternative (or additional) sources of growth, Chapter 1 showed that sectoral shifts permitted but did not initiate growth, while 'disembodied technological progress'—if such a thing exists—seems, according to the imperfect methods of measurement used in this field, to have been at its peak during investment booms. This would lend strong support to those who argue that most forms of technical progress are in fact 'embodied' and would reaffirm the pre-eminence of investment. Any examination of Japanese growth is therefore bound to start with a survey of the forms and sources of capital accumulation.

Following Harrod (and Domar), output growth is the product of the incremental output–capital ratio and of the average propensity to save. Japan's uniqueness resides in the fact that both the right hand terms of this identity were exceptionally high in the period under review.[1] The productivity of investment (see Table 1.3 above) was from 25 to 100 per cent higher than in other major economies while saving ratios have stood at world record levels since at least the mid-1950s. Other countries may have used their investment with a fair degree of efficiency (e.g. Italy) or allocated a sizeable share of their output to capital formation (e.g. Germany), but none seems to have been able to combine both a high saving propensity and a high productivity of capital. Moreover, not only were saving proportions already high in the 1950s, but they have been rising steadily since. And the efficiency of capital hardly declined until the early 1970s, despite massive investments.

Investment

That Japan's capital formation effort has been very high by international standards is well known. Table 4.1 shows that Japan invested roughly one-third of its GNP (at constant prices) between 1953 and 1972. This ratio is unparalleled by any of the

TABLE 4.1

Gross fixed investment ratios—1953 to 1972

	TOTAL FIXED CAPITAL FORMATION	EXCLUDING RESIDENTIAL CONSTRUCTION	TREND INCREASE IN TOTAL SHARE[1]
	PERCENTAGE OF GNP AT CONSTANT PRICES		
Japan	31·8	26·2	1·11
France	23·0	17·1	0.66
Germany	25·1	19·4	0·25
Italy	20·2	14·2	(0·03)
United Kingdom	17·3	14·1	0·40
United States	17·0	12·8	(−0·02)
Soviet Union	..	..	0·28[2]

1. Annual increase in share of total gross fixed investment in GNP obtained by fitting linear time trends to the data. Figures in brackets are statistically not significant at the 5 per cent confidence level.

2. Total fixed investment as a share of NMP (1950 to 1969).

Sources: E.P.A., *National Income Statistics*; O.E.C.D., *National Accounts of O.E.C.D. Countries*; U.N.(E.C.E.), *Economic Bulletin for Europe*, Vol. 18, No. 1, and *Economic Survey of Europe, 1968* and *1970*.

market economies shown in the table or, for that matter, by other high-investment countries like Norway or Switzerland; and it does not seem to have been reached even by socialist countries in which capital accumulation has clearly been a top planning priority.* Moreover, Japan's investment effort seems to have been concentrated, more than in other countries, in sectors in which

* Comparisons with Eastern European countries are made difficult not only by differences in national accounting definitions but also by the structure of relative (market) prices, which leads to an underestimation of investment shares. Indirect United Nations evidence (U.N.(E.C.E.), *Economic Survey of Europe in 1969*, Pt. I, p. 145), suggests that in 1965 the centrally planned economies of Europe invested perhaps 30 per cent of their GDP. More careful estimates made for the Soviet Union (A. S. Becker, *Soviet National Income 1958–1964*, Berkeley and Los Angeles 1969) show that at 1958 factor costs, the share of gross fixed investment in total output was 28 per cent between 1958 and 1964.

average capital–output ratios are low, notably manufacturing. Roughly 8 per cent of GNP went to capital formation in this branch over the period, as against 4 per cent in Britain and 6–7 per cent (including investment in the construction sector) in France and Germany. This is, of course, the reverse side of the preceding chapter's coin, namely the low priority given to investment in social infrastructure, and to some extent housing, where the measured additions to output in response to investment tend to be smaller.

The high productivity of Japan's capital stock can also be gauged by looking at the development of the economy's over-all capital–output ratio. In 1970, this stood at roughly 2·25, or 2·75, depending on whether the residential capital stock is excluded or included.[2] This seems to be a good deal lower than the figures of 3–4 which have often been advanced for developed countries. But such a finding must be highly tentative. International comparisons of changes in capital stocks through time are subject to very great uncertainties; and comparisons of absolute figures are probably impossible.

More remarkable seems to be the behaviour of the capital–output ratio over time. Between FYs 1955 and 1970, using potential output estimates as denominators (and excluding housing), the ratio seems actually to have declined slightly, from 2·3 to 2·2, whereas elsewhere ratios have more usually risen. This is somewhat surprising in the light of *a priori* reasoning, since a rising investment share, the increasing proportion of output accounted for by goods and services with an above-average capital–output ratio, as well as the capital-using nature of most forms of technological progress, would all tend to raise the economy's capital coefficient. That this did not happen is largely a reflection of the very rapid rate of technological innovation which accompanied the investment effort, and of the ensuing youth of Japan's capital stock. It was estimated that in the mid-1960s two-thirds of the capital in manufacturing, and over half of the total private capital stock, excluding housing, were less than 5 years old,[3] and the average age of the housing stock was put at 6·5 years in 1970.[4] Though not strictly comparable, average age figures for the Soviet Union, the United States, Germany, and Britain in the early 1960s varied between roughly 10 and 20 years.

It may be interesting to note at this stage that, in contrast with the development of the fixed capital–output ratio, Japan's ratio of accumulated inventories to GNP has been rising over time. Between 1953 and 1972, Japan devoted some 3·5 per cent of its GNP to investment in inventories, as against 1–2 per cent in most other market economies. The rising stocks–GNP ratio is surprising since it is usually argued that over the longer run growth should decrease the need for inventories in the wake of increasing economic concentration, improving transport facilities, growing rationalization in retailing and in the management of stocks, the increasing weight of services in output (and the declining share of agriculture), etc. Moreover, Japan experienced a falling dependence on raw material imports and a decreasing 'roundaboutness' of production (as measured by the ratio of intermediate to total, or to final, output in the 1955 and 1970 input–output tables). Yet, contrary to expectations, stock formation as a percentage of GNP has not declined, and the ratio of accumulated stocks to annual (potential) output has risen from roughly 0·25 to 0·5 over the period.

The fact that this ratio rises most rapidly in years of buoyant expansion (especially 1955–7 and 1966–70) suggests that the reasons for such rapid stock accumulation are to be found in the economy's high rates of growth of output and rapid technical progress which increased the volume of work in progress (notably in shipbuilding), in the variety of new goods, and, perhaps, in the need for precautionary stocks in the face of more violent cyclical fluctuations. Similarly, rapid rises in boom periods are also recorded by the fixed investment–GNP ratio, but the order of causation is likely to have been the opposite. Whereas high output growth induced stock accumulation, it was investment activity which generated rapid growth.

The reasons for Japan's high (fixed) investment propensities over the period are numerous and have probably changed in relative importance through time. No growth model can possibly account for them all, particularly because some go beyond the realm of measurement and involve more complex socio-economic factors. A rough distinction can perhaps be made between, loosely defined, exogenous and endogenous causes, with the former originating in external circumstances beyond the control of investors themselves, and the latter being more closely linked to business behaviour and expectations. Yet any hard and fast separation between the two is clearly impossible.

Among various factors which have been put forward as explanations of the high investment ratios at the outset of the period, two are frequently assigned an especially important role in the literature on Japanese economic growth—government policies and the availability of a stock of unexploited techniques. The role of economic policies is looked at in greater detail in Chapter 6 below. Suffice it to say here that action to foster investment was pursued by post-war governments, as it had been by practically all Japanese governments from the days of the Meiji restoration onwards. Some of the ways in which the government intervened in the economy have been mentioned earlier—e.g. preferential loan and tax treatment for large corporations, and the creation of a suitable infrastructure. Additional action took the form of choosing priority sectors for special treatment, screening the import of technology, drawing up annual investment plans, and, in the early days of exchange controls, allocating foreign currency. It could even be argued that the creation or development of many large industrial sectors was a direct response to government stimuli. This is most true of shipbuilding, steel, and electric power generation—the priority industries of the reconstruction effort. Stimulus from the government was also important in the machinery and petroleum branches, in which M.I.T.I. planning was crucial, and may now be playing a role in new sectors like computers and electronics. Indeed, of the success stories of Japanese industry, it is only the durable consumer goods industries (including, possibly, passenger cars) which experienced a largely unplanned growth of output.[5]

The initial technological backlog has also been stressed by many and is likely to have been important. The Japan of the early 1950s had been to a large extent cut off, for about twenty years, from scientific developments in the West—first by self-imposed isolation and later by war and reconstruction. Industrial output rose very rapidly in the late 1930s, stimulated by military demand, but according to most observers, the heavily protected Japanese industry of those days was not very efficient. The opening of the country to foreign influences after such a long time faced Japan with a double backlog in relation to foreign technology—new techniques perfected in the West in those branches in which Japan already had an established base (largely in the heavy industries), and new products, almost unknown in pre-war Japan, mainly in the chemical and durable consumer goods fields.[6] Backlog and the availability of foreign techniques are not sufficient conditions for

investment to be stimulated.[7] But the combination of technological backlog, on the one hand, with a trained labour force, a
relatively sophisticated and industrialized economic structure,
and a 90 million population, on the other, meant that Japan was
able to assimilate the West's more advanced technology rapidly
and on a relatively large scale. The favourable influences stemming from technical backlog, as well as from government intervention, were at their peak in the 1950s. But, like public policies,
the catching up with foreign technology went on contributing to
growth in the next decade as well, since rapid expansion of the
market made the adoption of progressively larger-scale foreign
techniques economical.

Yet a backlog of exploitable technology and government help
could not alone have been sufficient in the framework of a market
system, to push rates of capital formation to the levels they
reached. As has already been mentioned, the growth rates of
investment or capacity, during upward cyclical phases, may be
difficult for the Western observer to visualize. Between 1955 and
1957, investment in manufacturing rose by 130 per cent; in the
three years to 1961 it more than trebled (with 1960 alone recording a 70 per cent growth rate) and it nearly trebled again in the
four years to 1970. Industrial capacity, as represented by E.P.A.
potential-output estimates for mining and manufacturing, nearly
doubled every five years between 1956 and 1971; it rose by 94, 84,
and 80 per cent in successive quinquennia, investment cycles
notwithstanding. Some individual sectors' growth rates between
FYs 1965 and 1970 are even more striking—an over 100 per cent
increase in capacity for television sets and synthetic fibres, a near
trebling for ethylene, and a fourfold increase, in barely five years,
for passenger cars.[8]

It is clear that to initiate such investment drives, expectations
had to be highly optimistic. To some extent this optimism
stemmed from the economy's rapid growth itself, which went
back to the late 1940s. The speed of growth in the reconstruction
years had created a certain momentum, which it might have been
difficult to break subsequently, even if other circumstances had
not been favourable. But, in fact, additional exogenous stimuli
were present to sustain expectations. In the early 1950s it was the
Korean war, in the mid-1950s M.I.T.I.'s blueprints for the
growth of specific industries, in the early 1960s the government's
bullish longer-run projections of the economy, more recently the

threat of trade liberalization, and throughout the period the buoyant development of a market for durable consumer goods. The mechanism of favourable expectations encouraging investment, which promoted growth and reinforced expectations, is thus crucial to an explanation of Japan's investment drives. Investment would call forth new investment by creating consumer demand (through multiplier effects), export demand (thanks to rapid productivity growth), and demand for investment goods themselves (through forward and backward linkage effects). Supply was creating its own demand, if in a somewhat more roundabout way than postulated by Say's law.

Yet this 'virtuous circle' explanation is incomplete. Other countries have been able to enter similar virtuous circles, without experiencing the almost explosive growth rates of Japanese investment. The story of investment growth cannot be dissociated from the behaviour of Japanese firms.

As mentioned in Chapter 3, the structure of Japanese business is highly oligopolistic, yet the traditional caution typical of Western oligopolies seems to have been largely absent from the behaviour of Japanese firms. For one thing, the speed of growth itself (cause and effect of practically all the phenomena looked at in this chapter) made caution an almost impossible policy. Failure to expand capacity when the market was growing at 10–15 per cent per annum, and a lot faster in some sectors, almost inevitably implied large loss of market share. Conversely, being the first in the investment race in a rapidly expanding sector could mean sharp increases in sales and a swift climb to the top of the ladder of the leading corporations. Secondly, technological backlog meant that available techniques were open to all. This is not always the case in countries leading in the technological field, where new techniques are frequently developed by monopolistic firms which may even be reluctant to adopt them themselves before their existing capital stock has been entirely amortized. There were no such inhibitions in Japan. As the market expanded, larger and more efficient scales of operation could be, and had to be, adopted by all producers, since failure to do so by any individual firm meant a rapid decline in its market share. Established firms thus enjoyed advantages only for very short periods of time, since the optimum scale of operations as well as the number of new products entering the market kept on expanding.[9] Indeed, the faster the growth of a given sector, the more numerous were newcomers and the more frequent were the changes in rank among the top producers.[10]

Such action inevitably entailed a wholesale scrapping of relatively young equipment. To some extent this process was, if not helped, at least made less painful by the possibility of selling used machinery to smaller firms—usually sub-contracting enterprises. More importantly, extremely liberal depreciation allowances, which were a part of government policies, meant that amortization periods could be a good deal shorter than they would otherwise have been.

To complete this picture one may have to add one further and even less quantifiable factor. So far, investment has been seen largely as a function of expected market growth rather than of the more traditional concept of profitability. Seen from a macro-economic standpoint this approach may be debatable (the problem is taken up again in Chapter 8). But at the micro-economic level, it seems that the investment plans of individual corporations were governed, in the short run at least, not so much by considerations of profit maximization, as by the attempt to achieve as large as possible a market share. Sales maximization is not an unknown aim among Western corporations;[11] but it may have played a relatively more important role in Japan because of the country's particular social characteristics. As stressed in a number of works on Japanese society, the concept of ranking (itself part of the wider notion of hierarchy) is an extremely important component of social life.* Though such concepts cannot be assimilated to the mere achievement of larger market shares and involve more complex criteria, they none the less seem to have played a large role in intra-business relations.

Achieving first rank, or at least a high position, in a particular sector has been the ambition of any firm, newcomer or established alike, and dropping down an industrial 'league table', implies a form of social disgrace felt by both managers and employees. Nowhere is this phenomenon more evident than in the behaviour of the three giant *zaibatsus* '. . . for each group feels itself obliged, for reasons of prestige, to obtain a share of every new industry as it appears and to hold its own in all fields with the rivals.'[12] This

---

* See for instance C. Nakane's *Japanese Society*, Penguin Books 1973, pp. 90–107, in which the '. . . ever present consciousness of ranking [which] contributes to the encouragement of competition among peers', is considered a very important element of the society's overall structure.

judgement is confirmed by more direct evidence. Replies to a business survey among major firms, conducted by Kōbe University, showed that nearly 80 per cent of the companies surveyed considered maintenance or increases in market shares as a major factor determining investment, and nearly 50 per cent admitted that this preoccupation with market shares stemmed from the attempt 'to improve one's status in the industry'.[13] It is true that such behaviour had other motivations as well. It allowed a form of expansion which did not clash with the relatively strict anti-monopoly rules of post-war Japan and it made possible the achievement of external economies for the group as a whole. Yet the initial motivation seems to have had as much to do with not letting a rival step ahead as with estimates of likely future indirect benefits.

These investment races, in which capacity is being established not so much in function of the likely development of the market but so as to achieve the largest possible scale of operation which will in turn allow the achievement of a high share in an expanded market, even at the cost of some spare capacity, have often been criticized in Japan as forms of 'excess competition'. Yet if *ex-ante* they may have given this impression, they do not seem to have been excessive *ex-post*. Competition can be 'excessive' if it prevents all firms from reaching optimum scales of production or if it ends in the achievement of a monopoly position by the last, and most efficient, survivor.[14] But over the past twenty years, neither of these two things seems to have occurred. Though, *ex-ante*, fears may have been expressed for the economic viability of particular investment efforts, market growth has usually vindicated them *ex-post* and capacity has frequently been insufficient rather than over-abundant. There have, of course, been crisis periods, and during the brief but sharp recessions of 1958, 1965, and 1971, capital utilization rates fell drastically. But on these few occasions, the situation was saved by the government. Rather than seeing firms engage in cut-throat competition, each trying to preserve as large as possible a share of a shrinking market, the M.I.T.I. usually intervened by arranging temporary cartels which fixed prices and market shares. Interestingly enough, even these interventions were, in a sense, 'growth-promoting' since market shares were usually allocated as a function of existing capacity.[15] 'Excess' investors were thus doubly rewarded—in boom periods they were normally able to increase their market shares and in recession periods they were hit less than the more cautious firms.

The picture so far sketched is highly impressionistic. There are no hard and fast quantitative measures, no parameters or coefficients. But the dynamic interactions between expectations of market growth generating investments in highly efficient techniques which, in turn, create higher incomes justifying and renewing favourable expectations, with the sequence heightened by a very competitive oligopolistic structure, is not a process which lends itself easily to the rigours (and restrictions) of econometric analysis.

Savings

Paralleling the rapid rise of investment and its high share in output, is a similar development of savings. Gross national savings as a percentage of GNP in current prices, rose from 23 per cent in 1953 to nearly 40 per cent in the early 1970s, a share some 8–10 per cent above that of any other country. Table 4.2 provides an international comparison of saving ratios in major sectors of the economy. The coverage of Table 4.1 has here been

TABLE 4.2

Gross saving ratios—1953 to 1972

(percentage of GNP at current prices)

	TOTAL	HOUSEHOLDS[1]	CORPORATIONS[2]	GOVERNMENT
Japan	36·9	15·8	13·5	7·8[2]
France	25·0	10·2	10·4	4·3
Germany	27·1	9·6	11·2[3]	6·3
Italy[4]	23·4	12·6	9·7[3]	1·1
United Kingdom	18·3	5·0	8·8	4·3
United States	18·0	8·0	7·7	2·4[2]
Finland	28·4	10·0	9·6	8·9
Netherlands	27·1	9·1	12·9[3]	5·1
Switzerland[5]	28·3	12·6	10·2	5·4

Note: Detail may not add because totals include residual errors.

    1. Including unincorporated enterprises.
    2. Including public corporations.
    3. Includes depreciation allowances of unincorporated enterprises.
    4. 1961 to 1972.
    5. 1953 to 1969.

Sources: E.P.A., *National Income Statistics*, and O.E.C.D., *National Accounts of O.E.C.D. Countries*.

extended to include a few more countries which have recorded relatively high saving ratios in the post-war period; but it will be seen that, discounting small definitional differences, the average saving propensities of Japanese households, firms and government are higher than virtually all the corresponding figures in other countries, and by quite a wide margin in most cases. For the public sector, differences from the other high-saving countries of Northern and Central Europe are of the order of $1\frac{1}{2}$ per cent of GNP, for the corporate sector they average $2\frac{1}{2}$ per cent, and they reach 5 per cent or more for households. And as with the (constant price) investment ratio, the trend rise of the over-all Japanese savings ratio throughout the period is the highest in the sample. Despite the acceleration of inflation over time, savings have been rising consistently. By 1973 they represented 40 per cent of GNP and preliminary estimates for 1974 point to only a small decline.

Government savings as a percentage of GNP show very little upward trend through these years. The reasons for their high levels must therefore be found in more structural or institutional factors. Three seem to have been important. First, a generally cautious fiscal policy, exemplified by the long-held theory that budgets should be balanced; in fact, the central government budget was often in surplus.[16] Secondly, a high automatic elasticity of tax revenues to income, which ensured growing, and unforeseen, government receipts, and allowed both cuts in tax rates and generation of savings.[17] Thirdly, a high investment propensity on the part of the authorities, largely in order to help and stimulate the corporate sector's growth, which encouraged the allocation of revenue to capital rather than to current expenditure. Relatively small defence outlays were one means by which this policy was furthered; another was the low priority given to social welfare expenditures and to transfers to the household sector.

Savings in the corporate sector, on the other hand, were fairly low by international standards in the early 1950s. They rose very rapidly over the period, as well as showing some fairly marked pro-cyclical fluctuations. This suggests that they were mainly a result of the economy's growth and of the need to retain as large as possible a share of business income in view of the pressure to invest. But despite their size and upward trend, they remained insufficient to finance the corporate sector's investment requirements and massive recourse was made to the savings of households.

It is the size and growth of household savings which accounts for most of the differences between Japan and other countries. From 1953–5 to 1970–2 gross household savings rose from 11 per cent to 17 per cent of GNP, and from 15 per cent to 26 per cent of personal disposable income. This last figure is to be set against peaks of 15–17 per cent in France, Germany, or Italy. It should be stressed that the Japanese data here presented, which, as elsewhere, are obtained as a residual item in the national accounts, are in fact highly reliable. Very similar saving ratios are obtained by regular surveys of the incomes and expenditures of employees and of various categories of the self-employed population. But the same may not be true for other countries, and notably for Italy.

The list of factors which have been put forward to explain Japan's high personal saving ratio is impressive.[18] It covers almost all conceivable fields (economic, institutional, sociological, historical, demographic), and the weights assigned to these often reflect only personal preferences. A distinction may perhaps be made between, on the one hand, institutional or other more structural influences which, *ceteris paribus*, would make for a high share of savings in income compared to other countries and, on the other hand, voluntary motivations, or involuntary factors, which might have added to (or subtracted from) savings through the period. But the borderline between these two sets of influences is inevitably blurred, with 'permanent' and 'trend' causes interacting with each other.

The most usual 'structural' factor which springs to mind when looking at savings in an international context is the notion of 'thrift' or 'traditional behaviour', as a national characteristic. Shinohara, for instance, has argued that the high values attached to frugality and hard work in pre-1868 Japan have continued to influence behaviour in modern days.[19] It is usually difficult either to substantiate or to disprove such claims. Yet, before dismissing this hypothesis for lack of data, or faith, it should perhaps be mentioned that both in the 1930s and in the mid-1950s, times when *per capita* incomes were still relatively low, personal saving ratios in workers' households were clearly high by international standards—of the order of 11–12 per cent of disposable income. In addition, it has been shown that average saving propensities among urban wage or salary earners tend to be higher in relatively poorer or more 'traditional' regions, as well as in smaller towns, in which 'inherited' cultural characteristics are likely to be stronger.[20] But this element can throw little light on the reasons for an increasing saving propensity over time, since, with the spreading of urbanization, and with economic growth generally, 'traditional' behaviour, whatever it may have been, has presumably been gradually eroded.

Turning to more economic explanations, a factor often mentioned when looking at international differences in personal saving ratios is the importance of the self-employed sector, in the labour force or in national income. While it can be argued that this variable is partly a proxy for more complicated influences, it is undeniable that saving ratios among the self-employed tend to be higher than among wage-earners for two main reasons: the uncertainties attached to many of the activities of artisans and, even more, farmers, which raise the need for precautionary savings, and the investment requirements of the non-corporate sector. Since access to outside sources of finance tends to be restricted, investment funds have to be generated out of current income. This is confirmed by survey data which show, for 1965, the saving ratio of the self-employed to be roughly 26 per cent of disposable income for farmers and 33 per cent for non-farmers.[21] Such findings, confirmed also for other countries, throw some light on the relatively high figures for the personal saving ratios shown in Table 4.2 for Japan, as well as France, Italy, and Finland. Yet, while this factor is important, it should not be forgotten that figures for employees' savings are also very high by international standards.* In addition, the weight of the self-employed sector has been declining steadily over time. Both these considerations suggest that other forces are at work probably more important than the above-average propensity to save of a steadily declining sector.

Inequalities in income distribution have also often been put forward as explanations of international differences in saving ratios. The more skewed the distribution (be it of personal income or of factor shares) the larger the volume of savings, given

* Mizoguchi (*Personal Savings and Consumption*, p. 25), provides comparable figures for a number of countries for the late 1950s and early 1960s; these show that in most cases workers' saving ratios are of the order of 6 per cent of disposable income, with peaks of 13–14 per cent in Switzerland and the Netherlands, as against Japan's 16½ per cent.

that saving propensities are higher out of profits than out of wages and higher at the top of the income scale than at the bottom. The factor-shares, or Kaldorian, hypothesis applies to the economy's over-all saving ratio rather than to that of households, and will be considered in Chapter 8, which looks at Japanese income distribution in greater detail. As for the skewness of the personal-income distribution, anticipating the conclusions of that chapter it can be said that it contributes little, if anything, to a comparative explanation of Japan's high household saving ratio, given the relative equality of Japanese incomes.

Another frequently mentioned 'structural' element is the age structure of the population. Following Colin Clark, it is held that the younger such a structure, and Japan's is relatively young, the higher the average saving ratio since, traditionally, the young save and the old dis-save. This behaviour seems confirmed in Japan's case by attempts made to calculate the 'pure age effect' on savings, abstracting, that is, from the influences of income, number of earners, and household size on the saving ratio of heads of households.[22] Results show that, as with Western patterns, the desire to save rises up to the age of 39 and falls back rapidly thereafter. But the actual picture is complicated by the particular income life-cycle which, broadly, ensures that income, and therefore saving possibilities, rise with age. In practice, the combination of these two phenomena has meant that savings are fairly high for all age classes between the ages of 25 and 64, with only small variations among them. But while this fact may boost Japan's saving ratio at any point of time, it is unlikely to have made for increases in saving proportions over time, at least in more recent years. The progressive ageing of the population and the gradual, if slow, erosion of the traditional wage hierarchy by age may have had offsetting effects on average saving propensities.

Most of the factors looked at so far have provided some reasons for Japan's relatively high household saving ratio at the outset but, if anything, would have pointed to stability or even a decline of this ratio over time. There is, however, one further institutional factor which may be able to throw a good deal of light on both rate and trends. As is well known, a large share of Japanese wages is paid in the form of twice-yearly bonuses. In 1953–5, these accounted for 14 per cent of total wages, and 11·5 per cent of employees' household incomes; and their shares had risen to as much as 25·5 and 21·5 per cent respectively in the early 1970s.

Such figures can hardly be paralleled in other developed countries. Statistics show that savings, while positive in every month of the year are particularly high in June–July and December, when most of the bonuses are paid out, and intention surveys usually indicate that one of the primary destinations of bonus income is savings. The link between these two elements is also shown by their near parallel development as percentages of disposable income over time. Between 1954–6 and 1970–2, they both increased their share in employees' disposable income by roughly $10\frac{1}{2}$ per cent, and since 1956 annual savings have been a nearly constant proportion (about 88 per cent) of bonuses, with relatively few and small deviations.

The very lumpiness of bonus payments may well represent an encouragement to savings; and there have been a number of positive reasons for bonus income to be saved in Japan. At the outset of the period, there may well have been a desire to bring the ratio of liquid assets to income back to some more 'normal' (e.g. pre-war) level, after very rapid inflation through the late 1940s had wiped out all forms of financial savings. It has been plausibly argued that, be it for transaction or precautionary reasons, savings were first accumulated to restore some desired financial assets–income ratio.[23] Bonuses, which do not seem to have been important before the war,* provided a convenient source of, almost windfall, income out of which savings could be generated. And once a more appropriate level of liquid assets, in relation to income, had been reached, saving ratios did not fall back, partly because income had risen rapidly in the meantime making savings less of a burden, and partly because other motivations had entered the picture.

Among such new motivations, an important one, stressed by Blumenthal,[24] has been the 'consumption revolution'. Traditionally it has been argued (for instance by Nurkse or Shinohara), that Japan had succeeded in isolating itself from Western consumption habits while at the same time absorbing Western techniques.[25] The virtual absence of a 'demonstration effect' on consumption, combined with the presence of a strong 'demonstration effect' on investment, meant that relatively high saving and investment

* Bonuses are hardly ever mentioned in discussions of pre-war wage problems, suggesting that their importance was limited. One reference to them (Komiya, 'Supply of Personal Savings', p. 170), indicates that they were restricted to white-collar workers.

ratios could be maintained, in contrast to the experience of today's developing economies.

Such a thesis is probably valid if applied to pre-war or early post-war Japan. Ohkawa and Rosovsky estimated that as late as 1955 'indigenous' consumption expenditure (that is, expenditure on items which had been in general use in the 1860s), still accounted for 50 per cent of total private consumption and that three-quarters of household assets, including housing, were indigenous.[26] But such ratios are likely to have changed drastically over the following fifteen or twenty years, as Japanese households 'discovered' durable goods. Diffusion rates of most major modern appliances sprang from negligible proportions to ratios of 50 or 80 per cent in a matter of a few years.[*] But interestingly enough, the consumption of other goods, notably food but also clothing, furniture, and housing remained much more attached to traditional patterns.[27] On the one hand this permitted, as was seen earlier, the survival of many traditional small-scale firms, and on the other it actually encouraged saving to acquire durable goods. Consumer credit—available to only a very limited extent—was replaced in Japan by lumpy bonus payments. *Ex-post* savings were probably not very different as a result; but *ex-ante* it was not the corporate sector which extended credit to households but households which handed over their financial surplus to the banking system.

A final, and important, form of voluntary savings must have been made in order to supplement insufficient public welfare provisions.[†] This would seem to be a fairly natural reaction when it is remembered that 75 per cent of university places in recent years have required payment of fees and that pension payments, in a country of early retirement, accounted in 1966 for only some 10 per cent of total social insurance benefits and barely 0·5 per cent of GNP, against ratios in other developed countries ranging from 30 to 50 per cent and 5 to 9 per cent respectively.[‡] And

[*] The percentage of households owning electric washing machines, television sets, or refrigerators rose from practically nil in 1955 to roughly 40 per cent in 1960 and 90 per cent in 1970; passenger cars and stereo sets diffusion rates rose from zero in 1960 to 10 per cent in 1965, 20–30 per cent in 1970 and 30–40 per cent in 1972.

[†] Savings for house acquisition must also have been sizeable but are not discussed since the motivations behind them have probably been similar in all countries.

[‡] Jinushi, 'Social Security System', pp. 502–3. In the last few years Japan's ratio may have risen somewhat but so have those of most other countries and any international comparison would remain equally, if not more, unfavourable.

these *a priori* considerations are reinforced by surveys which show that 'provision against sickness', 'education of children', and 'security in old age' are the three strongest motives for saving.[28]

The picture sketched so far has not been very coherent. Various structural factors and motivations likely to influence savings have been indicated, but they have not been quantified or interpreted in the light of theoretical models. But quantification is probably impossible, in view of the complexity of the issue; and most theories have one main drawback—they tend to look at savings as a residual and focus their attention on consumption. The one approach which, prima facie, is most likely to throw some light on Japanese experience is Friedman's 'permanent income' hypothesis, which stresses differences between regular and transitory income and their respective allocations to consumption and savings. In many ways this theory seems very attractive. Given a system of pay-by-age, annual increments in regular income could be foreseen with a reasonable degree of accuracy and long-term consumption plans drawn up accordingly. And bonuses could be regarded, if not quite as windfalls, at least as exceptional income and therefore saved. The actual strong association between bonus income and saving was noted earlier; and a similar close link exists between consumption expenditure and 'non-temporary' income. Between 1956 and 1973, $92\frac{1}{2}$ per cent of household income, *excluding* bonuses and other 'temporary' income, of urban employees was consumed; and the ratio did not vary by more than $1\frac{1}{2}$ per cent in any year. It could therefore be argued that in Japan both savings and consumption decisions are voluntary, with regular and foreseeable income deciding the pattern of consumption and expected, but somehow special, bonus income being largely saved.

Yet in practice things may not be quite as clear cut. Though rising income could be expected over an individual's life-cycle, any more precise *ex-ante* forecast than that would probably be wide of the mark. The varying intensity of wage negotiations during 'spring rounds', or the much faster than expected growth of the economy over the period as a whole, meant that wage increases usually were well above *a priori* expectations. And it is even more difficult to associate bonuses with Friedman's transient income. The latter, as suggested by the terminology, is very much in the nature of a non-recurring windfall. Bonuses on the other hand, except in the early 1950s when they were an innovation, have long been regarded as a normal component of total earnings.

Though voluntary motivations clearly play a role in explaining both consumption and savings, these various considerations suggest that plans may frequently have been thwarted by unforeseen and unforeseeable income changes. Thus, involuntary forces must also have been at work. Rapid growth is the most obvious likely generator of involuntary savings. As argued by many theories of the consumption function, consumer expenditure (C) tends to lag behind the growth of income (Y). Rather than C_t being a unique function of Y_t, as assumed by Keynes, it may well be influenced by past consumption patterns (C_{t-1}) as well. The stronger the impact of the second factor and the faster the growth of income, the more rapid the increase in savings. It is almost impossible to dissociate the two elements in econometric estimates since both usually have high explanatory powers. But it would seem plausible to argue that in a very rapidly growing economy in which, in addition, growth forecasts have usually underestimated actual outcomes, lags in the adjustment of consumption to income could be particularly important.

Such lags may also provide a partial explanation for the more recent behaviour of the savings ratio which, contrary to what would seem to be rational behaviour, has been rising even more rapidly than before, despite a notable acceleration of inflation. In the mid-1960s, net savings, as a percentage of household disposable income, were about 17·5 per cent. They were 20 per cent in 1969–71 and rose yet further to 21 per cent in 1972, 22 per cent in 1973, and may have fallen back only marginally in 1974 despite an extremely rapid erosion of their real value.

To some extent such behaviour could reflect a positive relation between voluntary savings and inflation. If it is true that a part of savings is designed to compensate for an inadequate social security system, then inflation, by raising the price of present and future social services, would actually increase the need for savings.

But involuntary factors may have played an even larger role. A combination of the lag hypothesis advanced above and wrong expectations or 'money-illusion' type behaviour may have depressed real consumption below what it would otherwise have been. It is possible that in a situation of accelerating inflation households may have continued to increase their consumption expenditures in money terms at roughly the same pace as before without perceiving, at least in the short run, the erosion of their real consumption standards.

A very simple test shows that there may be grounds for this hypothesis. Taking the period 1964–72, during which both consumer prices and the saving ratio were rising, the standard deviation (and *a fortiori* the coefficient of variation) for quarterly seasonally-adjusted percentage changes in the value of consumption is a good deal lower than that for changes in volume. This could suggest that ratios of spending to income are more stable in money than in real terms and that changes in the volume of consumption may be a sort of residual. In the case of Japan such a conclusion may be more justified than elsewhere. In a very rapidly growing economy, tastes and patterns of demand are constantly changing and the concept of 'real' consumption may be inappropriate, if only because spending patterns are less fixed than in conditions of slower growth and the 'volume' of new goods (or, increasingly, services) consumed out of additional income cannot really be appreciated by the purchaser. In other words, money expenditure is raised regularly, as a function of both present disposable income and past money value of consumption; and, either because of money illusion or because of changes in consumption patterns, it is not perceived that these increases in nominal consumption result in smaller increases in real consumption. Thus, as incomes respond to inflation, because of trade union action or high corporate profits or both, they are increasingly allotted to savings.*

To sum up, the combination of motivations for voluntary saving, encouraged by the form of income payments and by the lack or insufficiency of certain social services, with the involuntary savings imposed by price rises or made inevitable by rapid growth seem to be the main factors behind the very high, and rising, share of savings in Japanese household income. Other factors also contribute, notably the employment and age structure of the population; but their explanatory power seems to be more limited.

* Some preliminary empirical confirmation of the validity of this hypothesis has been provided by the O.E.C.D. (*Economic Outlook*, December 1974, pp. 108–9), which has shown that, between 1956 and 1972, the difference between actual and 'expected' inflation exerted a highly significant (positive) influence on savings.

Interactions and prospects

So far, a fairly long list of factors has been reviewed making for either high, and highly productive, investment or for a large volume of savings. *Ex-post*, of course, these two magnitudes are equal. *Ex-ante*, however, they may differ and it is important to know by what mechanism, and following what causation, the two are equalized. In Japan, it was undoubtedly a Keynesian rather than a classical mechanism which was at work. High investment ratios stimulated growth and thereby pulled up savings, rather than high autonomous savings inducing an equivalent flow of investment. That investment was the main growth-stimulating factor seems to be beyond doubt. It is true that international cross-section analyses have often failed to detect a strong relation between investment shares and GNP growth-rates. But in Japan's case, the association seems overwhelming, for reasons that have been given already and will be only briefly mentioned again. Private fixed investment led the various cycles and has been the most dynamic component of total demand through the past twenty years. By embodying latest techniques, it allowed a progessive rejuvenation of the capital stock and the achievement of optimal levels of production and economies of scale. And in addition to enhancing supply, it continuously created new demand.

Savings were in many ways but a consequence of the income growth propelled by extremely high rates of capital formation. Corporate savings were able to increase rapidly, thanks to large profits made possible by successful investment drives. Government savings could be high because rapid income growth increased tax receipts at unforeseen rates. Household savings, even with a relatively large autonomous component, were boosted by over-all growth both directly and indirectly. A direct effect came through rapid personal income increases combined with lagged adjustments of consumption; an indirect inducement was provided by the rising share in total income of bonus payments, themselves largely a function of corporate profits. As argued by Ohkawa and Rosovsky, Japanese savings can be '. . . considered as an essentially dependent process whose key determinants are the rate of growth and the level of income'.[29] This being said, it is nevertheless obvious that without a high saving propensity, especially on the part of households, Japan's investment effort would not have been sustainable. The existence of a large and steadily growing volume of highly liquid personal savings, which were efficiently mobilized by the banking system and transferred to the corporate sector, clearly enhanced growth possibilities and facilitated the achievement of fixed investment ratios of the order of 30 per cent or more of GNP. To quote Ohkawa and Rosovsky again: 'The frequently repeated thesis concerning investment as the driving force of Japanese growth does not imply a minor role for savings.'[30]

Japan's future growth prospects are, therefore, heavily coloured by what will happen to both capital formation and saving propensities. The private sector's investment behaviour has, until recently at least, remained highly buoyant. Despite the uncertainties and shocks which followed a relatively long recession, two revaluations of the currency and an unprecedented rate of inflation, private non-residential fixed investment rose in volume by some 20 per cent in 1973. And forecasts for 1974, as well as business surveys (which had been made before the outbreak of the 'oil crisis' and the adoption of severely restrictive policies at the end of 1973), were pointing to further large increases.

It would seem, therefore, that forces stimulating investment are still strong. It is true that the encouragement to investment provided by the competition for market shares, as outlined above, may have lost some of its force. Concentration and oligopolistic collusions have been increasing, especially since the 1971 recession. Moreover, the entrance of newcomers has become progressively more difficult as the size of initial investment outlays has risen *pari passu* with market growth and new foreign technology is no longer freely available to the same extent as before. But the threat of foreign competition, consequent upon rapid trade liberalization in recent years and the currency's revaluations, may have partly offset the diminished intensity of domestic competitive forces; and new techniques developed at home may be progressively taking the place of the exploitation of foreign technological progress. Direct macro-economic evidence for this is not available, but such a tendency is strongly suggested by the acceleration of investment growth in the late 1960s (when, presumably, the 'technological gap' had already been greatly narrowed), the increasing share of research and development expenditure in GNP, the rising value of payments for patents and royalties received by Japan and, of course, by the innumerable articles of foreign journalists who marvel at the technical innovations to be found in many modern Japanese factories.

In addition, changing demand patterns are still providing new investment opportunities. Demand for durables is far from being exhausted despite saturation for some particular commodities, and changes in consumption habits towards services create new wants. More importantly, shifts in the composition of investment itself may have made for higher shares of capital-formation in total output. Anti-pollution investment has been representing a rising share of total outlays, not only because of direct government regulations but also because the installation of such equipment has become an almost indispensable condition for obtaining permission from local authorities to establish new factories.

Finally, the decline in the price of capital relative to that of labour has probably accelerated. Taking as a proxy for these two variables the real rates of return to capital and labour respectively (as estimated below, see Chapter 8 and Fig. 9), the relative price of capital which had risen until 1960–1 has been on a falling trend since then. An even more rapid and accelerating decline is shown by a very simple current-price proxy—the ratio of the average interest rate on all loans and discounts extended by the banking system to monthly wages in all industries. In a static framework, movements in relative factor prices should not affect total investment flows but only their composition. But in a dynamic economy, continuing rapid increases in labour costs and very stable costs of loanable funds in money terms (and, therefore, declining costs in real terms) may lift investment propensities above what they would otherwise have been. Be this as it may, it appears that labour-saving investment has been increasing in importance over time. The ratio of the total private capital stock (excluding dwellings) to the (potential) labour force, which had increased only slowly between 1954 and 1960, rose somewhat faster in the following decade and has shown a marked acceleration since 1969. More direct estimates of labour-saving investment also suggest that substitution of capital for labour has increased over time with nearly 40 per cent of FY 1972 investment in manufacturing being made specifically for that purpose.[31]

These tendencies suggest that the economy's over-all capital–output ratio may eventually increase and capital's productivity diminish. In other words, for any given growth rate of income, investment rates must increase from past levels, and therefore more savings must be generated or, alternatively, for a given level of investment, income growth will decelerate. Until the mid-1960s Japan was able to avoid both these alternatives since capital–output ratios were actually falling. And in the latter half of the 1960s, the share of investment in output increased sufficiently to more than offset the increasing amount of capital required for any annual increment of production. In the early 1970s, however, this did not happen and recent estimates of Japanese potential output show a marked deceleration of growth possibilities in the four or five years since 1970, despite roughly unchanged investment proportions.[32]

Ex-ante nothing ensures that it will be possible to continue matching high or rising shares of private investment in total output with an adequate volume of savings. On the contrary, should growth decelerate as a result of the purely technical factors just mentioned, saving propensities, which it has been argued are to an important extent a function of growth itself, might also fall or at best remain constant. Instead of high investment ensuring high rates of growth of income and therefore savings, high investment may be unable to contribute to the same high income growth as in the past and Japan's marginal propensity to save may decline. This could lead either to more frequent imposition of restrictive policies, which would dampen favourable expectations, and/or to permanent inflationary pressures. The latter in turn could have two negative effects on savings. First, they might in time lessen the impact of 'money illusion' among consumers, and thereby reduce involuntary savings (if it is accepted that there is a link between the two phenomena). Secondly, they might bring about a voluntary curtailment of savings should the present extremely rapid erosion of the real value of the 'stock' of savings continue.* And voluntary savings might also be reduced, or at least not increased further, should the government plans for the creation of a 'welfare-oriented' economy (on which more in Chapter 6 below), improve the levels of pensions and social security generally.

These arguments suggest that several of the factors which have

* Most savings are held in the very liquid form of cash or relatively short-term deposits with banks or the post office. In 1974, the rate of return on such deposits was of the order of 5–6 per cent; the rate of consumer price inflation of 20–25 per cent! However, savings have been losing their value for many years without any impact yet on saving propensities. Between 1960 and 1969, for instance, the annual real yield of deposits ranged from zero to −4·5 per cent, depending on degree of liquidity and on the price deflator used: E.P.A., *ESJ* (*1969–1970*), p. 122.

made for high savings until now might lose some force in the future. They should not, however, be taken as conclusive. While an increasing capital–output ratio seems inevitable, declines in Japan's saving ratio have been predicted all too often in the past and have not yet materialized. New motivations may take the place of old ones or offset the influence of decelerating growth. But the possibility of a negative process of interactions between private investment, output growth, and savings substituting itself for the hitherto virtuous circle cannot be discounted entirely. Before passing judgement, however, it would be well to look at likely future trends in government policies, labour supply, and income distribution, and leave a final consideration of longer-run prospects for the concluding chapter.

NOTES

1. S. Kuznets, 'Notes on Japan's Economic Growth', in L. R. Klein and K. Ohkawa (eds.), *Economic Growth—The Japanese Experience since the Meiji Era*, Homewood, Ill. 1968, pp. 410–21.

2. These figures are based on official estimates of the gross private and public non-residential capital stocks, as published in the *1973–1977 Basic Economic and Social Plan*, p. 159, and on very rough estimates of the residential housing stock.

3. E.P.A., *ESJ (1965–1966)*, p. 61 and O.E.C.D., *ESJ, 1970*, p. 39.

4. J.E.R.C., *The Outlook for a Trillion Dollar Economy*, Tokyo 1971, p. 76.

5. A vivid description of official intervention in these various fields, as well as of the private investment drives of the period, is given by Sautter, *Japon—Le prix de la puissance*, Ch. 3.

6. Ohkawa and Rosovsky, *Japanese Economic Growth*, p. 92.

7. Kuznets, 'Notes on Japan's Economic Growth', pp. 388–95.

8. E.P.A., *ESJ (1970–1971)*, p. 25.

9. Several of these points are developed in E.P.A., *ESJ (1964–1965)*, pp. 78–80.

10. S. Nishikawa, *Concentration under Rapid Economic Growth: Japanese Manufacturing—1955 to 1962*, E.P.A. Economic Research Institute 1969, p. 14.

11. See for instance W. J. Baumol, *Business Behavior, Value and Growth*, New York 1959.

12. Allen, *Japan's Economic Expansion*, p. 192.

13. H. Iyemoto, R. Mikitani, and K. Ohno, 'Survey of Entrepreneurs Investment Behavior: Some Results of the "Questionnaire" Study by Kōbe University Study Group of Money and Banking', in J. Yao (ed.), *Monetary Factors in Japanese Economic Growth*, Kōbe University 1970.

14. M. Bronfenbrenner, '"Excessive Competition" in Japanese Business', *Monumenta Nipponica*, 1–2, 1966.

15. Yamamura, *Economic Policy in Postwar Japan*, p. 85.

16. R. Tachi, 'Fiscal and Monetary Policy', in Komiya (ed.), *Postwar Economic Growth*, pp. 15–18.

17. H. T. Patrick, 'The Financing of the Public Sector in Postwar Japan', in Klein and Ohkawa (eds.), *Economic Growth*, pp. 330–1.

18. Two of the most complete expositions are T. Blumenthal, *Saving in Postwar Japan*, East Asia Research Centre, Harvard University 1970, and T. Mizoguchi, *Personal Savings and Consumption in Postwar Japan*, Tokyo 1970; interesting surveys can also be found in R. Komiya, 'The Supply of Personal Savings', in Komiya (ed.), *Postwar Economic Growth* and in Chapter 2 of Shinohara, *Structural Changes*. The following discussion draws heavily on all these sources.

19. Shinohara, *Structural Changes*, p. 66.

20. *Ibid.*, pp. 66–70; see also a somewhat different approach supporting these conclusions in Blumenthal, *Saving in Postwar Japan*, Ch. 5.

21. Mizoguchi, *Personal Savings and Consumption*, Ch. 2.

22. Blumenthal, *Saving in Postwar Japan*, pp. 46–53.

23. Shinohara, *Structural Changes*, pp. 60–1.

24. Blumenthal, *Saving in Postwar Japan*, Ch. 4.

25. Shinohara, *Structural Changes*, pp. 40–1.

26. K. Ohkawa and H. Rosovsky, 'The Indigenous Component in the Modern Japanese Economy', *EDCC*, April 1961, pp. 489–91.

27. Blumenthal (*Saving in Postwar Japan*, pp. 70–4), provides some examples of Japan's relatively skewed consumption patterns; see also Ch. 8 of Mizoguchi, *Personal Savings and Consumption*.

28. E.P.A., *ESJ (1966–1967)* p. 92.

29. Ohkawa and Rosovsky, *Japanese Economic Growth*, p. 172.

30. *Ibid.*, p. 212.

31. E.P.A., *ESJ (1972–1973)*, p. 20.

32. O.E.C.D., *ESJ, 1974*, p. 13.

CHAPTER 5

LABOUR

LABOUR market developments provide a fairly sharp contrast to the buoyant expansion of investment. While the economy's gross capital stock grew by 10 per cent per annum between 1953 and 1972, the labour force (employed plus unemployed) expanded at an annual rate of barely $1\frac{1}{2}$ per cent. This growth rate was only marginally faster than that witnessed in the major West European economies and slightly slower than those recorded by the United States or the Soviet Union. At a first glance, therefore, it does not seem that labour force developments can contribute much to an explanation of Japan's exceptional performance. It is true that the $1\frac{1}{2}$ per cent over-all rate hides some very divergent sectoral developments. Thus, employment in non-agricultural activities rose by over $3\frac{1}{2}$ per cent per annum, well above the record of other major economies. Re-allocation of labour from the primary to the secondary or tertiary sectors could therefore have made a substantial contribution to growth; but the crude measures used to illustrate the effects of inter-sectoral labour shifts do not usually show that these were very important. It is true that such results are based on simplifying assumptions and use a very static approach;* but they constitute a temptation to belittle labour's contribution to post-war growth, which is reinforced by the relatively limited attention paid to this factor in the literature.

Yet, while it is undoubtedly true that the main thrust in Japan's expansion came from capital formation, labour force developments also played some role, both direct and indirect. Even leaving aside such imponderable qualities as rapid adaptability to different tasks, hard work, strong motivations, and

---

* The assumptions which are made in this sort of exercise have a crucial bearing on the results. Hence the available estimates differ quite widely. A number of estimates put the contribution of labour shifts to growth of total output at 10 to 20 per cent of the output growth-rate between the mid-1950s and the late 1960s (e.g. Ohkawa and Rosovsky, *Japanese Economic Growth*, pp. 115–17, Michalski *et al.*, *Perspektiven der Wirtschaftlichen Entwicklung in Japan*, Stuttgart 1972, pp. 137–8, or E.P.A., *ESJ* (*1966–1967*) p. 54). Using the assumptions made by the O.E.C.D. (*The Growth of Output*, pp. 38–9) results, however, in a more pronounced contribution—of the order of 30 per cent, second only to that shown for Italy.

dedication, etc., which have often been bestowed on Japanese workers, the apparent discipline of the work force, as measured by the relatively small number of working hours lost through strikes in comparison with most other major market economies, must have helped, at least indirectly, to enhance the growth of output. A more important factor, mentioned several times already, has been the high educational level attained by Japan's labour force. International comparisons suggest that in terms either of years of schooling or of percentage of the population following higher education, the Japanese level is second only to that of the United States.[1] This is, of course, an incomplete comparison, since the impact of education on economic growth will greatly depend on the form and content of the learning imparted. Accounting for such factors would seem to be conceptually impossible. But lack of data should not lead to an automatic underestimation of the contribution to growth of labour's 'quality'. Without a competent and increasingly skilled labour force, a good deal of the investment effort might well have been wasted (or not undertaken in the first place).

Factor proportions and choice of techniques

One important feature of Japan's labour market which has a bearing on the country's economic performance is the existence, already mentioned, of a wide spectrum of wage differentials by scale of firms. The relevance of this phenomenon for the persistence of a dual economic structure was examined in Chapter 2. But wage differentials also influenced the relationship between labour supply and over-all growth, since they allowed a much wider choice of production techniques than would probably have existed under a more uniform wage structure. The existence of opposite differentials for capital costs, i.e. an inverse relation between firms' size and interest rates on borrowed funds, reinforces this argument since it provides a further encouragement to the adoption of very different combinations of productive factors depending on scale.*

A graphical presentation, using familiar isoquant curves, can perhaps best illustrate this point.[2] In Fig. 5 Panel A shows two relative factor price lines, p_1 and p_2, facing firms within a given

---

* It could be argued, however, that the frequent use of second-hand machinery by smaller enterprises lowers their purchase price of capital goods. Much, in fact, depends on what concept of capital costs one is looking at.

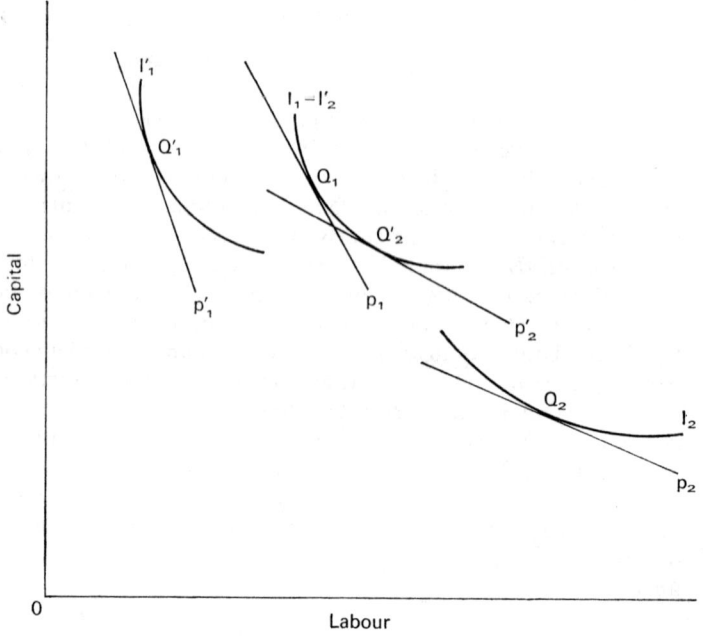

(a) Isoquants by enterprise scale

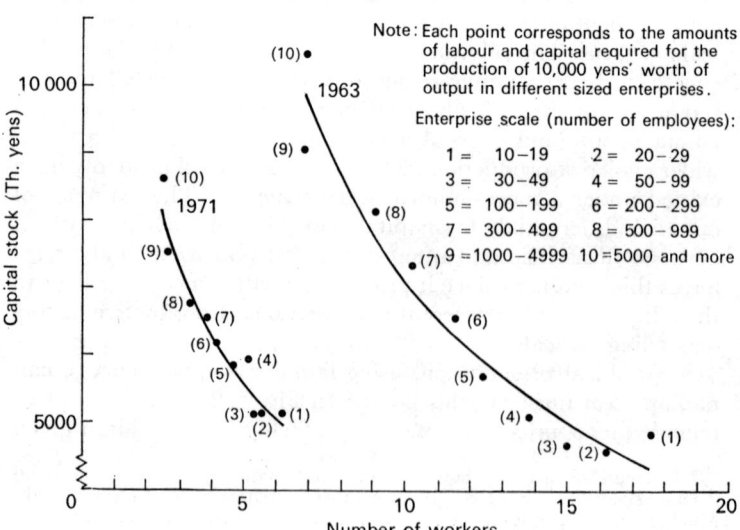

(b) 'Isoquant' for the manufacturing sector

Note: Each point corresponds to the amounts of labour and capital required for the production of 10,000 yens' worth of output in different sized enterprises.

Enterprise scale (number of employees):

1 =	10–19	2 =	20–29
3 =	30–49	4 =	50–99
5 =	100–199	6 =	200–299
7 =	300–499	8 =	500–999
9 =	1000–4999	10 =	5000 and more

Fig. 5. *Enterprise and industry isoquants*
Source: M.I.T.I., *Census of Manufactures*.

sector. The p_1 line will be relevant to large-scale enterprises for which labour is relatively more expensive than capital. Small firms, on the other hand, will be facing the p_2 line. The isoquants I_1 and I_2 represent two different technical possibilities, open to both firms, for the production of a given output volume. I_1, which will be chosen by the large firm, is a relatively capital-intensive method of production in which capital–labour substitution possibilities are fairly limited. I_2, a more flexible and relatively labour-intensive technique, will be selected by the smaller firm. Other isoquants and other factor price lines lying between these two can be imagined, corresponding to different production possibilities and to the various wage and interest rate differentials existing in the economy. The curve linking points Q_1 and Q_2 and other points of tangency between isoquants and factor price lines can be thought of as being a kind of 'sectoral isoquant'—with the important difference, however, that the various observed points along it are not potential but actual combinations of factors producing a given output.

Through time, the slope of both factor price lines will presumably become steeper, with labour appreciating in relation to capital. And the isoquants themselves are likely to move in a leftward direction as capital–labour ratios increase in both sets of firms for any given level of production. Large enterprises will continue to lead in the technological field, either importing or creating new processes. Their isoquant will move to I'_1. Smaller firms, on the other hand, can be assumed to be somewhat more passive and to adjust their investment and labour-hiring plans to given factor price relations. Their productivity may however improve, especially if they are able (or even forced) to adopt the equipment just discarded by the larger firms. In such a case they could move to isoquant I_1. The smaller firm would not, however, produce at point Q_1, but at some point to the right of it where its factor price line will be tangent to I_1. The new 'industry isoquant' line will now join points Q'_1 and Q'_2. In practice, of course, the more likely movement of individual isoquants, and therefore of the 'industry isoquant', is in a south-western direction as economies of labour and capital are achieved, for any given output, in both sets of firms.

For all this to be possible, three major conditions must be satisfied.[3] The first, already mentioned, is the existence of wage, or factor price, differentials by scale. The second is the availability of a whole array of techniques, ranging from very capital- to very labour-intensive methods of production. The third is the presence of sufficient demand for the output of the relatively labour-intensive firm, which may differ from that of the more capital-intensive firm. (This last condition need not hold, however, if one assumes that the two isoquants apply to firms within the same branch. In such a case, product differentiation may be relatively limited.)

It is usually argued that such conditions are seldom present in most of today's economies, whether developing or developed. Demonstration effects on consumption limit demand for 'traditional' goods; the factor price lines facing individual firms tend to be similar, and technological choice is frequently restricted to the processes developed in the more advanced economies. These in turn are strongly biased in a labour-saving direction. In fact, relatively simple models frequently assume that at any moment of time investors have hardly any choice. Whatever factor prices may be, most commodities can be produced with only one technology, i.e. factor proportions are fixed. The possibility of an alternative, highly labour-intensive technique is sometimes accepted in theory, but is usually dismissed as non-viable in open economies, in which only goods produced with the most advanced techniques can be competitive. The only exception to this rule could come from the existence of substantial wage flexibility; but in those dual economies in which wages are flexible to some extent, below-average labour costs are usually recorded in underdeveloped regions in which investment in more labour-intensive techniques is inhibited by the widespread presence of external diseconomies.

Japan may provide an exception to the general rule. The particular nature of its dualism means not only that it faces wide factor price differentials, but also that these occur within the industrial sector. And the seemingly inevitable limitations to technological choice may have been less binding than elsewhere, partly for historical and partly for economic reasons. At the outset, technical backlog presented the opportunity to import very capital-intensive methods for heavy industry or for production of new commodities, while the persistence of past consumption habits allowed the continuation of much more labour-intensive operations in the traditional sector.* Through

* As was mentioned in Chapter 4, goods and services used in pre-Meiji days still represented 50 per cent of private consumption expenditure in 1955.

time, and given very rapid economic expansion as well as a shrinking pool of under-utilized labour, progressively more capital-intensive techniques were adopted all along the scale of enterprises. Large companies continued to import foreign technology; smaller ones gradually abandoned 'traditional' lines of activity, entered into sub-contracting arrangements, bought second-hand equipment or switched over to processes discarded by the larger firms.

Extremely rapid growth probably facilitated this technological transfer. Competition and market expansion required frequent increases in capacity and adoption of continuously more efficient techniques by all enterprises. But the equipment which was obsolete for one sort of firm could, technically, be still perfectly appropriate for a different set of firms (e.g. sub-contracting enterprises), provided that recourse could be had to somewhat cheaper labour. In other words, Japan may have adopted what has been called a 'half-way technology' for its small firm sector.[4] Capital intensity was lower than in the largest firms, but a good deal higher than in the purely labour-intensive model sometimes used for developing economies; and this half-way technology also mitigated the contradiction between Japan's domestic factor endowments and the introduction of the very capital-intensive foreign techniques made inevitable by the reopening of the country to foreign trade after the war.*

That the various theoretical arguments so far developed have some connection with reality is illustrated in panel B of Fig. 5 which, assuming constant returns to scale, shows the various combinations of capital and labour used by different sized firms in manufacturing to produce 10,000 yens-worth of output in 1963 and 1971 (the first and last years for which full data were available in the *Census of Manufactures*). Because of lack of data, output and capital stock are expressed in current prices and no adjustment is made for different capital utilization rates as between firms. This latter statistical shortcoming is unlikely to alter the shift through time of the two curves, since over-all capacity utilization rates in the two years were roughly similar;

---

* This was not the only way in which the requirements of modern industry were made to match domestic factor proportions. As pointed out by Ohkawa and Rosovsky (*Japanese Economic Growth*, p. 90), other methods were the selection of branches most suited to a relatively intensive use of labour (e.g. light machinery and small electric durables), or the fullest possible use of capital equipment by multi-shift work.

it is impossible to say whether differing utilization rates by scale of firms affect individual points on either curve. Use of current price data clearly distorts the through-time comparison. Since output prices rose faster in smaller firms than in larger ones, and faster than prices of investment goods, the 1971 curve should probably be both closer and somewhat more parallel to the 1963 line than shown here. But the general leftward shift, as well as the shortening of the observed curve, due to the closing of factor price differentials and to the adoption of more capital-intensive techniques by all firms, remain largely unaffected.

The validity of the diagram depends crucially on the assumption of constant returns to scale, and this is one of the limitations of the argument. Another may come from excessive aggregation. The 1963 and 1971 curves have been drawn for the whole of the manufacturing sector. It is possible that for individual branches, notably those in which production functions are discontinuous from an engineering standpoint, the very wide choice of techniques here suggested is not, in fact, present. But the existence of small firms in such instances is also less likely. More generally, and subject to further more detailed and comparative examination, it can be argued that Japan was able to innovate, or at least adapt existing technology to its factor endowments, more successfully than most other countries which had smaller wage or interest rate differentials and in which slower growth may not have permitted as rapid a switch of techniques.

There is one other major country which, like Japan, utilized '. . . the most advanced technology while at the same time economizing the scarcest inputs—capital and skilled labour', namely the Soviet Union. There are both similarities and differences in this aspect of Japanese and Soviet industrial development. The latter involved 'selection of a mixed or dual technology employing advanced Western technology with a high capital–labour ratio in the basic production processes and old-fashioned methods with a low capital–labour ratio in auxiliary and subsidiary processes', and 'extensive multiple-shift operation of plant with equipment typically kept in operation long after what would be its retirement age in the more advanced countries of the West'.[5] As in Japan, a given output was thus achieved with a relatively larger use of labour and a smaller use of capital than would have been the case almost everywhere else. As Japan and the Soviet Union were both 'capital-scarce' countries over most of the period of their industrial development, this was clearly a great advantage and, *inter alia* ensured virtual full employment of the labour force.

The links between these relatively static arguments and Japan's growth record are not immediate. Wage differentials and the availability of a wide spectrum of techniques allowed a resource allocation pattern which, given the relative scarcity of one factor, may have been a lot closer to textbook ideals than that of many other countries. But *per se*, this only enhances the volume of output at a given moment of time. However, over time, the possibility of adopting a large number of techniques and, more importantly, of keeping both factors of production fully employed, meant that the country was always close to the outer bound of its (short-run) production possibility curve.

'Unlimited supplies of labour'

The most important form in which labour contributed to Japanese economic growth was by being 'abundant'. This may seem paradoxical in view of what was said above on the small over-all growth of the labour force. The latter, however, is a statistical fact which does not reflect the underlying demand–supply relations on the labour market. In fact, a vast Marxian 'reserve army of the unemployed' or, more aptly, of the under-employed, existed in Japan at the outset of the period. Large numbers of people receiving well below average wages or no wages at all were active either as self-employed and unpaid family workers (mainly in agriculture),* or as employees in very small firms (mainly in industry and services). The gradual absorption of many such workers into more modern and better-paid forms of employment had no statistical effect on the over-all growth of the labour force. But seen from an economic standpoint, their existence suggests that the supply schedule of labour to the modern sector was a good deal more elastic than is suggested by the aggregate figures.

It is usually assumed that an abundant labour supply can contribute to growth either directly, by allowing a highly labour-intensive development, promoted for instance by the state, or indirectly, and more appropriately in the case of an already

---

* Nearly 60 per cent of the total labour force in the mid-1950s, as against rates elsewhere of, at most, 50 per cent (Italy) and more usually 20–35 per cent (United States, Germany, or France).

partly industrialized economy, in a Marx–Lewis mechanism of capital accumulation. In the Lewis framework,[6] the economy is divided into two sectors—modern and traditional (or, for simplicity, industry and agriculture). In the latter, labour supply is excessive and labour's marginal productivity lies below the subsistence wage level. In the former, profit maximization is assumed and workers will be employed only if their wage falls short of marginal productivity. As long as surplus labour exists, the modern sector, through (capital-widening) investment, will be able to increase its employment at a wage close to the subsistence level, by drawing labour from agriculture. The increase in output achieved thanks to the shift of labour is nothing but 'surplus value'. Some will accrue in agriculture and some in industry. The former may or may not be channelled to the modern sector; the latter, however, can be expected to be reinvested and will thereby increase industrial employment yet further. This process continues until 'unlimited supplies' are exhausted, that is until labour's marginal productivity in agriculture rises above the subsistence level of wages (because of the diminished number of farm workers or improved technology or both). After this 'turning point', both sectors adopt profit maximization criteria and increases in labour's marginal productivity through (capital-deepening) investment will be accompanied not by rising employment but by rising wages. The share of profits in total income will now either rise or stay the same or even fall, compared to the pre-turning point position, depending on the nature of technological progress and on the elasticity of substitution between labour and capital.

These arguments are clearly very simplified. Despite a number of attempts made to fit a Lewis-type mechanism to Japan's economy, it is doubtful whether post-war developments closely conform to the simple accumulation model just described. For one thing, real wages were rising through time, rather than being constant; and capital–labour ratios were also increasing, in contrast to what happens in the simple model which assumes only capital-widening forms of investment. But increasing real wages can be accommodated by the model, and the distinction between capital-deepening and capital-widening is almost impossible to draw in practice, given that any new investment usually involves both extensions of capacity and more sophisticated machinery. Other features of the model are, however, more difficult to reconcile with reality. Chapter 2 showed that a major characteristic of the economy was not so much duality between agriculture and industry, as a differential structure within industry. And the modern sector (i.e. large scale firms) was not faced with near subsistence wages, but, for a number of reasons, had to pay its workers rates well above those set in the traditional and small-scale sectors.

Yet despite these difficulties, some features of the Lewis model can be illuminating—notably that of abundant labour setting some sort of ceiling to wage rates or, in a dynamic setting, to wage increases. The existence of wage differentials made it impossible for the modern sector to employ labour at the subsistence wage, but it provided a strong incentive to workers to move from low-pay to high-pay enterprises. Simplifying, each set of firms, except the smallest, could face almost perfectly elastic labour supplies at its particular wage level. Through time this meant that relatively small wages increases were sufficient to satisfy labour requirements. The over-all share of profits in income was lower than it would have been in a purely Lewis-type mechanism, but it could grow through time relatively unhindered by wage pressures. The fact that the growth of productivity consistently outstripped that of real wages (by roughly 1 to 1·5 per cent per annum between the mid-1950s and the early 1970s[7]) strongly supports this conclusion. At home these developments allowed high rates of profits. Abroad, they made possible continuous falls in the prices of Japanese goods relative to those of competitors. Both factors stimulated investment, the latter by creating an increased demand for Japanese goods, the former by engendering further expectations of high profits. Whatever other motivations there may have been behind business investment propensities, it is clear that a high rate of return on capital, achieved through this relatively easy mechanism, could only contribute to buoyant capital formation.

This process cannot, of course, last for ever. Unlimited, or simply abundant labour in self-employment or in small-scale firms must eventually be absorbed, especially in an economy like the Japanese one which has had no recourse to immigration.* It

* The 600,000 Koreans living in Japan can hardly be assimilated to an immigrant labour force of the West European type (except in so far as they are similarly discriminated against). They were mostly brought to Japan before or during the war and there have been no moves to increase their number since then.

is tempting at this stage to push the analogy with the Lewis model a bit further and try to detect (or forecast) some 'turning point', following which labour will become scarce rather than abundant. Fairly rigorous proof of the existence of such a turning point in the late 1950s or early 1960s has been provided by Minami.[8] The main drawback of his analysis is, however, that agriculture is used as a proxy for the labour-abundant sector; and this may not be sufficient in Japanese conditions, since many small-scale enterprises in industry and services can also be assimilated to the traditional economy. Ohkawa is probably closer to reality when he proposes the introduction into the Lewis model of an intermediate stage between perfectly elastic and perfectly inelastic labour supply—a stage in which labour is forthcoming not so much from agriculture as from small-scale industrial firms and only at rising real wages.[9] In Japan, in fact, according to him, the two first stages practically overlap. The pure Lewisian phase of falling agricultural employment begins in the mid-1950s;* the 'semi-limited supplies of labour' phase of closing wage differentials begins in the late 1950s and has not yet ended.

Throughout the period under observation, therefore, it seems that labour supplies were abundant, but not infinite. Changes have occurred between the 1950s and the early 1970s but they have not altered this pattern fundamentally. It is true that open unemployment has decreased, that job offers have recently out-stripped the number of job-seekers, that the growth of the aggregate capital–labour ratio has accelerated through time and, of course, that wage differentials by scale of firms have closed somewhat. But labour is still forthcoming to the modern sector, if at a rising wage rate. Its supply elasticity, while clearly not infinite, is certainly not zero, notwithstanding some sectoral bottlenecks. Most likely it is slowly decreasing. Evidence for this is provided by the already mentioned wage-productivity gap, whose existence throughout the period points to relatively abundant labour supplies. Its changes within the period (from nearly 3 per cent in the 1950s to barely 1 per cent in the 1960s) suggest that labour's supply elasticity has been declining.

---

* Before that date, and excluding a few exceptional post-war years, the agricultural labour force had remained roughly constant from the beginning of the century.

A shortage of labour?

An abundant labour supply, by affecting wages and wage differentials, allowed a relatively wide choice of techniques and contributed to high profit and investment ratios in the corporate sector. Both these mechanisms seem to have been permissive, rather than absolutely indispensable, components of growth. But the disappearance of abundant labour supplies could change this picture and bestow on labour the much more crucial role of ultimate factor of production which it has reached in most of the fully employed economies of the West. The frequent references in recent writings on the Japanese economy to impending labour shortages suggest that some such turning point into a third phase of zero labour supply elasticity is indeed imminent, and that labour force developments rather than capital accumulation (or balance of payments constraints) will be setting the ceiling to future growth possibilities.

Demographic factors *per se* are clearly making for a slower expansion of the labour force. The over-all growth of population, which has varied little over the last twenty years, is not expected to decelerate very markedly over the decade of the '70s. At 1–1·1 per cent per annum, it would still lie at the upper end of the scale for developed economies. But the age composition of the population has been changing. In the mid-1950s, the share of the population aged 15 to 64 (61 per cent), was the lowest among major countries. By the early 1970s, it had risen rapidly, contrary to developments elsewhere, and at 69 per cent was the highest. But this upward movement had stopped by the end of the 1960s and recent figures, as well as projections for the future, point to a reversal of the trend. The combination of a roughly constant growth rate of population and less favourable age structure will, *ceteris paribus*, reduce the rate of increase of the labour force in the 1970s.

In addition, participation rates may continue their longer-run decline. Throughout the period under review, Japanese participation rates (defined as the ratio of the total labour force to the population in the 15 to 64 age group) have been among the highest in the capitalist world. This is especially true for women, whose activity rates are second only to those of a few high-income and high-welfare Scandinavian countries. But trends through time in Japan, as in the case of most maturing economies, have been downwards. Lengthening education periods have been diminishing the participation rates of the young, while the gradual exodus from the countryside has brought about the well-known fall in female participation in the labour force. Unlike trends elsewhere, it is only among the older age group (40 to 64 years), that there has actually been a small increase in participation (taking men and women together), possibly because of the gradual extension of the retirement age beyond 55.

The future behaviour of participation rates is not easy to predict. Usually, they have tended to decline in the transition period from semi-development to economic maturity. But once the latter stage is approached, trends are subject to contrasting influences. This is shown, for instance, by the relative stability of some countries' participation rates through the 1960s (e.g. Germany or Britain), and the rising trends in others (like the United States, Sweden or Belgium), with earlier retirement or longer education being offset by a higher propensity for women to seek work in very highly industrialized societies. Present Japanese forecasts, contained for instance in the official plan for FYs 1973–7 or prepared by private institutions,[10] point to further declines, if at a slower rate than was recorded through the 1960s. On balance, this would seem the most likely outcome. Combining these various population, age, and participation-rate assumptions, results in an annual growth of the labour force from 1972 to 1980 of 0·8 per cent, less than half as large as the rate recorded in the 1950s and two-thirds of that witnessed in the 1960s.

These various trends and hypotheses are brought together in the following table, which tries to isolate the effect of each of the three factors examined by assuming for each in turn that the other two remained constant at their initial year levels. The sum of the three effects is equal to the total recorded change in the labour force.

A further factor which could bring about a deceleration in the growth of the total labour supply would be a more rapid fall in hours worked than has been recorded so far. This has been frequently forecast, in expectation of a gradual extension of a five-day working week. Until recently it has not materialized, and though working hours have been decreasing, their decline has been both slow and regular (from 0·75 to 1 per cent per annum since 1960). But the basic reorientation of Japanese economic priorities (on which more in the following chapter),

Components of labour force change[1]
(annual average changes in thousands)

	1953–61	1961–72	1972–80[2]
Population effect	420	520	600
Age effect	290	300	−200
Participation rate effect	0	−250	−50
Total change in labour force	710	570	350

1. The labour force is defined as the total number of employed and unemployed.
2. Based on Health and Welfare Ministry projections of the future population and on J.E.R.C. forecasts for the two other components (*The Structure of a Three-Trillion Dollar Economy*, p. 6).

Source: O.E.C.D., *Labour Force Statistics.*

should, if successfully implemented, induce an acceleration of this trend for a few years and bring the length of the working week in 1980 closer to European levels—35·4 hours in 1980 are forecast by the J.E.R.C. as against 43·3 in 1970.

Quantifiable trends, in so far as they can be predicted, seem, therefore, to point to a relatively sharp deceleration in the growth of Japan's labour force over the coming decade. But 'abundant labour' in the past, as has already been noted, was not merely a function of the development of the total labour force as recorded in the statistics. It reflected, in addition, the pressure on wage levels of an underemployed army of unpaid family members and other agricultural and small-firm workers. Over time, this source of supply has clearly been diminishing. Agriculture accounted for almost 40 per cent of the labour force in 1953–5; its 1971–3 share was below 15 per cent. The proportion of self-employed and unpaid family workers fell from 58 per cent to 32 per cent. It is true that in both percentage and absolute terms, falls in these two, partly overlapping, segments of the labour force were actually at their peak in the years 1969–72, with average annual decreases of 600,000 in the numbers in each category. But in agriculture, at least, these declines must have been due more to withdrawals from the labour force than to switches to industrial employment, in view of the rapid ageing of the farming population. And over the longer run, Japan can hardly expect to go on witnessing similarly large absolute declines in either of these two components of its work force.

Yet labour reservoirs still exist elsewhere. Surveys show that

persons without jobs wishing to work totalled 8½ million in
1971—or three million more than fifteen years earlier—
supplementing a labour force (employed, *plus* unemployed) of
some 52 million. Women represent the bulk of this potential
supply, but it also included 1½ million men. Moreover, among
the employed, low-wage and low-productivity jobs are still
widespread. Nearly one-quarter of the workers in manufacturing
were, in 1970, earning 80 per cent or less, of the sector's average
wage (and 60 per cent or less of the average wage paid in large
firms). The services sector could provide an even larger labour
supply. Community, social, and personal services accounted for
18 per cent of Japan's total employment in the early 1970s as
against shares of the order of 15 per cent in many other countries.
More important than this rather mixed category, which shows
large intercountry variations, is the share of employment in the
more homogeneous and better-defined commerce and catering
sectors. At 20 per cent in Japan this is far higher than in any
Western developed country for which data are available. Even
Japan's relatively efficient financial institutions or public administration would seem largely overstaffed to the foreign observer.[11]
The progressive conversion to a more service-oriented economy
would therefore not necessarily require large shifts from manufacturing employment, since increasing demands for services
could to a large extent be met with existing labour resources.

These few considerations suggest that, barring a sudden (and
unlikely) acceleration in the demand for workers, Japan's looming
labour shortage may not be as dramatic as it is often made out to
be. In fact, the much-publicized shortage, said already to be
afflicting the economy, is largely a shortage of young labour. It is
true that the young form a particularly crucial segment of the
labour force, especially in Japanese conditions. Young workers'
wages are below average and their skills are probably above
average, given the very rapid obsolescence of earlier training in
conditions of swift technological progress. But the desirability of
employing young workers is likely to decline. Demographic
factors will slowly bring about a further relative appreciation of
their wages and force firms to tap the reservoir of (older) workers
in smaller firms or tertiary activities who for the moment are
fixed in their jobs. These two movements must eventually lead
to a narrowing of wage gaps between age groups and between
different sized firms. But as long as such gaps continue, and

recent trends do not in fact point to much narrowing, physical shortages of labour are unlikely to exist.

Bringing together these various considerations, it seems that, on balance, the future outlook is for a continuing positive, but slowly declining, supply elasticity of labour. The 1970s will be witnessing somewhat less favourable labour supply trends than in the past on all accounts—an ageing population structure, further falls in participation rates and in hours worked, and an inevitably smaller contribution from the traditional to the modern sector. An offset to some of these trends will come from the continuing substitution of capital for labour, but such a development is, to some extent at least, limited by the relatively labour-intensive nature of some of the service activities to which demand has been, and will be, shifting. Labour is unlikely to become the bottleneck factor to future growth, which it already is in economies like the United States, Britain, or even Germany (in view of the inevitable limits to immigration). But its positive contribution, in the form of downward pressures on the wage level, and therefore abundant profits, is likely gradually to diminish. Wage costs per unit of output have been rising appreciably in the last few years and even without the 1973–4 inflation, and the inflationary expectations it induced, pressures from the side of labour would have been felt on the level of profits and/or prices. For the future of Japan's physical growth-potential, the dangers inherent in labour scarcity are, as yet, slight. But for the mechanism of accumulation through which this growth potential had been realized in the past, the future uncertainties are a good deal more serious.

NOTES

1. U. Kaneko, 'Employment and Wages', *DE*, December 1970, p. 460.

2. Similar, but not identical, arguments have been developed by Ohkawa, *Differential Structure*, pp. 61–76, and K. Miyazawa, 'The Dual Structure of the Japanese Economy and its Growth Pattern', *DE*, June 1964.

3. R. S. Eckaus, 'The Factor-proportions Problem in Underdeveloped Areas', *American Economic Review*, September 1955.

4. K. Bieda, *The Structure and Operation of the Japanese Economy*, Sydney 1970, p. 189.

5. N. T. Dodge and C. K. Wilber, 'The Relevance of Soviet Industrial Experience for Less Developed Economies', *Soviet Studies*, January 1970, p. 332.

6. W. A. Lewis, 'Economic Development with Unlimited Supplies of Labour', *Manchester School*, May 1954.

7. The 'real wage' is here defined as the total return to labour (divided by

employment), as calculated in Chapter 8 below. Similar results are obtained by using employee compensation per employee, deflated by the consumer price index.

8. Minami, *The Turning Point*.

9. Ohkawa, *Differential Structure*, pp. 145–59.

10. For instance, the J.E.R.C., *The Structure of a Three-Trillion Dollar Economy—The Japanese Economy in 1985*, Tokyo 1974, p. 6.

11. According to business surveys, manufacturing firms have also complained about the excessive number of their clerical or administrative personnel; E.P.A., *ESJ (1967–1968)*, p. 145.

CHAPTER 6

ECONOMIC POLICIES

GOVERNMENT intervention has been a crucial factor throughout Japan's modern economic history. In this respect Japan is not exceptional. Most of today's developed economies owe much of their early industrial growth to direct or indirect official encouragement. In fact, England's unplanned industrial revolution is very much the exception rather than the rule. But it could be argued that the degree of intervention practised by successive Japanese governments has lasted longer than, and has gone beyond, that witnessed in most other countries (with the obvious exception of the centrally planned economies).

It was public action which set modern economic growth in motion a century ago, founded several of the major industries of the time, accounted for over half of the capital formation undertaken in the years 1890–1940,[1] and kept a close and uninterrupted scrutiny of the economy ever since.* Since the war, many of the more direct forms of intervention experimented with in earlier days have been avoided, partly because defence spending was reduced from some 6 per cent of GNP in 1900–36 to less than 1 per cent in 1953–72. But the government's indirect involvement has remained very strong and has made a fundamental contribution to shaping Japanese economic development over the last twenty or thirty years. Discussions of Japanese government policies during those years often concentrate on the (very successful) counter-cyclical record; and short-run action of this nature will be briefly looked at below. But more important for the purpose of throwing light on Japan's performance are the longer-run measures and instruments which the authorities used to maximize the growth rate and direct the course of the economy.

---

* Indeed, public involvement goes back to pre-Meiji days. Throughout the Tokugawa period, the government exercised '. . . some degree of control over almost every aspect of economic life'; E. Sydney Crawcour, 'The Tokugawa Heritage', in Lockwood (ed.), *The State and Economic Enterprise*, p. 42.

The cyclical record

Chapter 1 has already briefly shown that economic policy was highly effective, over most of the period, in steering the economy through cyclical fluctuations. This is especially true of monetary policy. Turning points in economic activity have usually followed very closely upon changes in the Bank of Japan's stance, at least until the mid-1960s. The last decade has witnessed some apparent erosion of the effectiveness of monetary policy, but this has been partly compensated by a more flexible use of fiscal policies. Institutional factors are paramount in explaining the large measure of success which counter-cyclical policies, and notably monetary policies, have had in Japan. But it is not proposed here to describe in detail the monetary and fiscal system of the country, since several works on the subject already exist.[2] The following paragraphs will provide only the very brief and broad outline of some important institutional features necessary for an understanding of both the cyclical and the structural roles of public policy.

The most important reason for the efficiency of monetary action lies in a double set of dependences—a high dependence of corporations on the banking system and a high dependence of the latter on the Bank of Japan. Firms depend on the commercial banks for outside finance to a larger extent than in most other major economies,* for two main reasons—rapid economic growth and lack of alternative sources of capital. In the early days of the reconstruction period, internal supplies of funds were clearly insufficient to finance vast investment needs and outside capital had to be obtained from the banking system (or, in those days, directly from government financial institutions); and rapid growth then perpetuated the dependence on external financing. Though both profits and depreciation funds were usually large, the financial requirements of very rapid investment growth regularly outstripped availabilities of internal funds. The gap was filled by the banking system, since a proper capital market has never really gained a firm foothold in Japan. Share issues have been an unattractive way of raising funds because of their

* Through the 1960s, Bank of Japan figures show that roughly two-thirds of the corporate sector's financial needs were covered by internal funds in France, Germany, and the United States, but less than half in Japan.

high cost to firms,* while bonds have usually been purchased by the banks themselves, thus providing no real offset to the strict dependence of enterprises on banking tutelage.† It should perhaps be added that this dependence is two-way, at least for larger firms and major commercial banks. Corporations were forced to rely on banks to satisfy their needs for funds, but the latter were themselves hardly in a position to turn down such requests since they were frequently linked to the demanding companies in the framework of one of the giant conglomerates.

To satisfy their clients' demand for funds, the commercial banks (in fact the dozen or so major 'City banks'), were in turn closely dependent on credit from the Bank of Japan. This dependence on central bank loans stemmed largely from the near-absence of alternative sources of 'high-powered' money. Money creation through the foreign sector never played a large role, since balance of payments surpluses were small through most of the period and usually concentrated in slack periods of relatively abundant liquidity. And the post-war policy of balanced budgets, pursued until the mid-1960s, limited money creation through central government operations. By the same token, this policy prevented the accumulation of a post-war public debt (the large pre-war debt having been wiped out by inflation) and severely restricted the scope of central bank purchases and sales of securities.

At all stages, therefore, the indirect links common in a number of Western monetary systems were replaced by more direct channels of transmission. Not only was the Bank of Japan the most important source of money for the economy (just as the commercial banks taken together were the largest supplier of funds to the corporate sector), but its funds came through loans to financial institutions rather than through the mechanism of open market operations. Similarly, the financing of long-term investment through the capital market was replaced by direct bank advances. 'Overloan' is the term which has frequently been

---

* Shares have been issued at (low) issue prices rather than at (much higher) market values and dividend payments, unlike interest payments on borrowed funds, have been subject to taxation.

† In the 1960s, private credit institutions directly supplied nearly three-quarters of the external financing needs of the corporate sector. They also purchased 90 per cent of its bond issues and nearly 30 per cent of its stocks. Direct and indirect dependence thus amounted to some 80 per cent; O.E.C.D., *Monetary Policy*, pp. 16–17.

used in Japan to describe this system. By 'overloan' are really meant three things—the high dependence of enterprises on bank loans, the banks' high dependence on Bank of Japan loans and, given strong demand by the enterprises and controlled supply by the Bank, the tendency of the large City banks to grant loans in excess of deposits.[3]

The Bank of Japan's crucial position as virtually the sole lender, rather than 'lender of last resort', assured it of a high degree of supervision over the City banks to which it advanced funds. In addition it had at its disposal some further and far-reaching instruments of control. Thus, through most of the period, it also set detailed quantitative limitations, euphemistically called 'guidance lines', on City bank loans to the corporate sector. These, in turn, ensured that credit extended by other financial institutions (local banks, credit associations, long-term credit banks, etc.), which were less strictly supervised by the central bank, would follow the latter's guidelines.[4] Moreover, most interest rates were pegged, notably those on longer-term loans, allowing market forces little play except on the short-term end of the money market.

It is not surprising that in these conditions, resort to the more traditional instruments of monetary policy was limited. Minimum reserve requirements were unnecessary in view of the permanent indebtedness of the City banks to the Bank of Japan. Interest rate policy was used only very intermittently. Action on the money supply was replaced by the much more direct (and less dubiously effective) control of credit availability. And, as already mentioned, open market operations were hardly practicable before the mid-1960s, given the small amount of government bonds and bills. Over the last decade the Bank of Japan has been more active in buying and selling securities, but the impact of these operations has, by and large, been limited to evening out seasonal fluctuations in availabilities of funds.

Control of its own advances, control of the loans extended by major banks, interest rate pegging and strict regulations on capital imports and exports, in conjunction with the institutional peculiarities noted above, allowed the Bank of Japan to act swiftly and efficiently not only on monetary variables but also on those real variables which most depended on bank credit—particularly stockbuilding and private fixed investment. Since the latter were the two most important elements producing fluctuations in over-all activity, the course of the business cycle could to a large extent be mapped by the authorities—easy monetary policy until a balance of payments deficit arose, or price inflation threatened, credit restrictions from then onwards until private investment activity subsided and the trade balance swung back into surplus, or the growth of prices decelerated, and credit relaxations thereafter.

This mechanism has been somewhat impaired, but not destroyed, in recent years. Partly this has been due to a diminished sensitivity of investment to easier monetary policies, partly to a less severe imposition of restrictive policies and partly to other factors which will be looked at in the concluding section of this chapter. But a more rigorous credit crunch, like the one imposed in 1974, seems to have restored to monetary policy some of the effectiveness it had exhibited until the mid-1960s.

The cyclical role of fiscal policy looks pale in contrast. Fiscal policy suffered through most of the period from three major constraints—the budget had to be balanced or in surplus (a legacy from the United States occupation reforms), it was felt unadvisable to raise the share of taxation above 20 per cent of GNP, and little flexibility was allowed to government expenditures once a budget had been voted, apart from the possibility of one annual supplementary budget.[5] It is not surprising that in these conditions fiscal action contributed but little to demand management. A comparative study following a method developed by B. Hansen for a number of O.E.C.D. countries showed that the net stabilizing effect of total budget policy (changes in revenues and expenditures) on short-run fluctuations between FYs 1955 and 1965 was very small, smaller than that witnessed in Germany, Italy, or the United States and not much larger than that recorded in France or Britain; and even this result seems to have been obtained thanks to automatic rather than discretionary changes.[6]

Changes have, however, taken place over time. As already mentioned in Chapter 1, an easy monetary policy was insufficient to stimulate demand during the 1965 recession. With a flexibility characteristic of much of Japanese economic policy making, the balanced budget principle was abandoned and expenditures increased well beyond the limits set by current revenues. A similar policy was followed in 1971 and 1972, while in 1974 expenditure cuts were used to dampen demand. Indeed, estimates similar to the one quoted above, covering more recent years, show that the counter-cyclical record of Japanese fiscal policies has improved over time, with relatively large stabilizing effects coming from discretionary changes in years of recession.[7] In fact, fiscal and monetary policies have progressively become more complementary over the last decade. Rather than the whole burden of adjustment falling on monetary policy, the budget has taken its share of counter-cyclical action even if, on balance, the Bank of Japan tends to play a somewhat more important role in restrictive phases and the Ministry of Finance in expansionary phases.

Over the period as a whole, therefore, the government was able to keep a close watch over the economy thanks to a mixture of institutional factors (some fortuitous, some encouraged) and a fairly tight network of controls. On balance, its counter-cyclical record seems to have been positive—though this is not to say that it was perfect. There were some failures to recognize turning points; and the very ample fluctuations in growth rates of output, *per se*, suggest some miscalculations. But it should also be remembered that these fluctuations had little influence on the level of open unemployment. Indeed, the virtual absence of an unemployment constraint, as well as of a full employment ceiling, contributed powerfully to an uninhibited use of policies whenever required. In a relative sense, therefore, and taking as a standard of comparison the record of other major market economies, an over-all judgement tends to be favourable. The direct contribution of such a positive short-run performance to longer-run growth is not immediately evident. Indirectly, however, as argued convincingly by some,[8] the knowledge that powerful and efficient instruments existed which could be relied upon to break the momentum of growth whenever needed, meant that at other times (in fact usually) the economy could be left unbridled.

It is surprising, in these circumstances, that in addition to some autonomous trends tending to diminish the counter-cyclical efficiency of government policies in the recent past (on which more below), official pronouncements themselves indicate the preference of the authorities for a somewhat different monetary system. Influenced perhaps too strongly by foreign (notably Anglo-American) examples, the Bank of Japan has frequently argued in favour of the creation of a developed capital market, a freer interest rate policy, and much higher self-financing capacities for enterprises.[9] Yet, as was said quite appropriately in an otherwise debatable book, '. . . it makes little or no difference to the productivity of a machine whether [the] money is debt or equity capital',[10] and even less, presumably, whether the money has come from a commercial bank or through bond issues. But it would make a lot of difference to the powers of intervention of the authorities if they had to cope with a large capital market, numerous financial intermediaries, and much more independent banks or firms—as the post-war record of monetary policy in Britain or the United States sufficiently shows. To be sure, the present system does not ensure 'perfect resource allocation'; but it may be doubted whether adherence to the precepts of (static) neo-classical analysis, had it even been possible, would ever have allowed growth rates of GNP of the order of 10 per cent per annum.

Policies for growth

The foregoing discussion, by stressing the counter-cyclical policies of the Bank of Japan, and to a lesser extent of the Ministry of Finance, and their successes in restrictive phases, might give the impression that the authorities' main task was that of dampening vigorous private demand. Yet, over the longer run, the opposite was the case. Throughout the period under observation, economic policy was, in fact, overtly expansionary. Deteriorations of the balance of payments, or more recently accelerating price inflation, imposed a need for restrictive policies from time to time; but such action was always regarded as a temporary and unfortunate departure from a consciously growth-promoting longer-run stance. Any analysis of the latter is hampered by its frequently elusive nature. Restrictive monetary action or public expenditure cuts are relatively easy to date and assess, and their impact on other variables can be traced with some degree of confidence. The workings of longer-run policies are frequently diffuse and indirect, and their effects cannot always be isolated or detected. Moreover, in Japan's case, economic policies have tended to rely on '. . . an extraordinary amount of consultation, advice, persuasion and threat',[11] knowledge of which is not usually forthcoming.

One way of measuring the government's direct impact on economic growth is to look at its contribution to the expansion of total demand as measured by the share of public spending on

goods and services in gross national expenditure (see Table 6.1).
Excluding defence, this has stood at some 14–15 per cent of
GNP throughout the period, with little growth in the share over
the years suggesting that direct demand stimulation was not the
prime concern of the authorities. By international standards, the
share was high in the mid-1950s but relatively low in more recent
years, and the same is broadly true if the investment of public

TABLE 6.1

Share of government expenditure in GNP[1]

(percentages, based on data at current prices)

	TOTAL	CONSUMPTION	OF WHICH: INVESTMENT[2]	TRANSFERS[3]
Average 1953 to 1955				
Japan (FYs)	17·8	8·9	4·6	3·7
Five major countries[4]	23·6	8·6	2·9	8·5
Average 1970 to 1972				
Japan (FYs)	19·6	7·9	6·0	4·5
Five major countries[3]	32·7	12·4	3·6	12·4

1. Excluding defence.
2. Excluding nationalized industries and public corporations.
3. To households and private non-profit making institutions.
4. Unweighted average of ratios for France, Germany, Italy, the United
Kingdom, and the United States.

Sources: E.P.A., *National Income Statistics*, and O.E.C.D., *National Accounts of
O.E.C.D. Countries*; Japanese figures on defence spending in FYs 1953–5 have
been estimated with the help of budget data.

corporations and nationalized industries is added to general
government expenditure. Allowance for transfers, however, rele-
gates Japan to a much lower position in relation to other countries
and throws more light on the type of policies followed.

Within its total outlays, the government consciously selected
those activities in which measurable returns and external economies were likely to be highest. Political circumstances made it
possible to refrain from military outlays while economic choices
led to a neglect of expenditures for social welfare purposes. Given
rapidly rising revenues, this policy of 'neither warfare nor welfare'
allowed high savings and investment, notably investment in the
sort of infrastructure needed by the private sector. Thus, public
capital formation, including that of public corporations, accounts
for the highest share in total government spending among major

economies while the opposite is true for both government consumption and transfers. The combination of a very low and stable
share of current disbursements and an above-average and rising
share of investment, while hardly optimal from the welfare point
of view, must have been beneficial to the corporate sector and to
the economy's growth rate. It absorbed fewer resources than
would have been the case elsewhere, where government current
expenditure usually rose as a percentage of GNP, while at the
same time providing the infrastructure needed to sustain private
investment drives.[12] In other words, since there was no need to
provide a direct stimulus to demand, which was kept high by
buoyant business investment, the government restricted its direct
role to enlarging supply in those areas in which it had a clear
advantage over private activity.

A more complete view of the government's fiscal operations
can be obtained by considering both the direct and indirect
effects of changes in revenues and expenditures on longer-run
growth. Approaches of this sort are usually subject to numerous
caveats and have to rely on a number of restrictive assumptions.
They can nevertheless provide some insight. An attempt, avoiding
the use of econometric models and showing some interesting
international comparisons, was made for the period 1952–67.[13]
Growth rates of potential output were compared to growth rates
of actual output and of a 'pure cycle' output—the last being a
hypothetical GNP derived by subtracting from recorded GNP the
estimated effects of all budgetary changes. Results showed that,
over the fifteen years, fiscal policy was consciously expansionary
in all years but one and stabilizing (i.e. trying to bring the
economy close to its potential ceiling) in all but three. Indeed, in
terms of the longer-run stabilization-*cum*-growth-fostering effect,
Japanese budgets were noticeably more successful than those of
other major market economies between the mid-1950s and the
mid-1960s.[14]

Evidence for the stimulating role of fiscal policy is also provided
by estimates of 'full employment budget balances' for the central
government. Since FY 1961 actual budget deficits have been consistently larger than those required to ensure full employment.[15]

Turning now to the less measurable but perhaps even more
important indirect effects of fiscal policies, it seems that these
exercised an important stimulating influence on private investment demand. Tax concessions to the corporate sector took

various forms—lavish depreciation allowances, creation of tax-free reserves, preferential tax treatment for large-scale firms, low indirect taxation on goods whose production was to be stimulated, etc.[16] The common element in most of these interventions was the desire to foster private investment, and notably investment in large-scale firms and in particular key sectors.

An equally, if not more, important instrument used by the government to shape its economic policy was the Fiscal Investment and Loan Programme (FILP). This large quasi-budget (equivalent to almost 50 per cent of the central budget's general account) administers the funds of numerous government institutions, is virtually free from parliamentary control, and has been the main means of circumventing the rigid balanced-budget principles laid down after the war. It uses funds collected by the government, largely through savings deposits with the postal system and pension contributions, to finance a whole array of activities, from the investment needs of public corporations (railways or telecommunications) to welfare schemes (housing or environment) and agriculture. But the two crucial roles played by the FILP have been in helping basic industries and exports, on the one hand, and smaller enterprises on the other. Lending to key sectors was at its peak in the early 1950s, when it absorbed perhaps 30 per cent of FILP's funds; support to small business has increased through time; and export promotion (including aid to developing countries) has consistently accounted for some 8–10 per cent of FILP lending, even in the early 1970s.

Monetary policy used two main instruments to foster longer-run growth—interest rate pegging and central bank credit creation. As already mentioned, the Bank of Japan set most interest rates at given levels by decree. The aim of such operations was to keep long-term interest rates relatively low so as to provide a further encouragement to investment, as well as to reduce costs to firms which were highly dependent on bank loans. International comparisons do not, however, suggest that long-term rates were particularly low. In fact, throughout the period, Japanese longer-term rates seem to have been slightly above those of other major economies. But it is doubtful whether much weight can be attached to such comparisons, partly because of the difficulty of choosing appropriate rates and partly because numerous other factors, notably the economy's growth rate and 'overloan' situation, should also enter the picture. The artificial pegging of long-term interest rates is best shown by the domestic divergence between long- and short-term rates, the latter being represented by the call rate on the money market—virtually the only rate which was not directly managed by the Bank of Japan. In phases of monetary restraint, this rate shot well above longer-term rates, and over the period as a whole it stood, on average, somewhat above the nominal interest cost of long-term loans.

More important than this rather artificial state of short-term rates being above most longer-term rates was the use of interest rates, in conjunction with some other elements of government policy, to help transfer resources from the household to the corporate sector. The intentional or unintentional insufficiency of social security provisions was, as argued earlier on, one of the factors making for high savings. The intentional or unintentional lack of a capital market meant that the bulk of such private savings had to find their way into relatively liquid deposits held with either private or public financial institutions. In the latter case, the government could use the funds directly for investment in industrial infrastructure or for re-lending to private business. In the former case, the banking system would channel private savings to corporations. In both instances, an essential ingredient would be the artificial compression of interest rates on such deposits to very low nominal (and frequently negative real) rates. This allowed, in turn, the levying of a relatively low rate on loans to business and, of course, a much higher rate of return on the final investment. Not only was financial intermediation highly successful for institutional reasons, it was also highly profitable to the corporate sector as a whole for policy reasons.

Yet, not unlike the situation in most other countries, credit availability probably mattered even more than credit cost; and this is where the Bank of Japan played a crucial role. Though it restricted its credits to City banks and limited the latter's loans to business in phases of retrenchment, over most of the period its policy was in fact very expansive. As mentioned in Chapter 4, *ex-ante* investment demand usually exceeded *ex-ante* savings; and this gap was consciously filled by the central bank through credit creation. *Ex-post*, a large enough income would be generated out of which sufficient real savings would flow to re-establish the savings-investment balance. But the whole process was made possible by the central bank's operations. Had it not stepped in to meet requirements for investment finance (as well as a rapidly rising demand for transaction money), many of the investment drives previously described might never have materialized.

It is difficult to say whether the authorities' credit creation was excessive or insufficient. It was clearly excessive in the easy-policy phase of the early 1970s, when it combined with a huge balance of payments surplus to increase the economy's liquidity to such an extent that the commercial banks were able to lessen their dependence on the Bank of Japan by repaying most of their debts, while firms could engage in purely speculative transactions which reinforced inflationary pressures. But through the period as a whole, it could be argued that credit policy was broadly appropriate. It was sufficient to finance a volume of investment which permitted a long-run 10 per cent growth rate, while at the same time insufficient to diminish the chronic state of 'overloan' and the financial system's dependence on the Bank of Japan.

Apart from these major fiscal and monetary interventions, examples abound of other instruments used to foster economic growth. An important case in point is provided by foreign trade policy. It should not be forgotten that rapid growth was usually subject to external constraints. Hence the growth aim was always combined with the goal of making Japan competitive in international markets. From this followed the constant preoccupation with protection, economies of scale, technological progress, and price competitiveness—all seen not only as fostering domestic expansion but also as strengthening the balance of payments.

Over the years, therefore, Japan's administration constructed a '. . . system of strict, extensive, and minutely prepared measures for promoting exports and restricting imports' which has few, if any, equivalents abroad.[17] On the export side, direct help came in the form of a variety of tax concessions to exporting firms,[18] and indirect help by way of subsidized export credits. Similarly, the whole programme for aid to developing countries, which 'even by the degraded standards used in this field' has been very small so far,[19] was little more than an export promotion programme; and the same was true of reparations.* An even larger role in the foreign trade field was played by protection. By all standards, Japan was a highly protected country until not very long ago. An

---

* In negotiating reparations, '. . . the government actually preferred the services of businessmen to those of the Foreign Office, because it was essential that the negotiations be based on realistic business arrangements', C. Yanaga, *Big Business in Japanese Politics*, Yale University Press 1969, p. 204.

abundance of tariffs, quotas, and indirect restrictions allowed the birth and development of most major industrial sectors, while strict controls on capital inflows kept out virtually all forms of foreign direct investment. Estimates of the height of tariff barriers against manufactures in 1962, made by Balassa, showed that Japan's effective rate of protection was some 50 per cent higher than that of the United States or the E.E.C.,[20] while the number of items subject to quota restrictions at the end of the 1960s was some 2–6 times larger than in the major European countries.[21] It should be added, however, that the early 1970s witnessed a very significant progress towards liberalization, and at present the level of protection in Japan is probably not significantly different from that in other major market economies.[22]

Yet, interestingly enough, protection against the outside world went hand in hand with the almost opposite policy of encouraging (or at least not discouraging) competition at home. The competition which was being allowed was of course not the atomistic competition prescribed by textbooks and favoured by the American occupation authorities. It came as a by-product of a policy which fostered large-scale enterprises and oligopolies in the knowledge that keen rivalry existed between the various conglomerates. It is true that the M.I.T.I. promoted rationalizations and the creation of large units or anti-recession cartels, and that the Bank of Japan favoured the major banks. But neither institution was apparently trying to create monopolies. Both credit and licences for importing foreign technology (two of the essential conditions for success) seem to have been distributed as equally as possible to each City bank or to each large corporation.[23]

Such a 'dual economic policy', of fostering both protection without and competition within,[24] may well be one of the keys to understanding the general attitude of Japanese policy-making. The foreign observer is often struck by the simultaneous presence of fairly detailed guidance on the one hand and seemingly uncontrolled market forces on the other. Yet the latter were given a free rein only within an over-all framework which remained subject to continuous supervision as well as safeguards. Competition was allowed as long as it manifested itself in investment drives and output expansion; and competition of this kind was at all times protected by a safety net. Both the major banks and the larger firms felt that their weak financial positions, be they due to 'overloan' or to over-investment, would never represent a fundamental danger, and that the authorities would always bail them out if a major crisis occurred.

Little mention has so far been made of formal economic planning, which has had a long but chequered history since the war. Plans abounded, but hardly any of their targets ever had much to do with reality; and instead of trying to steer the economy in the direction foreseen by the plans, governments usually scrapped the plans, replaced them by new ones which tried to take account of more recent developments, and scrapped these, in turn, a few years later. To some extent this was due to poor forecasting (the average under-estimation of real GNP growth in the five plans from FYs 1956 to 1971 was of the order of $3\frac{1}{2}$ per cent per annum); but in addition, and more seriously, the planners were unable to implement any of the resource allocation targets set for the variables under direct government control—public consumption and public investment.[25]

There are many reasons for this, some of which are political and will be looked at in the following section, and some of which are purely institutional. The two most important economic policy-making ministries, the Ministry of Finance and the M.I.T.I.,* went on carrying out their own planning irrespective of the wishful thinking, to which they had formally subscribed, contained in the official planning documents. The former did so in the framework of budgets and of the FILP; the latter through annual investment plans for key industries agreed upon with business, and through longer-term sectoral blueprints. Not fortuitously perhaps, one of the few targets which seems to have been attained at times was that for the distribution of various branches within industry as a whole.[26] Over-all industrial growth was substantially under-estimated, but the relative shares of iron and steel, chemicals, or machinery were not too far out of line with what the plan (in fact the M.I.T.I.) had wanted. Otherwise, the contribution of plans was at best limited, as it was in most other Western economies, to the frequently argued role of providing a suitable and relatively optimistic background for private investment decisions. The best-known example of this is the investment boom which followed the publication in 1960 of the, then very ambitious, income doubling

---

* The Bank of Japan, let alone the E.P.A., have been far less important. The latter has played a purely consultative role. The former, whatever outward appearances may be, has in fact been rather firmly subordinate to the Ministry of Finance for all its major policy decisions.

plan for the 1961–70 period. It is said that in most branches individual firms took sectoral production plans as government guaranteed minima and attempted to obtain a disproportionate share of the new markets.[27]

The contribution of the various planning influences and policies to growth is impossible to measure, let alone compare with what has been done in other countries. However, it seems to have been sizeable. Japan, and notably its business community, wanted growth and probably wanted it more than other market economies. The country's governments therefore used most of the means at their disposal to foster that aim and brought them to bear on one element—investment—which, partly as a result, became the most dynamic component in total demand in the economy. Capital formation was encouraged in all possible ways— by the Bank of Japan's permissive, or more aptly downright expansionary, credit policies; by the Ministry of Finance's tax and other financial stimuli; by the M.I.T.I.'s investment guidance, insistence on protection, and selection of key sectors and infant industries. The ministries directed growth; the central bank financed it. Whatever the short-run dissensions between government institutions, or the semantic discussions on who was being restrictive or expansionary, basically they pursued similar aims and used complementary methods to achieve them.[28]

Japan is not, of course, the sole example of a government using the whole array of direct and indirect instruments in its hands to stimulate both over-all growth and a particular sectoral allocation of resources. France springs to mind as a country where a similar course of action was followed. But among market economies Japan may well have been at the top of the scale for both the comprehensiveness and the efficiency of its governments' interventions.

Economic policy at the crossroads

As with developments in several other economic fields, the basic framework within which Japanese policies were formulated through the 1950s and 1960s has witnessed some fairly drastic changes in more recent years. Some of these changes are institutional, and have altered the day-to-day workings of monetary or fiscal policies. Others are more fundamental and have involved a full-scale reappraisal of the basic aims of government intervention. Both sets of changes have one characteristic in common—

they are unlikely to facilitate the future tasks of Japanese policy-makers. The institutional changes are impairing the previous effectiveness of traditional instruments. The reconsideration of aims is raising new targets which the traditional instruments may not always be suited to achieve and for which alternative tools must be found.

At the operational level, monetary policy in particular is likely to find its thrust progressively blunted. Several of the features which contributed to its effectiveness in the past have been modified of late, and the process is likely to continue.[29] For one thing, the earlier effectiveness owed a lot to a ruthless application of restrictive policies whatever their social costs. Now there is increased concern for the fate of smaller enterprises, which used to bear the burden of adjustment. Also, a rising dependence of housebuilding on loans from the banking system (partly replacing the earlier financing of residential construction mainly by personal savings), implies that new social constraints are likely to limit the scope of Bank of Japan interventions. And even if such considerations were bypassed (as, to some extent, they were in 1974) technical difficulties might well hamper the successful working of some of the central bank's instruments.

Smaller financial institutions less directly subject to Bank of Japan supervision have slowly improved their position at the expense of City banks. Budget deficits and balance of payments surpluses have become a good deal more common than in the past, and their contribution to increases in money supply has correspondingly risen. This limits the direct impact of central bank credit-extension or -restriction, and it may also impose an additional constraint on interest rate policy or open market operations, should the Bank of Japan wish to maintain orderly conditions in a growing market for government bonds. The lessened dependence of the banking system on the Bank of Japan is paralleled by a somewhat diminished dependence of firms on banking funds. Self-financing ratios have been rising and in the early 1970s were not far from the rates recorded in other major Western economies. Finally, the movement towards greater freedom for capital movements adds a further degree of uncertainty, by allowing both banks and enterprises to resort to foreign sources of finance. In this field, however, powers of intervention have not been relinquished and, should the need arise, will probably be used again.

Future fiscal policies may suffer from fewer constraints than monetary policy, especially now that the principle of balanced budgets has been rejected. But the possibility of using budgets for counter-cyclical purposes can create new difficulties since short- and long-run desiderata may frequently clash, as they did in 1974. On the one hand, the government may wish to expand public works and social welfare programmes; on the other, increasing such expenditures (and especially the former) tends to have a strong inflationary impact. Curbing the public investment effort results in some dampening of price increases, but only reinforces the lack of basic facilities and creates even greater needs for increased government spending in the next phase of expansion. Japan is not the only country facing a conflict between growing and increasingly sticky public expenditure requirements and the difficulty of satisfying them in times of generalized inflationary pressures. The whole Western world is, to a greater or lesser extent, faced with the same dilemma. But in Japan the problem is probably heightened by the relative neglect of welfare considerations for so long.

It is true, however, that Japan may face fewer constraints on the revenue side than most other countries. The share of taxation in GNP is very low by international standards (some 20 per cent) and has hardly risen over the last twenty years. This should make it easier for the government to increase the fiscal burden without generating inflationary pressures in the form of the 'after-tax' price-setting or income-bargaining practices which have, apparently, become more common in a number of West European countries.

Yet the major problem facing Japanese policy-making is not that of reconciling short-run cyclical and longer-run structural needs, but that of achieving the frequently proclaimed goal of a welfare-oriented society. This is not an easy task. It requires a careful definition of what this aim actually means and it implies devising a whole new set of instruments which could direct the economy towards the new targets. For a number of years, planning documents and political speeches have been filled with vague statements on the needs for less pollution, a better environment, a comprehensive social security system, an improved housing stock, more leisure, etc., as well as diminished reliance on private investment and exports.

Yet results so far have been disappointing, to say the least.

Apart from some successes in combating pollution and a concerted, but temporary, effort to increase the social overhead capital stock during the 1971–2 recession, the traditional pattern of Japanese growth, led by investment in boom periods and supported by exports in downswings, has largely been maintained over the last cycle (and this despite the currency's revaluation). Business investment was the most dynamic component of demand in 1973; exports took over that role in 1974. And even measures ostensibly designed to change traditional priorities have often backfired. Thus, in the early 1970s a plan for economic decentralization and decongestion led to massive land speculation in areas selected for future growth, while the public investment effort just mentioned was one of the causes of subsequent inflationary developments. The growth of public investment was therefore halted in the FY 1974 budget, but consumers were granted the largest tax cut in post-war history—a measure which could only stimulate private consumption and, indirectly, private investment. It does not look as if Japan's exceptional record, of having the lowest share and the lowest elasticity with respect to GNP of public revenues and expenditures, is coming to a close.

Strangely enough, the issues at stake may at least have been clarified, if not solved, by the 1973–4 explosion of primary product prices and the oil crisis. These showed that Japan's future requirements were of a twofold nature: not only a more welfare-oriented society, but also a more diversified and less heavily industrialized economy. So far, issues of pollution and pensions, education or environment had often been grouped together; now they could be separated. The vague pronouncements on the need for a changed industrial structure were suddenly given a sense of immediate urgency (as witnessed by the importance devoted to this issue in the FY 1974 Economic White Paper). A new and unforeseen constraint, similar in many ways to the earlier balance of payments 'ceiling', had come to the forefront. If past performance is any guide to the future, it can be expected that M.I.T.I.'s planning (and market forces, in view of a 50 per cent increase in the relative price of energy) will be successful in shifting the weight of Japanese industrial production away from the relatively raw-material-intensive activities encouraged in the past (e.g. iron and steel or chemicals) towards high-value-added sectors like machinery or scientific equipment. This is likely to entail additional significant progress in the fight against pollution and may even have some beneficial side-effects on environmental and regional-location problems.

But attainment of the older goal of more welfare and leisure looks more distant than ever. The 1973–4 inflation slowed down yet further an already slow rate of progress; but it could be argued that far-reaching changes in priorities cannot be accomplished over a few years. However, there are reasons for the apparent lack of success so far which go well beyond technical problems or time lags and involve more complex political issues. The creation of more welfare and leisure would seem hardly to be possible without a substantial degree of government involvement in the economy (notably in land-pricing and ownership) and fairly large transfers of resources, for subsequent redistribution, from the private to the public sector. As already said earlier, Japanese governments have not refrained from direct intervention and have helped to bring about massive transfers. But the type of intervention followed, and the kind of transfers encouraged, in the past are almost the opposite of those required for the present purpose. Direct action over the last twenty years has been largely investment-fostering and therefore, inevitably in a private economy, in favour of the corporate sector. The same was true of the mechanism, illustrated above, through which resources were transferred from households to business. And though some redistribution took place within the personal sector, largely thanks to a progressive income tax system inherited from the American occupation, redistributive effects have been diminishing through time.[30]

The strategy that would now be required to provide better housing, larger pensions, or more leisure is practically the opposite of the one followed for the past twenty years. It would require transfers of resources from corporations to households and, within the personal sector, from richer to poorer. *Per se*, this may not seem impossible. Other countries have, over time, succeeded in redistributing income and resources; and on the surface, it may seem that Japan could well be ripe for a similar change. The amount of public discussion of these issues, the concern felt about the problems, and the almost daily reiterations of government statements in favour of such changes recall the kind of consensus which in the past surrounded income-doubling and other growth-maximizing targets.

It could, therefore, be expected that 'in the interest of the people', the government would change the basic orientation of its policies. Such a view is often expressed in Japanese discussions of economic policy. But implicit in this attitude is the idea that '. . . the State is a purely rational agent . . . willing and capable to perform the tasks attributed to it'[31]; and it is precisely this willingness which can be questioned. Most observers of the Japanese economy agree that Japan's government is far from being a neutral and impartial agent. It is difficult to be precise about the interrelations between government, business, and the bureaucracy—the three repositories of post-war power. At a superficial level opposition and disagreements appear daily; and neither business nor the bureaucracy themselves present united fronts—factions exist among both.[32] But bureaucracy, politicians, and business '. . . share . . . a basic consensus in support of the existing structure of power. If necessary to preserve it, elements of all three groups might go far to abridge parliamentary rule.'[33]

Ultimately, as in all capitalist societies, and Japan does not seem to be fundamentally different in this respect, the 'consensus' and the basic rules of the game are mapped out not so much by democratic procedures as by the pressures emanating from ruling interests, in this instance the business community. The working of the system has a logic of its own which it imposes on the political decision-making process. If anything, this influence may be more pervasive in Japan than elsewhere and there may be fewer countervailing powers—for complex historical and socio-logical reasons which can hardly be investigated in this context.

Seen in this light, it would appear that a government which for the last twenty years (or, for that matter, the last century) has been primarily devoted to furthering the interests of one part of society is ill equipped to alter its course by 180 degrees. Whatever political pronouncements may be made, the relations of power within the ruling élite would seem to be such as to prevent more than minor tamperings with the existing situation, in the short run at least. Over the longer run, it can be argued, most capitalist economies have accepted progressively greater inroads into their workings and have adapted themselves to more welfare and some measure of redistribution, and Japan could do the same. But it is arguable whether Japan can wait for very long. The whole point about unbalanced growth is that it can maximize growth rates provided shortages in bottleneck sectors are eventually relieved. It is doubtful whether in Japan's case such relief can come merely from a more efficient use of fiscal or monetary policies, or from a likely shift towards production of 'knowledge-intensive' commodities. It would seem to involve a more drastic overhaul of much of the present economic system, something which would seem only possible through political change.

NOTES

1. H. Rosovsky, 'Japanese Capital Formation: The Role of the Public Sector', *Journal of Economic History*, September 1959.

2. Bieda, *The Structure and Operation of the Japanese Economy*, provides a useful survey of both monetary and financial institutions. For more detail on the monetary side see O.E.C.D., *Monetary Policy in Japan*, 1972 and Bank of Japan, Economic Research Department, *Money and Banking in Japan*, London 1973. For the fiscal side, M.o.F., *The Budget in Brief*.

3. Shinohara, 'Causes and Patterns', p. 351.

4. Econometric evidence, presented in O.E.C.D., *Monetary Policy*, pp. 93–7, shows a very close correspondence between credit extended by major banks and by other financial institutions.

5. Patrick, 'Cyclical Instability', pp. 595–8.

6. W. Snyder and T. Tanaka, 'Budget Policy and Economic Stability in Postwar Japan', *International Economic Review*, February 1972. See also H. Ishi, 'Cyclical Behaviour of Government Receipts and Expenditures—A Case Study of Postwar Japan', *HJE*, June 1973.

7. O.E.C.D., *ESJ, 1974*, pp. 61–5.

8. Cf. Allen, *Japan's Economic Expansion*, pp. 70–1.

9. See for instance B.o.J., *Money and Banking*, p. 58.

10. H. Kahn, *The Emerging Japanese Superstate*, London 1971, p. 216.

11. W. W. Lockwood, 'Japan's "New Capitalism"', in Lockwood (ed.), *The State and Economic Enterprises*, p. 503.

12. Patrick, 'The Financing of the Public Sector', pp. 327–30.

13. Snyder and Tanaka, 'Budget Policy and Economic Stability'.

14. *Ibid.*, p. 103.

15. E.P.A., *ESJ (1971–1972)*, p. 60.

16. Yamamura, *Economic Policy in Postwar Japan*, Ch. 8.

17. T. Murano, 'International Currency Realignment and the Yen', *DE*, December 1972, p. 350.

18. Described in some detail in L. Hollerman, *Japan's Dependence on the World Economy*, Princeton 1967, pp. 185–95.

19. J. Halliday and G. McCormack, *Japanese Imperialism Today*, Penguin Books 1973, p. 29.

20. B. Balassa, 'Tariff Protection in Industrial Countries—An Evaluation', *Journal of Political Economy*, December 1965.

21. Murano, 'International Currency Realignment', p. 352.

22. E.P.A., *ESJ (1972–1973)*, p. 83.

23. Y. Miyazaki, 'Rapid Economic Growth in Post-war Japan', *DE*, June 1967, pp. 347–9.

24. Shinohara, 'Causes and Patterns', p. 354.

25. K. Ohkawa, 'Problems of Plan Implementation', in *Economic Planning*, pp. 102–4.

26. Y. Kogane, 'The Objectives and their Attainments in Long-term Planning in Japan', pp. 20–3.

27. Allen, *Japan's Economic Expansion*, p. 39.

28. Patrick, 'Cyclical Instability', p. 558.

29. O.E.C.D., *Monetary Policy*, pp. 67–9.

30. E.P.A., *ESJ (1971–1972)*, p. 138.

31. C. Castoriadis, 'Comments on "Planning and Politics"', in *Economic Planning*, p. 518.

32. Allen, *Japan's Economic Expansion*, pp. 43–7.

33. Lockwood, 'Japan's "New Capitalism"', p. 514. A very complete survey of the relations between government and business can be found in Yanaga, *Big Business in Japanese Politics*.

CHAPTER 7

FOREIGN TRADE

FEW subjects in Japan's economic history have attracted more attention abroad than the spectacular development of the country's foreign trade. The performance of exports has, predictably, been the most discussed aspect, but recently the increasing inroads made by Japanese demand on world supplies of raw materials have also received some publicity. Yet, despite an abundant literature on the subject, misconceptions abound. Accusations of dumping and of prohibitive visible and invisible protection have long been levelled against Japan; it is commonly thought that production for export is the primary occupation of most Japanese firms; and foreign trade is frequently seen as the engine which propelled the country's economic growth. But many of these arguments, especially those concerning exports, tend to stem from pressure groups in America or Europe defending particular sectors threatened by Japanese competition, rather than from economic analysis. After a brief survey of the country's trade structure, this chapter will try to shed some light on the frequently misunderstood relations between Japan's economic growth and its foreign trade. The focus will be on exports, notably on the question whether they played a fundamental role in stimulating rapid growth of output or were largely a consequence of domestic developments.

Trends and structure

For a nation supposedly devoted almost solely to foreign trade, the weights of exports and imports in total output are surprisingly low. Table 7.1, which presents data for a number of comparable major countries, shows that Japan's share of foreign trade in GNP is well below that of the other countries for which figures are provided. Indeed, within the O.E.C.D. area, only the United States has lower foreign trade proportions. Outside the O.E.C.D., a few more examples can be found but, apart from the Soviet Union, these are all developing and relatively large economies (e.g. Argentina, Brazil, India, China). Thus, despite the fact that Japan has become the world's single largest importer of raw materials and the third largest exporter, it remains one of the countries least dependent on external transactions, when 'dependence' is measured in this relatively simple statistical manner (other technological, and more far-reaching economic, aspects of trade dependence are examined below).

TABLE 7.1

Foreign trade ratios—1953 to 1972

	EXPORTS[1]	IMPORTS[1]	TREND INCREASE IN COMBINED SHARE[2]
	PERCENTAGE OF GNP AT CONSTANT PRICES		
Japan	11·3	10·2	0·33
France	15·2	14·8	0·42
Germany	20·8	18·3	0·85
Italy	17·0	16·2	0·93
United Kingdom	21·3	21·2	0·32
O.E.C.D. Europe[3]	21·2	20·9	0·67

1. Goods, services, and factor income.
2. Annual increase in the average of the export and import shares in GNP obtained by fitting linear time trends to the data.
3. At 1963 prices and exchange rates.

Sources: E.P.A., *National Income Statistics,* and O.E.C.D., *National Accounts of O.E.C.D. Countries.*

It may be interesting to note that Japan's trade dependence may, in fact, be 'too low' by international standards. Income and size have long been considered as two fundamental determinants of a country's foreign trade proportions.[1] A simple test of this proposition was carried out for a sample of forty market economies (half of them developed and half developing) for the years 1968–70. The average share of exports and imports in output was regressed on income *per capita* (in U.S. dollars) and either population or area or total output (the latter three variables standing as alternative proxies for an economy's size). The explanatory power of the resulting equations was not very high, suggesting that a number of other factors influence the share of foreign trade in output; but the coefficients for the variables chosen were usually significant. The predicted values of Japan's foreign trade proportions varied between 18 and 25 per cent of GNP, against the 10 per cent actually recorded—one of the largest examples of overestimation in the sample.[2] Geographical distance from the world's main trading regions, as well as exclusion from all customs unions and free trade areas, is partly responsible for Japan's relative 'underspecialization', but other factors looked at below are probably equally, if not more, important.

Trade dependence has increased only marginally through time, and this despite a twentyfold increase in the volume of foreign transactions (on a customs basis) since 1953 and a rise in the share of world trade (in value terms) from some 2 per cent in 1953 to $6\frac{1}{2}$ per cent in 1973. This slowly growing trade dependence also contrasts with developments elsewhere. Throughout the post-war period, trend growth-rates of exports and imports in the developed world have been well above those of GNP, and foreign trade shares in GNP have risen rapidly and consistently almost everywhere, even in nearly self-sufficient countries like the United States or the Soviet Union. While Japan is not an exception to the general rule, the increase in export or import shares it recorded over the period as a whole is one of the lowest witnessed among industrialized economies.[3] This is the more surprising since pre-war Japan depended to a much larger extent on foreign trade (from 1905 to 1936 the average share of exports and imports in total output was of the order of 18–19 per cent) and a return to earlier foreign trade proportions might have been expected.

Anticipating somewhat on the later discussion, the relatively sluggish growth of the share of foreign trade in output, as well as its comparatively low level, may owe a lot to the nature and the speed of the growth of output. The speed of growth implied that, fast as exports developed, total output more or less kept pace. The nature of growth, centred as it was on manufacturing, meant that needs for finished imports were never very large, while needs for raw material imports hardly increased, thanks to import-saving production processes and shifts in consumer demand away from import-intensive commodities.

While in volume terms the shares of both exports and imports in GNP rose slightly, there is no increase whatsoever in current price terms. Both flows have represented roughly 11 per cent of GNP over the twenty years and the ratios have, if anything, shown a slight downward trend from 1953 to 1972, thanks to gently falling, or roughly stable, foreign trade prices.* On the

* There are some statistical problems in measuring Japanese foreign trade prices, the three available indices giving widely different results. Thus, the (trend) terms of trade improvement between 1953 and 1973 implicit in the

import side, until recently, Japan benefited more than any other
O.E.C.D. country from stagnation of primary producers' export
prices. Prices of Japanese imports fell steadily from the mid-1950s
to 1972 and even in 1973 were not much higher than twenty years
earlier. On the export side, Japan's price competitiveness is well
known and needs little illustration. Between 1953 and 1971,
export prices remained roughly stable. Since then they have
climbed rapidly in foreign currency terms as a consequence of
both revaluation and domestic inflation, but their international
competitiveness does not seem to have suffered too seriously.
O.E.C.D. estimates show that Japan's *relative* export prices had
fallen by some 20 per cent between 1955 and 1971; and even in
1974, according to preliminary calculations, they had barely
risen back to the level prevailing at the turn of the 1950s.

Fierce competition for market shares, which has often called
forth accusations of dumping, is clearly one factor behind such a
performance. To be sure, wholesale prices rose somewhat faster
than export prices over the period as a whole; but this cannot be
taken as immediate proof of differential pricing. It is well known
that there is a general tendency for domestic prices of all goods
and services together to rise faster than the domestic prices of
goods only, and that the latter in turn have tended to rise faster
than the prices of internationally traded goods alone, at least for
those countries—and they are the majority—which are not price
givers on the world market. Since the relative stability of Japan's
wholesale price level was impressive by international standards
(cf. Table 3.2), it is not surprising that its export-price performance should have been similarly remarkable. Dumping has little
to offer by way of explanation, except perhaps in particular
cyclical phases. What did matter were the same factors that
ensured the near-stability of wholesale prices—very rapid investment and productivity growth on the one hand, and the wage lag
on the other. Wages rose extremely fast by international standards
but still less fast than productivity. It is this dynamic factor which
allowed stable or falling prices both at home and abroad and

E.P.A.'s national accounts deflators (for goods and services) is 15 per cent; that
shown by the Bank of Japan's price indices is 8 per cent; while the Ministry
of Finance's unit value indices show a 2 per cent deterioration. In the following
discussion, unless explicitly stated otherwise, the B.o.J. index will be used, since it
is the one most frequently quoted in Japanese economic discussions; qualitative
judgements, however, will take into account the development of the two other
indices as well.

determined Japanese export successes, rather than a static situation of low wages or artificially reduced export prices.

Despite the rough stability of its export prices, Japan could still record a large terms-of-trade gain through the period, thanks to the steep fall in its import prices. Between the mid-1950s and the early 1970s the (trend) ratio of export to import prices rose by perhaps 8 per cent, an increase which seems to be second only to those of Germany and France among major market economies, and Switzerland among the smaller ones. This gain was, of course, wiped out in 1973 and 1974, as were the comparable gains of the whole industrialized world. But even the spectacular increase in primary product prices in those two years is unlikely to have fully offset the earlier improvement in Japan's (single) factorial terms of trade (the quantity of imports which can be purchased per unit of domestic labour input). E.P.A. estimates show that, thanks to the growth of productivity in export industries, these had improved by over 100 per cent between 1955 and 1965 as against a (barter) terms of trade rise of, at best, 10 per cent.[4] The discrepancy between the two indices shows that Japan shared some of its welfare gains with the rest of the world. Though regional terms of trade indicators are not available, it can be suggested that this gain went largely to developed countries, in view of the commodity composition of Japanese exports and imports by main areas.

If the structure of trade is examined, a further difference from other major trading nations lies in the very asymmetrical (and unique) commodity composition of foreign trade flows—an overwhelming, if slowly declining, share of primary products* in imports (almost 90 per cent in the early 1950s, roughly 75 per cent twenty years later) and an equally overwhelming, and increasing, share of manufactures in exports (rising from 80 per cent to 95 per cent over the same period). The former reflects straightforward comparative advantage, or in fact just absolute advantage, in view of the natural-resource poverty of the Japanese islands. The latter stems largely from two factors already mentioned—protection at the outset, as well as through most of the period, and the competitiveness of Japanese goods. Geography largely explains the market composition of Japanese sales, with South-east Asia and the United States alone absorbing almost 50 per cent of exports throughout the years 1953–73.

Partly because of the non-competitive nature of most of its

---

* Defined as S.I.T.C. sections 0 to 4 plus division 68 (non-ferrous metals).

imports, partly because of the dual nature of its outlets (a large developed and a large developing market), partly because of the dual nature of many of its exports (highly labour-intensive commodities produced by small firms, highly capital-intensive commodities produced in large-scale enterprises), as well as an increasing share of electric or electronic machinery and consumer goods whose factor intensity it is difficult to determine, no precise answer exists to the question whether Japanese exports are relatively capital- or labour-intensive. Some studies have suggested that, relative to the structure of import-competing activities, Japanese sales abroad are capital-intensive; and they have therefore argued that Leontief's paradox (in reverse) can also be applied to Japan.[5] This finding may, as in the United States case, reflect the natural resources content of Japanese foreign trade as well as the geographical distribution of its exports. Indeed, the earlier of the two works quoted in note 5, as well as studies on American trade,[6] show that, for United States–Japanese bilateral trade relations, factor intensities seem to be closer to the two countries' relative factor endowments.

In any case, the conclusion that the country's over-all trade pattern is 'paradoxical' assumes that Japan is a capital-scarce and labour-abundant economy. A rigorous examination of this conclusion, even if possible, may have to wait upon a detailed examination of Japan's input–output tables over the period as a whole. At a superficial level, there seems to be some supporting evidence in the 1950s and, perhaps, in the 1960s (the studies noted were based on input–output and trade relations in the 1950s); but more recent years may have witnessed a change. The very rapid and accelerating shift towards a higher capital–labour ratio in the economy as a whole was mentioned earlier; and although this says nothing about Japan's relative factor endowment, it can be supposed that the shift has lately been more rapid than elsewhere. Moreover, and partly in consequence, factor prices have come closer to international levels recently. Wages in large-scale enterprises, at least, are now similar to European levels while long-term interest rates have been declining over time, in contrast to patterns elsewhere. Such comparisons do point, however shakily, to some tendency towards factor price equalization with other mature economies, and to a factor-intensity pattern which, relative to the rest of the world as a whole, may have reversed itself in the last decade.

A somewhat different, and indirect, piece of evidence suggesting a change in Japan's factor proportions *vis-à-vis* other countries comes from the liberalization efforts made in the recent past and from the revaluation of the yen (which can be assimilated to a wholesale tariff cut-*cum*-import subsidy). International trade theory indicates that protection increases the return to the relatively scarce factor, while free trade generally favours the relatively abundant factor.[7] While there were outside pressures on Japan to liberalize its trade in the early 1970s, the Japanese government's willingness to respond may have reflected a belief that this would, *inter alia*, promote some shift in income distribution towards capital—a belief that could be held only if a change from capital to labour scarcity was indeed taking place in the economy.

Foreign trade and growth

The interactions between foreign trade and growth are numerous and complicated and the literature on the subject abounds with theories and models of varying degrees of refinement (and unreality). This discussion will concentrate on a few relatively simple approaches. Analysis of the effects of Japan's economic growth on imports or exports will be limited to a discussion of foreign trade proportions and of the importance of income or substitution effects in changing these proportions. But no similarly simple approach can examine the effects of trade on growth. At a very elementary level, Keynesian theory has stressed the favourable effects of exports on activity in advanced countries, while the theory of economic development has underlined the importance of imports for growth in developing countries. Keynes's short-term multiplier has been extended to the longer run in 'export-led' models of growth, while the notion of imports as a crucial bottleneck has been incorporated in linear programming models in which foreign trade is looked at as one of several alternative production processes. It is not intended to test such models against Japanese experience, but comments will be offered on some aspects of them—especially on the more interesting, and debatable, significances of export growth.

But brief attention must first be given to imports. In Japan's case, a judgement on the role of imports in the process of economic growth is relatively straightforward: they were absolutely indispensable. But the nature of the link between growth and imports has changed over time, with an earlier economic dependence giving way to a strictly technical dependence. In pre-war days, imports fulfilled a role similar to that hypothesized by the theory of economic development. They were a 'highway of learning'[8] through which new products, capital equipment, and technical progress entered the country. In the post-war period, the inflow of technology continued, more through the purchase of patents and licences than through the introduction of prototypes for subsequent copying; but imports of finished goods were much less important. The essential role of imports was no longer to lead industrial development but to provide it with the raw material inputs Japan could never have supplied for itself.

One should not be misled by the low over-all ratio of imports to total output; their share in supplies of most raw materials is extremely high, though it is lower for food products (other than cereals) partly because of a high level of protection. Dependence on overseas supplies is over 60 per cent for coal and lumber, and virtually complete for natural rubber, raw textiles, non-ferrous metal ores, iron ore, and, of course, oil. The degree of self-sufficiency in total energy was barely above 10 per cent in 1971— way below that of any other industrialized country.[9] In these conditions, any shortfall in the supply of a key commodity could seriously dislocate the economy. Though over-all import dependence in statistical terms has declined from pre-war days, technological dependence has probably risen to a level above that of most other countries. Lack of imports in the earlier part of the century would have slowed down growth; today it would probable lead to sizeable falls in output and welfare.

The effects of economic growth on imports have been twofold. On the one hand, growth has tended to reduce primary product requirements per unit of output in most lines of activity and has led to shifts of demand away from raw-material-intensive commodities. On the other hand, it has, together with liberalization, increased demand for manufactured imports. Western Europe and the United States have had a very similar experience. In these areas, however, a high income elasticity of demand for foreign manufactures has more than offset the low income elasticity of demand for primary products. In Japan, given the initial proportions of the two flows in total imports, the two effects have been roughly equal. Import saving was most visible in the early 1960s and gave ample confirmation of Nurkse's analysis of the longer-run trend of the income elasticity of demand for primary products.[10] Shifts in the industrial structure away from import-intensive activities, substitution of synthetic for natural products, savings of raw material inputs thanks to technological progress, even rationalizations in the management of inventories all led to a diminished reliance of industrial production on raw material imports. M.I.T.I. calculations, using the 1960 and 1965 input–output tables, show that shifts in final demand and the lowering of technological coefficients combined achieved an approximate 1·5 per cent per annum reduction in total imports.[11]

Lately, however, this picture has changed somewhat. A similar comparison between the 1965 and 1970 input–output tables shows that import dependence has risen again.* This is not due to a reversal of previous shifts in demand. On the contrary, use of the 1965 demand structure and of the 1970 import coefficients results in a theoretical ratio of imports to final demand some 5 per cent above the actual ratio. It is the direct and indirect import coefficients per unit of final demand which have been rising, notably in manufacturing. It is unlikely that the previous technical import-saving trend has been reversed; nor does the change seem to be due to the shift towards foreign energy sources, which was already evident in the earlier 1960s. The most plausible explanation is that increased recourse has been made to manufactured imports for final consumption (for instance of textiles and miscellaneous consumer goods, but also of machinery). In other words, substitution in production and consumption, which had hitherto depressed import requirements, was more than offset in recent years by strong income effects, encouraged by liberalization. This trend should, if anything, have been reinforced in the early 1970s by the yen's revaluation.

The inter-relations between exports and growth are far more complex. It can, of course, be argued at a very simple level that since rising imports were indispensable to growth, so were rising exports, given that Japan's borrowing capacity, however large, could not have been sufficient to finance the increase in the import bill. But this says little on whether the primary stimulus to growth came from the domestic or from the export side. In a short-run, cyclical perspective, it seems that the latter hypothesis

* There are some problems regarding the comparability of the two tables, notably in their treatment of re-exports. In addition, calculations were made on current price data (in contrast to the 1960–5 M.I.T.I. comparison), and therefore reflect not only changes in demand and technology but also relative price shifts.

is more realistic. Exports frequently played a Keynesian output-stimulating role in depressions. But this was not due to auto-nomous, and fortuitous, changes in foreign demand. On the contrary, Japanese recessions, especially in the 1950s, tended to coincide with those abroad, given the dependence of Japan, and of the whole Western world, on fluctuations in United States activity. A fall in Japanese exports produced a deterioration in the balance of payments which called forth restrictive policies and consequent domestic recession. During the 1960s dependence on the U.S. economy was lessened, but none the less, the 1962 and 1971 recessions closely followed upon, or coincided with, slow-downs in the growth of world trade. It seems that the essentially counter-cyclical pattern of exports was a function of Japanese business behaviour.

Chapter 2 pointed out the relatively high share of fixed costs in total production costs in Japanese enterprises. Recessions at home, by curtailing output, increased unit costs of production, and by dampening demand exerted downward pressures on prices. This happens in all countries, but the resultant reduction in profit margins may have been larger in Japan than elsewhere, given its relatively competitive product markets and relatively sticky wage and capital costs. Moreover, the early phases of recessions usually coincided with monetary squeezes. For the frequently over-borrowed Japanese firms, these could entail great difficulties in repaying debt, or simply in financing running expenditures; and increased sales abroad could solve, or at least alleviate, several of their problems—for instance, by spreading fixed costs over a larger output and providing firms with badly needed liquidity. Exports were therefore stimulated, through both increased sales efforts and price cuts. Theory-of-the-firm economics states that in the short run, faced with a shortage of demand, firms can cut prices to the point where only variable costs are covered. Japanese firms are unlikely to have gone that far, given the relatively low share of variable costs in their total costs; but the export (and wholesale) price reductions of 1954, 1958, 1962, 1965, and, to some extent, 1971 suggest that their behaviour may have been close to what simple theory would predict. The prompt re-establishment of Japan's balance of payments following monetary restrictions at first, and recession soon after, owes much not only to the direct impact of weaker domestic demand on imports, but also to concerted and vigorous export drives.

If exports play the short-run output stimulating role that has been suggested, this does not, of course, imply that total production is kept constant or grows steadily at a constant rate, with only the direction of sales shifting, or that changes in the growth of output and exports should be negatively correlated.* Both the relative severity of the domestic recession and conditions on foreign markets matter in determining how much a firm is forced to curtail the growth of its output and how much it can sell abroad. Hence direct evidence of this mechanism is not easily forthcoming unless recourse is made to a very detailed sector by sector analysis. Indirectly, it could be claimed that if this mechanism is indeed significant, it should figure in econometric relationships explaining Japanese exports. But one encounters here a common econometric pitfall. Variables proxying (absolute) demand pressures in the economy are frequently correlated with Japan's relative export prices. In the choice between a statistically significant price elasticity and a statistically significant coefficient for a business cycle variable, the econometrician tends to favour the former.[12] Thus, among the major quarterly forecasting models of the Japanese economy, some include such a variable in their export equations (e.g. the E.P.A.'s Economic Research Institute 'Master Model' or the Electric Corporation model used in the 'Link' project), but others do not (e.g. the J.E.R.C. or the Bank of Japan). Few firm conclusions can be arrived at on this basis.

On the other hand, some indirect, but more convincing evidence of the existence of this mechanism is provided by O.E.C.D. estimates of Japan's export performance. These estimates show that the largest annual gains in market shares (in volume terms) over the last fifteen years were recorded in 1959, 1962, 1964, 1965, 1969, and 1971—all (except for 1969) years coinciding with, or just following domestic recessions. On the strength of this, and recalling the earlier consideration of firms' cost structures, it can probably be concluded that exports did replace domestic demand in slack periods and fulfilled '. . . a useful demand-stabilizing task'.[13] Moreover, by lifting the floor of the business cycle and shortening the time necessary for return to balance of payments equilibrium, they must have contributed not

* These relationships have been postulated as conditions necessary for proving this mechanism by T. Blumenthal ('Exports and Economic Growth: The Case of Postwar Japan', *Quarterly Journal of Economics*, November 1972, pp. 626–7). They seem however, too restrictive, since they put all the onus of proof on supply mechanisms and ignore demand factors entirely.

only to evening out short-run fluctuations, but also to further longer-run growth.

Export-led growth or growth-led exports?

The counter-cyclical mechanism just outlined provides no clue, however, to whether the initial factors stimulating the longer-run growth of exports lie at home or abroad. If the latter were true, Japan's experience might well fit the sort of export-led models of economic growth which, originally developed for primary producing countries like Canada or Australia (and perhaps Japan in the silk days), have received renewed attention in the 1960s following the rapid growth of trade and output in Western Europe. In the modern version of such models, rapid increases in exports (due, for instance, to an undervalued rate of exchange) affect growth in two ways—by permitting economies of scale they encourage investment in particular sectors, and by ensuring a strong balance of payments they reduce the need for restrictive policies, bolster longer-run confidence, and stimulate over-all investment ratios. Productivity thus increases relatively fast, thus further stimulating exports and leading the country into a virtuous circle of high growth and favourable trade balances.

Econometric tests of the model have not proved very conclusive, partly because of statistical difficulties; but it has none the less continued to attract attention, in Britain for instance (which has clearly not found its way into a 'virtuous circle'), and also in Japan which, it can be argued, may be the best example of the model's validity. Thus, the extremely rapid rise in Japan's share of world trade, its change from a deficit to a surplus country, its massive investment effort might all be evidence for the existence of an export-led growth mechanism.[14] It is true that Japan's share of exports in total output is very small and has hardly risen over time but '. . . lack of a rising ratio of trade to income is no proof that export-led growth is inoperative; on the contrary, a sufficiently strong growth stimulus stemming from the export sector could raise income sufficiently to leave the export ratio unaltered'.[15]

Testing the theory is no easy matter since it is extremely difficult to disentangle the lead–lag pattern of exports and output growth. At the most aggregate level, Caves suggests an indirect and very simple test, based on familiar demand and supply curves. If the disturbance, or initial stimulus to export growth, comes from the (foreign) demand side, then export prices and quantities should both shift in the same direction. If the disturbance originates from the (domestic) supply side, the movements of prices and quantities should be in opposite directions.[16] It was shown above that a twentyfold increase in the volume of Japanese exports over the period went hand in hand with virtual stability in the absolute export-price level (and rapid falls, until the early 1970s in relative prices); such evidence suggests that downward shifts of the supply schedule played a much more important role than upward changes in demand.

A similar conclusion can be drawn by looking at the market- and commodity-composition of Japanese exports. A 'favourable' composition, that is an initial concentration on products or outlets which subsequently experienced very rapid growth, would provide some support for an export-led-growth model. It would allow a relatively easy expansion of sales (because of high foreign income elasticities of demand) and, by raising domestic incomes, would then further stimulate output growth. Yet all the evidence suggests that the opposite was the case. The growth of Japan's main export markets remained sluggish until the mid-1960s, relative to both world trends and Japanese domestic demand. Between 1955 and 1964, Japan's outlets grew (in volume terms) at an annual rate of 5 per cent as against a market growth for the O.E.C.D. area as a whole of $6\frac{1}{2}$ per cent per annum, and a growth in Japanese domestic demand of the order of 9 per cent. Japan hardly benefited from the buoyant expansion of Western European trade and had to rely on the comparatively slow growing United States and South-east Asian markets.

The initial commodity composition of Japanese exports seems to have been even more unfavourable than their market orientation. E.P.A. and N.I.E.S.R. calculations show that Japan's exports in the mid-1950s were heavily concentrated on commodities for which demand rose subsequently at rates well below the growth rate of total world trade.[17] This was in stark contrast to the experience of all other major trading nations. 'Growth commodities' accounted for barely 20 per cent, and 'stagnant commodities' for over 60 per cent of Japanese exports in 1955, against ratios of the order of 50–60 and 30–5 per cent respectively for the United States, Germany, France, Italy, or the United Kingdom.

Through time, Japan's foreign trade structure has, of course, improved; but it is only during the last ten years that the initial disadvantages have been fully overcome and the growth of its regional, and perhaps also commodity, markets has paralleled or even outstripped that of world trade. The over-valuation of the dollar and the economic effects of the Vietnam war boosted the growth of Japan's two largest markets—the U.S.A. and South-east Asia—while efforts at diversification, primarily in the direction of Western Europe, were made by Japanese exporters. On the product side, domestic supply shifts have allowed Japan to increase the concentration of its exports on those commodity markets which have expanded most rapidly; and already by 1964 the proportion of 'growth commodities' in total exports had risen from 20 per cent to 40 per cent. But initially, and for the first ten to fifteen years of the period under review, the external conditions surrounding Japanese exports were hardly favourable, even if one disregards 'voluntary restrictions' and other protective barriers set up against the country's products.

At a more disaggregated level, examinations of the growth of production and exports, or of exports and technical progress, by industrial sectors show that these are strongly correlated with each other. This has led Blumenthal to stress the above-average speed of technical advance in export industries[18] and Kanamori to point to the close relation between sectoral output and export growth.[19] The conclusions reached are, however, diametrically opposed. Blumenthal suggests that exports played a significant role in stimulating domestic growth because of their high technical progress content. Kanamori, on the other hand, argues that domestic demand stimulated mass production which, by reducing costs, led to subsequent growth of exports. But neither actually provide evidence of casual links. Neither the high rate of technical progress in export industries nor the concomitant rapid growth of exports and output prove whether foreign or domestic demand initiated the process of export growth.

Firmer conclusions, at a micro-economic level, may be arrived at only by looking at developments through time of exports and output in particular sectors. An approach of this type had already been developed in the 1930s by K. Akamatsu.[20] His theory is similar to, but was developed earlier than, the import substitution models discussed by Nurkse, Hirschmann, or Chenery, in which rising imports point to the existence of internal demand

and lead to the establishment of domestic units of production which, with time and economies of scale, first displace imports and later generate exports. Akamatsu showed that in several major instances in pre-war days (cotton yarn and fabrics, bicycles, textile and electric machinery), the development of imports, output, and exports closely followed this sequence. He called the process 'the wild geese flying pattern of foreign trade' (see Fig. 6) because the shape of the output, export, and import curves he had plotted reminded him of the inverse V pattern of wild geese flying in partly overlapping formations.

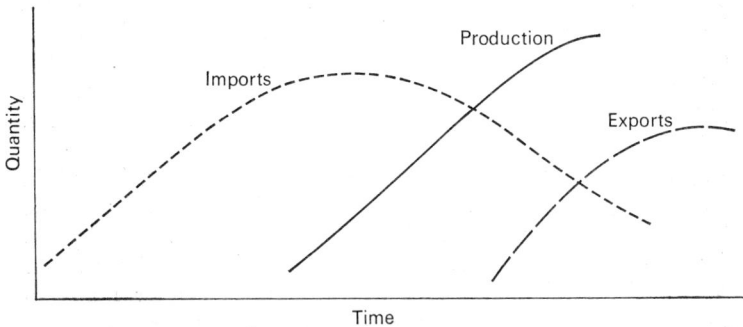

FIG. 6. *The 'Wild Geese Flying Pattern' of foreign trade*

Source: K. Akamatsu, 'A Theory of Unbalanced Growth in the World Economy', *Weltwirtschaftliches Archiv*, 2/1961, p. 206.

A more rigorous extension of the analysis showed that over the 1890–1962 period, out of 38 new export industries, 32 were import substitutes.[21] But an application of the Akamatsu scheme to the post-war years alone might not produce similarly telling results. For one thing, the period is relatively short. The study just mentioned showed that it took on average from 20 to 60 years (depending on whether commodities were produced by light or heavy industry), between initial imports and the stage at which Japan became a net exporter.[22] Secondly, income effects may have been sufficiently strong in the recent past to offset import substitution. Thirdly, a new pattern might have been expected for some of the products for which the Akamatsu scheme had worked in the earlier part of the century—a gradual decline of exports as sales of labour-intensive commodities from developing countries displace Japanese goods abroad, followed by an increase in Japanese imports from such countries and, finally, a decline of domestic production.

Figure 7 illustrates the development of imports, exports, and production of a number of commodities which have experienced very rapid export growth in the post-war period. It seems that evidence for a supply-led model of exports is forthcoming, at least for the products here shown. In practically all cases, production starts and reaches a very high level well before the beginning of sales abroad; and two commodities seem to conform quite closely to the Akamatsu pattern: motor cars and poly-ethylene. Here imports lead the way, but are quickly replaced by production at home, and this despite extremely rapid growth of demand, while exports follow only several years later. For the other commodities shown, there is hardly any trace of imports, at least since the war, but a clear lag between output and exports.

Though the six products given in the figure represent only 12·5 per cent of the value of total exports in 1973 (against nil in 1953 and 3 per cent in 1963), in several instances they can be taken as proxies for the exports of wider sectors—e.g. polyethylene for the field of new chemical products, machine tools for a whole range of capital goods, and television receivers for many of Japan's very successful consumer goods. In most cases the pattern has been the same—export drives are embarked upon only after production has reached a volume at which significant scale economies have been achieved and costs have been sufficiently reduced to withstand international competition. Moreover, and also in keeping with Akamatsu's analysis, products are first exported to developing countries and only later to the developed world, once distribution networks have been established and sufficient supplies are forthcoming to satisfy a rich market's potential demand.[23] Even at this stage exports do not account for a major share of output. In stark contrast with the heavy dependence on imports of a few commodities, export dependence ratios (in this case ratios of exports to output), with some

---

FIG. 7. *Production, exports and imports of selected commodities* (Volumes; five year moving averages; log scale)

Sources: B.S., O.P.M., *Japan Statistical Yearbook*; B.o.J. *Economic Statistics Annual*; M.o.F., *The Foriegn Trade of Japan* and *Japan Exports and Imports*; M.I.T.I., *Kikai Tōkei Geppō* (*Monthly Report on Machinery Statistics*).

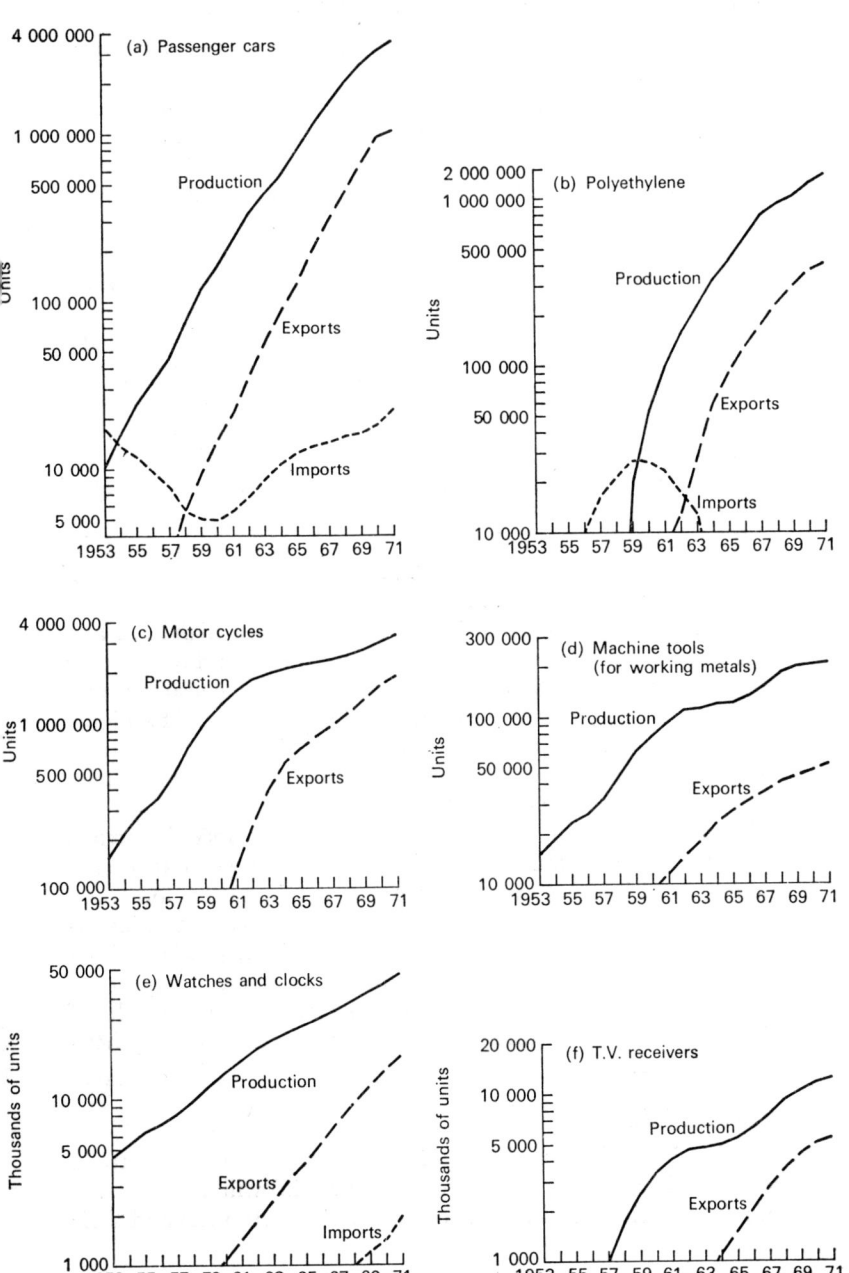

exceptions, are on the low side—of the order of 10–30 per cent on average.

Of course, these results were not achieved solely by market forces. The government's industrial policies played an important role. Many of the successful export sectors had been selected for specific encouragement, partly because it was felt that world demand for their output would grow rapidly. But production for domestic consumption has remained the primary occupation of most Japanese exporting firms, in line with the theories which suggest that countries export those goods which fit the standard of living already reached by broad numbers of their own popula-tion.[24] This seems also confirmed by the cotton yarn cycle—Akamatsu's first product. Following the rise in living standards which has taken place over the past half century, the last stage of the cycle has begun—exports have been declining from the mid-1960s and imports outstripped exports at the beginning of the 1970s.

The foregoing analysis seems to confirm the judgement by Ohkawa and Rosovsky that '. . . Japan's rate of growth of exports has been high . . . because the rate of growth of its economy and especially of its industry has been high . . . , and not vice versa.'[25] Exports were very much a resultant of domestic growth—of the growth of a large market for consumer and investment goods on the one hand, and of the growth of a highly productive capital stock (constantly embodying new techniques) on the other. Both these allowed the attainment of scale economies and cost reductions, which in turn permitted a successful growth of exports. Even in those periods of domestic recession when exports directly stimulated renewed growth, it was not foreign demand but internal supply which was the initiating force. To be sure, rapid export growth must also have encouraged invest-ment—directly through demand effects and indirectly by raising business confidence. But the over-all contribution of exports to economic growth (abstracting, of course, from their role of financing import requirements), does not seem to have been fundamental.

The trade balance

Following Johnson, changes in a country's balance of trade with another country (or the rest of the world) will be a function of relative price trends, the two countries' growth rates and their price and income elasticities of demand for imports.[26] The difficulties of estimating price elasticities are well known. For Japan's imports the elasticity must have been rather low, in view of the non-competing nature of most of the country's purchases abroad. Even assuming that this low value was more than offset by a relatively high price elasticity of demand for Japanese exports, it is unlikely that the sum of the two elasticities could have been much above one in the period under review. Given a (trend) terms-of-trade improvement, the model would suggest some (trend) deterioration in the trade balance. But any tendency to deterioration could only have been moderate, and was in any case swamped by the improvement implicit in the values of the two income elasticities of demand. The latter can be put at, roughly, 1 for imports and 3 for exports.[27] Despite the fact that Japan's growth rate of output was roughly double that of the rest of the world, the disparity in the two income elasticities was sufficiently large to provide Japan with an inherent tendency towards surplus on the trade account.

This, of course, is only an *ex-post* statistical account of what happened. The real reasons behind the yen's undervaluation at the beginning of the 1970s are to be found, as already said, in the nature and speed of domestic growth. It is the latter which 'generated' the particular values of the two income elasticities. It is true that at the outset protection was important in limiting the imports of most manufactures and stimulating infant industries. But from then onwards it was rapid growth which perpetuated, through various forms of import saving, Japan's low dependence on the rest of the world and, through the mechanism just outlined, created the conditions for a successful penetration of Japanese goods abroad. In contrast with the frequently held theory that high demand pressures and rapid growth tend to worsen a country's balance of payments, exactly the opposite consequence followed, over the longer run, in Japan. The improvement was no doubt helped by external circumstances. In the later 1960s the growth of Japanese export markets began to outstrip that of world trade as a whole, thanks to the geographical and commodity diversification noted above. But the underlying trend towards improvement could be traced already to the mid-1960s, if not earlier.

The improvement of the trade balance also reflected nearly infinitely elastic supply schedules—for raw materials on the import side and for Japanese exportables on the export side. Both these were assured over most of the period, Japanese demand never impinging sufficiently on world supplies to effect prices significantly and foreign demand for Japanese exports never amounting to a very large share of Japanese production of most commodities. The second condition remains broadly fulfilled at present; but the first does not hold any longer to the extent that it did in the past. The sharp deterioration in the terms of trade in 1973-4 had momentous effects on both inflation and the balance of payments, effects larger, probably, than those felt by any other developed economy. It could be argued on the strength of this, assuming that the increase in world primary-product prices is not merely temporary, that Japan's rise to the status of a 'structural surplus' country, hailed in the early 1970s, was perhaps only a very short-run phenomenon, and that the country will now relapse into its earlier precarious balance of payments situation.

But this prospect remains uncertain, since the world's future balance of payments configuration is too difficult to foresee. Too many imponderables colour the prospects for international monetary reform, exchange rate flexibility, energy prices, the amount and direction of capital flows between North America, Europe, and the developing world, etc., for any meaningful forecast to be possible. All that can be ventured at the present stage is a view on whether Japan's export competitiveness can continue in the future, assuming roughly unchanged rates of exchange and absence of protective measures abroad. The preceding discussion suggests the answer. If Japan is able to grow at a rate above that of its main competitors and, *a fortiori*, is able to alter its industrial structure towards high-value-added activities, it should continue to remain among the world's most dynamic exporters.

This seems to be the forecast implicit in the J.E.R.C.'s view of the 1985 world. Its, very optimistic, projections for that year foresee a Japanese share of world exports (13·2 per cent) almost double the present level, following a growth rate of GNP of more than 9 per cent between now and then.[28] Conversely, however, a permanent deceleration of growth to a rate much lower than that witnessed in the past would in all probability seriously impair Japan's longer-run competitiveness. In that case to re-establish equilibrium in its trade balance, Japan could well rely on a greater degree of exchange rate flexibility, which seems now to be an accepted part of the international monetary system. But other factors affecting the balance—future import needs and their cost, as well as the possible climate for foreign trade in a world perhaps subject to much larger disequilibria than hitherto—raise as yet unanswerable questions.

NOTES

1. S. Kuznets, 'Quantitative Aspects of the Economic Growth of Nations: IX.—Level and Structure of Foreign Trade: Comparisons for Recent Years', *EDCC*, October 1964.

2. A discrepancy of the same order of magnitude results when using a similar United Nations calculation made for 23 East and West European countries for the 1963–7 period: U.N.(E.C.E.), *Economic Bulletin for Europe*, Vol. 21, No. 1, p. 50.

3. For comparative trends, see *ibid.*, p. 45, and O.E.C.D., *The Growth of Output*, p. 60.

4. E.P.A., *ESJ (1966–1967)*, p. 76.

5. M. Tatetmoto and S. Nishimura, 'Factor Proportions and Foreign Trade: the Case of Japan', *RES*, November 1959; S. Naya, 'Natural Resources, Factor Mix and Factor Reversal in International Trade', *American Economic Review*, May 1967.

6. Tatemoto and Nishimura, 'Factor Proportions'; R. E. Baldwin, 'Determinants of the Commodity Structure of U.S. Trade', *American Economic Review*, March 1971.

7. W. F. Stolper and P. A. Samuelson, 'Protection and Real Wages', reprinted (from *The Review of Economic Studies*, November 1941), in American Economic Association, *Readings in the Theory of International Trade*, London 1950.

8. Lockwood, *Economic Development of Japan*, p. 320.

9. O.E.C.D., *Economic Outlook*, December 1973, p. 16.

10. R. Nurkse, *Patterns of Trade and Development*, Stockholm 1959, pp. 19–27.

11. N. Namiki, 'Growth of Japanese Exports', *DE*, December 1970, pp. 484–9.

12. This point was suggested in conversation by Hidekazu Eguchi of the Bank of Japan.

13. Ohkawa and Rosovsky, *Japanese Economic Growth*, p. 177.

14. Shinohara has argued strongly that pre-war growth was export-led; for the post-war period his attitude is not as clear-cut and he stresses the interactions between investment-led and export-led growth patterns (*Key Factors in Japan's Long-term Economic Growth*, E.P.A. Economic Research Institute 1971, pp. 7–13); for a recent restatement of the importance of exports for Japanese growth see Blumenthal, 'Exports and Economic Growth'.

15. R. E. Caves, 'Export-led Growth and the New Economic History', in J. N. Bhagwati *et al.* (eds.), *Trade, Balance of Payments and Growth* (Papers in Honour of C. P. Kindleberger), Amsterdam 1971, p. 425.

16. *Ibid.*, pp. 426–7.

17. N.I.E.S.R., 'Fast and Slow-Growing Products in World Trade', *Economic Review*, August 1963; E.P.A., *ESJ (1965–1966)*, p. 84.

18. Blumenthal, 'Exports and Economic Growth', pp. 618–22.

19. H. Kanamori, 'Economic Growth and Exports', in Klein and Ohkawa (eds.), *Economic Growth*.

20. Only two articles of Akamatsu have been translated into English: 'A Theory of Unbalanced Growth in the World Economy', *Weltwirtschaftliches Archiv*, 2/1961 and 'A Historical Pattern of Economic Growth in Developing Countries', *DE*, March–August 1962.

21. W. V. Rapp, 'A Theory of Changing Trade Patterns under Economic Growth: Tested for Japan', *Yale Economic Essays*, Fall 1967.

22. *Ibid.*, pp. 134–5.

23. GATT, *Japan's Econom : ·Expansion and Foreign Trade—1955 to 1970*, 1971, pp. 35–7.

24. S. B. Linder, *An Essay on Trade and Transformation*, Stockholm 1961.

25. Ohkawa and Rosovsky, *Japanese Economic Growth*, p. 173.

26. H. G. Johnson, *International Trade and Economic Growth*, London 1953, pp. 94–115.

27. Values of 1·23 and 3·55 were found for the 1951–66 period by H. S. Houthakker and S. P. Magee, 'Income and Price Elasticities in World Trade', *RES*, May 1969, p. 113.

28. J.E.R.C., *The Structure of a Three Trillion Dollar Economy*.

CHAPTER 8

INCOME DISTRIBUTION

COMPARED with other topics, the subject of income distribution seems to have been one of the least researched in the Japanese economy. This relative neglect may well have been due to rapid growth, which monopolized the attention of most economists. Moreover, when output increases continuously, and by unexpectedly large amounts, concern about its distribution is much less pronounced than when total income is stagnant or rises only slowly. But the lack of a profuse academic or government literature does not mean that the subject is without importance. For one thing, it may be interesting to see how income distribution evolved in the course of very rapid economic growth. For another, a look at Japan in an international context, however tentative and imprecise, may throw light on some characteristics of the country's economy. More fundamentally, it may be felt, in the tradition of classical economics, that '. . . the theory of distribution holds the key to an understanding of the whole mechanism of the economic system'.[1]

In what follows, distribution will be looked at from two different aspects—the distribution of personal incomes among households and the distribution of national product between factors of production. Both these approaches raise serious statistical and/or conceptual difficulties, notably in any attempt at international comparisons. It can hardly be claimed that these difficulties are overcome in the present chapter; and the conclusions reached on the degree of 'equality' in Japanese income distribution and on the effect of distribution on economic growth therefore remain very tentative.

Distribution of personal income

Investigations of personal-income distribution tend to face major statistical problems, compared with which the conceptual issues are relatively minor. It is usually accepted that included in 'personal income' should be income from work (both wages and salaries), from independent entrepreneurship and from capital assets held by households. Whether transfers, imputed rents, realized capital gains or incomes in kind should be added to, and direct taxes deducted from, such a total remains an open question and conventions vary. Once a particular concept is adopted and data are available for individual (or, preferably, household) incomes, a number of statistical devices allow comparisons of distribution over time and across countries and can be used, with caution, to draw some conclusions on relative degrees of equality. The real problems are statistical, since the availability of basic data is often limited and coverage can differ widely. Short of very complete population census results, the most often used sources are tax returns, or tax assessment figures, and special household surveys. Of these, the former are frequently deficient; they tend to underestimate incomes at the upper end, because of tax evasion, and do not always cover lower income brackets not liable to taxation. Household surveys are, in principle, superior; but sampling methods, coverage, and accuracy of replies may vary widely across time and space.

In the wealth of Japanese statistics, some fairly reliable survey data can be found which allow an assessment of changes in income distribution through time. But any international comparison must be heavily qualified since even when survey data are available elsewhere, definitions of incomes and/or income-receiving units are far from uniform. No attempt is made here to investigate in detail the distribution in various countries. Secondary sources are used and the conclusions reached on comparative degrees of equality remain tentative. No precise definition of 'inequality' is offered, since to do this would go well beyond the scope of a brief economic survey focused on one country. Similarly, no position is taken on the advantages and disadvantages of various measures of inequality. For the sake of simplicity and convenience, one single indicator of skewness of income distribution is used throughout—the Gini coefficient of concentration.* This coefficient has been subject to numerous criticisms, notably because it is insensitive to the location of income distribution differences (for instance whether they occur at the upper or lower ends of the income scale). It remains, none

* Very broadly, the Gini coefficient measures the difference between a completely equal distribution, in which each household receives the same income, and the actual distribution. The smaller its value, the closer is the distribution to perfect equality. For a description of the Gini coefficient and of some of its defects, see M. Bronfenbrenner, *Income Distribution Theory*, London 1971, pp. 45–50.

the less, one of the most widely used single indicators of equality or inequality in personal distribution of income.

These qualifications—and others not spelt out—should be borne in mind when considering Table 8.1, which presents Gini coefficients, generally for the mid-1960s, assembled from a variety of sources for a number of developed high-income countries. A preliminary and somewhat surprising conclusion is that the distribution of total personal incomes seems more equal in Japan than in any other market economy shown;* and this conclusion is reinforced by the data covering income from employment (or the income of households whose head is engaged in paid employment) only. Indeed for employment income alone Japan's degree of equality parallels that of some of the socialist countries of Eastern Europe, if one is bold enough to attempt comparisons in such a difficult field.

This relative equality of Japanese income distribution has been noted in earlier works, notably by Komiya and Mizoguchi in their investigations on Japanese savings.[2] Komiya's judgement that '. . . the Japanese distribution seems one of the most equal in the entire world'[3] supports the evidence presented here. Yet, a priori, such findings seem highly surprising and perhaps even suspect. Chapter 2 has shown that Japan's economy is characterized by scale-wage differentials greater than those recorded in most (if not all) advanced economies, as well as by sizeable disparities in regional income levels. Household incomes should presumably reflect such large differentials unless offsetting factors exist, or statistical biases make the household-income data misleading. It is unfortunately not possible to test for one obviously possible bias by checking the consistency of the household income figures with the personal income data of the national accounts statistics, since the *Family Saving Survey* used here does not distinguish between types of incomes. Hence an underestimation of, for instance, property incomes, which are likely to be less equally distributed than income from work, may be one reason for Japan's low Gini coefficient. But it is impossible either

* It should be pointed out, however, that, depending on the sources used, results for Japan differ and higher Gini coefficients can be found. Thus the figures given in T. Ishizaki ('The Income Distribution in Japan', *DE*, June 1967, p. 356), result in a Gini coefficient for all households in 1962 of 0·40. It is felt that the data shown in Table 8.1 are among the more reliable of those available, but the possibility of biases cannot be excluded.

to prove or to disprove this point; and in any case, other countries' data could be similarly biased.

There are, however, a number of other statistical and economic problems which need to be borne in mind in such comparisons and for which some qualitative or quantitative allowance can be made. First, all the figures in the table are based on pre- rather than on post-tax incomes. As argued by Kuznets,[4] the former need not be independent of the latter. It is, for instance, quite plausible to think that in a country with a very progressive tax system, the pre-tax distribution may be more skewed than in a country in which the redistributive effects of taxation are relatively small. Comparisons of the progressiveness of income tax structures and of their equalizing effect are not easy. An E.P.A. estimate showed that Japan's system had a somewhat higher equalization effect than that of the United States, but a much lower one than that of Britain.[5] A very impressionistic judgement would extend the Japan–United Kingdom conclusion to most of the countries shown in the table. It could, therefore, be argued that the apparent pre-tax superiority of Japan's income distribution would be reduced in a post-tax comparison or, alternatively, that other countries might also find themselves closer to Japan's distribution patterns if they had less progressive tax systems. A similar conclusion would probably be reached if one could take into account public goods, whose consumption is likely to be fairly equally distributed, but whose availability in Japan is limited in comparison with most of the countries shown in the table.

A second shortcoming of the Japanese survey data is the exclusion of agricultural and single-person households. The first omission is perhaps not as serious as one might imagine. By the mid-1960s, the average income of an agricultural household was only marginally below that of an urban household. Unless income distribution in the countryside was much more skewed, it is unlikely that the incorporation of farming families into the sample would greatly alter the results shown here.* The absence of single-person households is probably more serious, since their incomes tend to be below average. A very simplified calculation, adding to the original sample a number of households equal to the ratio of

---

* A calculation for 1963, which integrated the results of an agricultural household survey with those for wage and salary earning families, obtained a Gini coefficient of 0·35: H. T. Oshima, 'Income Inequality and Economic Growth—The Postwar Experience of Asian Countries', *Malayan Economic Review*, October 1970, pp. 12–14.

one-person households to total households in 1965, and attributing to these the incomes of the bottom 2 per cent of the non-farming distribution, would raise the Gini coefficient to 0·35. This may exaggerate the amount of correction needed. It none the less suggests some under-estimation of inequality in the original figures.

A third point is related to incomes in kind, which are excluded from the data shown in the table. Non-pecuniary benefits are probably more important in Japan than elsewhere in the industrialized world in view of the widespread existence of company-run housing estates, medical insurance schemes, leisure activities, etc. Their distribution should therefore be taken into account. In so far as company benefits are frequently a direct function of company size they accentuate rather than reduce money-income differentials. And a similar effect is achieved by a particularly important Japanese institution—the expense account. Business consumption expenditures specifically devoted to 'entertaining' represented in 1965 an amount equal to $4\frac{1}{4}$ per cent of private consumption expenditure and 3 per cent of personal income. The distribution of this sum must have been concentrated at the very upper end of the income scale, among the managers and executives of the larger corporations. While the effect of all indirect benefits cannot be measured, the quantitative importance of this last factor can be tentatively assessed. Surprisingly, perhaps, it does not amount to much. Increasing the total income of the household sample used by 3 per cent, and attributing the whole of this increase to the top 5 per cent of the household distribution hardly changes the Gini coefficient.

The various arguments advanced so far suggest that, on balance, some upward adjustment of Japan's figures in Table 8.1 may be warranted. But a number of points militate in an opposite direction. At a purely statistical level, it is well known that the calculation of Gini coefficients can be sensitive to the number of observations used, as well as to their bunching. The smaller the number of observations, the greater the bias towards under-estimating the coefficient. The results shown here are usually based on decile income groups, but the data for Japan cover sixteen groups. A very simple recalculation, based on decile groups read off a diagram showing the original Lorenz curve, obtains a 0·30 Gini coefficient for total household income rather than the 0·32 shown in the table. Secondly, the use of a single year for an international comparison may not be warranted since cyclical influences on distribution may distort results. Most of the market economies covered in the sample recorded at least average, and usually above-average, demand pressures in the particular year shown, with the notable exception of Japan which, in 1965, was in full recession. On balance, inequalities tend to increase in slumps, especially for wage and salary earners. Thirdly, the sources for

TABLE 8.1

'Gini coefficients' for personal income distribution in selected countries

	YEAR	ALL INCOMES	WAGE AND SALARY INCOMES
Japan	1965	0·32	0·21[1]
France	1962	0·52	0·35
Germany	1964	0·47	0·28
Italy	1966	0·37	..
United Kingdom	1963/4	0·40	0·27
United States	1964	0·40	..
Australia	1967/8	0·34	..
Canada	1969	0·38	..
Finland	1962	0·47	..
Netherlands	1962	0·44	0·40
Norway	1963	0·36	..
Sweden	1963	0·40	0·36
Czechoslovakia	1965	0·24	0·19[2]
Hungary	1967	0·26	0·25[2]

Note: Figures are far from comparable. For further detail see text. Income receiving units are households except for Germany, the United Kingdom, Finland, the Netherlands, Norway, and Sweden, where they are individual taxpayers. Data for the Scandinavian countries are based on tax assessment figures.

1. Total incomes of workers' households.
2. Wage and salary earners in socialist sector, excluding transfers.

Sources: Japan: unpublished E.P.A. calculations, based on data in B.S., O.P.M., *Family Saving Survey* and *Annual Report on the Family Income and Expenditure Survey.*
Italy: P. Roberti, 'Le variazioni nella distribuzione personale del reddito in Italia, 1948–1966', *Rassegna Economica*, July–August 1971.
Other Western European Countries: U.N.(E.C.E.), *Incomes in Post-war Europe,* Geneva 1967.
United States: Survey of Current Business, October 1974.
Australia: N. Podder, 'Distribution of Household Income in Australia', *Economic Record,* June 1972.
Canada: J. R. Podoluk, 'The Size Distribution of Personal Wealth in Canada', *Review of Income and Wealth,* June 1974.
Eastern Europe: J. W. Michal, 'Size-Distribution of Earnings and Household Incomes in Small Socialist Countries', *Review of Income and Wealth,* December 1973.

the data here used are not always uniform. Several of the figures in Table 8.1 are, in varying degrees, based on tax returns. As already argued, Gini coefficients calculated from such data tend to give a spurious impression of equality since the two extreme tails of the distribution are covered only imperfectly or not at all.

Finally, there are some other not solely economic arguments which really preclude, or at least impair, any direct comparison of income distribution patterns between different societies. The somewhat more traditional nature of Japan's society and some of the peculiar characteristics of its labour market provide a case in point. Individual wages may vary between firms of different size by more than they do elsewhere, but higher female participation rates, the virtual absence of open unemployment, and the widespread tendency for part-time occupations (by industrial workers in agriculture or vice versa) can have offsetting effects. In addition, as suggested by Kravis,[6] pension arrangements and family structures can also influence size distributions. In Japan's case, the near-absence of adequate retirement benefits forces older people to live with their children, a tendency favoured by the traditional (albeit rapidly disappearing) family structure. In the West, by contrast, because pension levels are somewhat higher and/or family structures have changed, older people are much more frequently found in independent households often clustered at the lower end of the income scale. But such arguments, though they qualify earlier conclusions, do not necessarily invalidate them. The factors just mentioned may reflect specific Japanese characteristics, but they also imply that the distribution of household income and other elements in welfare together (given that the Japanese household is more extended in terms of both its members and income earners) may still be more favourable than in the West.

Impressionistically assessing the various considerations set out above, therefore, a tentative conclusion might not be very different from the one originally proposed. Assuming that the international data assembled are reasonably reliable, Japan's personal income distribution, while not necessarily the most equal in the world, is among the more equal ones in developed countries, despite the 'dualism' of the economy. And Japan's degree of equality is particularly evident at the bottom of the income scale. The share of income obtained by the top 5 or 10 per cent of households is not very different from that in other relatively 'egalitarian' market economies like Australia or Norway. But differences are striking at the lower end of the scale. The bottom 20 per cent of Japanese families receive 8½ per cent of total income as against figures commonly around 4–5 per cent elsewhere and, at most, 6½ per cent. The absence of single-person and agricultural households from the sample clearly gives too favourable a picture for Japan; but the figures nevertheless suggest that absolute poverty and destitution may be less common than in most other market economies, with the probable exception of the high-welfare Scandinavian countries.

To the explanations of these findings already given, two further important reasons may be added—the relative absence both of under-privileged minority groups and also of a concentration of saving and wealth in the upper income brackets, which are probably the factors most responsible for large inequalities elsewhere. The dismantling of a number of huge corporations, the sweeping agricultural reform, and the runaway inflation of the early post-war years wiped out much of the great pre-war concentrations of wealth; and the very high saving propensities in most income brackets during the last twenty years, as well as the uniformly low rates of return on most savings, meant that the reconstitution of wealth was probably less unequal than was the case elsewhere. A simple comparison with Norway (a relatively egalitarian country), can best illustrate this point. The top 20 per cent of households own 43 per cent of all wealth in Japan and some 75 per cent in Norway.[7] It is true that the Japanese figure is based only on wage- and salary-earning households and hence may underestimate the degree of concentration for the country as a whole; but it nevertheless suggests that wealth is likely to be more evenly distributed than in most other market economies. As for under-privileged minorities, the racial homogeneity of the population, and the country's social structure may well have prevented the appearance of the three groups which form the bulk of the poor in Western countries—racial minorities, immigrants, and the old.

Indeed, the frequently invoked cultural and social homogeneity of the Japanese population may be related in more than one way to income distribution structures. A homogeneous population may imply not only relatively equal incomes but also relatively equal consumption patterns. The latter point is brought out by a test used by Lockwood for pre-war Japan.[8] Plotting, as in Fig. 8, yearly incomes and expenditures for (wage- and salary-earning) households distinguished by income brackets, it can be seen that there is a very close linear relationship between the two variables. Correlation coefficients are 0·999 for savings and for expenditures on clothing and on miscellaneous goods and services, and increase to 0·99 for expenditure on food and housing, once the three lowest income brackets are excluded. In other words, marginal propensities to save and consume, at a point of time, seem very similar

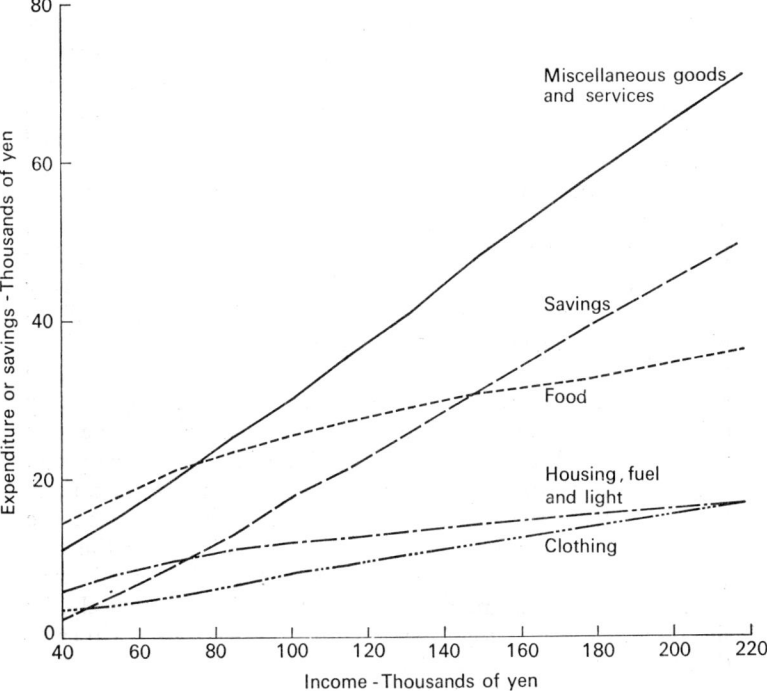

FIG. 8. *Monthly savings and consumption expenditures by income groups* (Workers' households; average 1969 to 1971)

Source: B.S., O.P.M., *Annual Report on the Family Income and Expenditure Survey.*

for all households, irrespective of incomes. Over time, the fit is not quite as good. Marginal propensities estimated for five income brackets over the 1963–72 period, while very similar for clothing and miscellaneous expenditures, show some relatively pronounced differences for food consumption and savings.* Yet the over-all

* The marginal propensity to consume food in workers' households declines from 0·26 to 0·14 going from the bottom to the top income quintile while the

evidence suggests a fairly homogeneous pattern of consumer behaviour not necessarily present elsewhere.

Secondly, opinion polls made by official bodies show that '. . . the majority (of people) harbour the middle-class consciousness under the impact of the equalization of incomes. The ratio of those people to the entire population climbed year after year, and in 1967 it reached nearly 90 per cent.'[9] One can be legitimately suspicious of such surveys. The way questions are formulated may almost dictate the answer. They none the less suggest that class consciousness among Japanese households may be a good deal less pronounced than in, for instance, Europe. Relatively similar tastes and, especially, incomes may well be linked to this.

Through time, it seems that equality has increased. Precise comparisons between the pre- and the post-war period are marred by statistical deficiencies, but the over-all conclusion seems fairly straightforward. Pre-war income differences were apparently very large.[10] For some of the reasons enumerated above, they diminished greatly after the war and the trend continued, at least throughout the 1960s. In this Japan's experience may have differed from more recent developments elsewhere. Fragmentary evidence for Western Europe suggests that after some definite progress towards equalization in the immediate post-war years, there has been little change, or even a reverse movement, since the mid-1950s or early 1960s. Had Table 8.1 been filled with more recent data, Japan (whose 1970 Gini coefficients for the two columns were 0·28 and 0·19 respectively) might well have appeared in an even more exceptional position. Conversely, its situation in the mid-1950s would probably have been closer to that of the sample as a whole.

Functional distribution

A study of functional income distribution does not encounter as many statistical problems, thanks to the availability of reasonably reliable and internationally comparable national accounts figures. But it raises several conceptual difficulties. Thus the definition of economic sectors implicit in national accounts does not necessarily correspond to the economic concept of productive

---

marginal saving propensity rises from 0·14 to 0·26. The very high levels of the latter two propensities are worth noting.

factors. An even more intractable problem arises from the existence of a category of workers (the self-employed) who earn income by combining their labour with their capital assets. Any attempt to calculate the total shares of labour and capital in national income thus involves splitting entrepreneurial income between its two components, with the inevitable consequence that the results obtained will be based on arbitrary assumptions. Moreover, the conventions usually adopted for this purpose cannot be indiscriminately and uniformly applied to all countries. The shares of capital and labour in entrepreneurial, or 'mixed', income are likely to be very different in a largely agricultural or artisan type economy, in which the self-employed sector looms large, from those in a highly developed and industrialized country in which entrepreneurial income is increasingly appropriated by members of the professional classes. International comparisons in this field between countries which are not homogeneous are, therefore, extremely difficult and will not be ventured here. An attempt will, however, be made to estimate the returns to labour and capital in Japan's 'mixed' income and, therefore, in the economy as a whole.

But first, some more limited international comparisons are possible which, while not involving estimates of total factor returns, still permit some generalizations on the likely trends and structures of factor-income distribution across countries. Table 8.2 presents data for a number of relatively developed market economies, for which statistics were available, for two major categories of income—the sum of compensation of employees and 'mixed' income* (this sum called 'participation' income by Kuznets and 'proletarian' income by Bronfenbrenner),[11] and a proxy for the share of capital assets in corporate sector income.† Both these two indicators present statistical problems. The first includes returns to both labour and capital, if in very different proportions, while the second includes some household property income, not originating in the corporate sector, and general government income. Exclusion of these items would have been more appropriate, but would have restricted the number of

* Analysis of either of these two components separately almost invariably shows rises in the former's share and falls in the latter's, largely because of labour force shifts from independent to corporate employment.

† Household, corporate (including public corporations) and general government income from assets as a share of national income minus the income of unincorporated enterprises.

TABLE 8.2

Selected income categories—1953 to 1972

	WHOLE ECONOMY		'CORPORATE' SECTOR	
	'PARTICIPATION' INCOME [1]		INCOME FROM ASSETS[2]	
	AVERAGE PERCENTAGE SHARE	TREND[3] INCREASES IN SHARE	AVERAGE PERCENTAGE SHARE	TREND[3] INCREASES IN SHARE
Japan	77·1	−0·59	29·6	0·46
France	85·7	−0·39	18·9	0·39
Germany[4]	90·9	0·16	12·1	−0·28
Italy[5]	87·2	(0·08)	18·0	(−0·28)
United Kingdom	85·5	0·34	15·7	−0·34
United States	81·8	(0·07)	20·6	−0·10
Average of seven other countries[6]	83·2	0·06	22·0	−0·19

1. Defined as employee compensation and entrepreneurial income of unincorporated enterprises as a percentage of national income at factor cost.

2. Corporate and government income *and* household income from property as a percentage of national income at factor cost excluding the entrepreneurial income of unincorporated enterprises.

3. Annual increase in share of items in national income (or in national income excluding the entrepreneurial income of unincorporated enterprises) obtained by fitting linear time trends to the data. Figures in brackets are statistically not significant at the 5 per cent confidence level.

4. 1960 to 1972.

5. 1961 to 1972.

6. 1954 to 1969; unweighted average of shares for Austria, Belgium, Canada, Finland, Ireland, Spain, and Switzerland.

Sources: E.P.A., *National Income Statistics* and O.E.C.D., *National Accounts of O.E.C.D. Countries.*

observations. In addition, employee compensation includes wages received by workers in unincorporated enterprises; an earlier estimate for Japan had put the share of employee compensation paid by the unincorporated sector at 3·9 per cent in the 1953–62 period.[12] But while such imperfections may lead to some inter-country distortions, the figures in the table can still be broadly compared.

The picture is striking. For both the categories of income chosen, Japan's shares are well below or above (depending on which share one is considering) those of any other country in the table and they show the highest single deviations from the (unweighted) averages of the whole sample (84 per cent and 20½ per cent respectively). The same divergence can be seen when looking at trends through time. Japan has recorded a strong, and statistically significant, movement away from 'participation' income towards income from assets throughout the period, in contrast to other countries which usually witnessed either no net movement or trends in the opposite direction. Only two economies in the sample approximate some aspects of the Japanese experience—Finland (not separately shown), whose absolute shares (79 per cent and $25\frac{1}{2}$ per cent) are a good deal closer to Japan's than they are to the international average, and France, whose trends are very similar to those shown for Japan. But in Finland's case it is the trends which go in the opposite direction while France's levels are well above (below) the sample's mean.

The trend figures also show that the exceptionally large weight of capital in Japan's income distribution has developed over the last twenty years. The 1953–5 unweighted average for the countries for which long series were available are 84 per cent and $21\frac{1}{2}$ per cent for 'participation' and 'asset' income respectively. Japan's figures at that time (86·3 per cent and 21·6 per cent) deviated only little from the average and, in one instance, in the opposite direction from the deviation at the end of the period. By 1970–2 the gaps between Japan's shares and the average had grown to 8 and 10 percentage points. Explanations for Japan's rather exceptional figures and trends may thus have to be sought in the country's pattern of growth during the last twenty years, rather than in any structural and unchangeable differences.

Before passing to some tentative explanations, it may be advisable to try to define more accurately the total shares of labour and capital in national income, by splitting the return to entrepreneurship. As already said, various methods exist for allocating entrepreneurial income. Those most commonly used impute to labour, or to capital, in the non-corporate sector the average return to the corresponding factor in the corporate economy and obtain the income of the other factor as a residual.[13] More detailed variants of these two basic approaches split returns to labour or capital in the corporate economy by individual industries (e.g. agriculture, various manufacturing branches, etc.) and then apply them to the corresponding breakdowns in the non-corporate sector. The main problem with an application of the 'labour' approach to Japan, as was pointed out by Ohkawa,[14] is that multiplying the number of self-employed and unpaid family workers by average employee compensation not only results in an estimated labour income in the non-corporate sector well in excess of that sector's total income, but also in a total labour income for the economy in excess of national income, at least in the 1950s.

The alternative, or 'capital' approach, which has been used by Ohkawa and Rosovsky in their recent work,[15] does not encounter this objection but can be questioned on its assumption of an equal return to capital in both sectors. This assumption may be valid for economies with highly developed capital markets and very efficient and sophisticated independent entrepreneurs. It seems much less warranted in the case of Japan, in which a large part of the non-corporate sector is composed of (slowly disappearing) very small family establishments earning well below average incomes.

It was long ago argued by Kuznets that for such economies the capital markets for the corporate and non-corporate sectors are far from being the same: '. . . there are two different markets for capital goods: in one the capital goods are relatively free to seek the highest return . . . , the other is a market for capital goods that are closely tied to the way of making a living, by combination with some specific type of labour services. The mobility of this type of capital goods is low, and the market for it tends to be a distress market—the goods becoming available for sale when, due to some untoward event, their tie to the productive service is dissolved. The specific returns assignable to such capital goods are largely a matter of convention, but they are clearly below those assigned to freely moving capital funds.' And '. . . equity is held on to despite low or zero returns, because possession of land, or of a few tools, or of a small commodity inventory means a larger income than could be secured by reliance on employment alone.'[16] Similarly the frequently above-average age and below-average skills of workers in the non-corporate sector imply that '. . . for a substantial proportion of the entrepreneurial group any defensible estimate of the value of their labour services must be lower than the per unit rates of compensation for the full-time, primary labour force in the free employment market.'[17]

Since it is felt that many of Japan's non-corporate activities conform to a greater or lesser extent to the picture just drawn, it would seem plausible to try to use in this instance a somewhat different imputation method, which would ascribe to both capital and labour in the 'mixed' sector returns lower than those recorded in the corporate sector. One approach which would usually ensure such an outcome would be to split total entrepreneurial income in the same proportions as total corporate income. But arithmetical convenience apart, there is little *a priori* economic justification for such a procedure. Hence, an alternative method will be used.[18]

In contrast with the usual hypothesis that capital is more homogeneous and mobile than labour, it will be assumed that the opposite is the case in Japan's non-corporate sector, and that it is unpaid family workers and the self-employed who can move with relative ease to paid employment, if wages in the corporate sector make it attractive to do so. The same is hardly true of their capital assets, often very specific to their jobs, which it may be difficult to sell and whose proceeds would hardly be used for investment in the capital market. In these conditions, the return to labour could be some sort of 'opportunity wage' or the return which could be (and is) obtained by the usually unskilled workers in the non-corporate sector when they first move to paid employment. The best proxy for this would seem to be the wages received in very small firms (with 1 to 29 employees), which, as was seen earlier, still account for a sizeable proportion of corporate employment—somewhat more than a third for the period as a whole. The return on non-corporate assets, on the other hand, may well be assimilated to a residual which, if insufficient to cover depreciation plus some small margin to keep total income above that which could be earned in small-scale enterprises, would eventually lead to the termination of independent activity. Such an approach, called 'marginal' for want of a better term, could, of course, be refined by distinguishing independent entrepreneurs from unpaid family workers, or by calculating different returns to labour depending on the self-employed workers' original sector of activity. But it is unlikely that such additional complications would greatly alter the final outcome.

The results obtained are shown in detail in the Annex table to this chapter and the various assumptions used are spelt out in the notes to that table. For the period as a whole, the return to labour in the non-corporate sector, which has risen through time in parallel with the longer run closing of wage differentials between different sized firms, has been estimated at some 60 per cent of that in the corporate sector. The rate of return on the capital stock, on the other hand, is much lower. It works out, on average, at only 10 per cent of the rate earned in the corporate sector and is negative on a net, though never on a gross, basis in several years of the period. This may seem low, and may be artificially depressed by some data deficiencies mentioned below, but it does not seem implausible in Japanese conditions.

The statistical problems which should be borne in mind when looking at both the results of the imputation and the final figures for the capital and labour shares in the economy, shown in Table 8.3, concern the coverage of the various series. All personal

TABLE 8.3

Returns to capital and labour—1953 to 1972

	AVERAGE PERCENTAGE SHARE OF CAPITAL INCOME IN NATIONAL INCOME		CONSTANT PRICE RATES OF RETURN[1]	
	CURRENT PRICES	CONSTANT PRICES	CAPITAL[2]	LABOUR[3]
Average 1953 to 1972	23·2	22·9	12·3	395·8
trend growth rate	0·73[4]	0·98[4]	0·052[5]	0·071[5]

Note: For definitions of capital and labour income, see text.

1. At 1965 prices, deflated by the private fixed gross investment deflator for capital and the private consumption expenditure deflator for labour.
2. Percentage return on gross private capital stock, excluding housing. Arithmetic average of annual rates of return.
3. Return to labour per employed; average of annual figures; thousands of yen.
4. Annual increase in item's share in national income obtained by fitting time trends to the data.
5. Log trends.

Sources: E.P.A., *National Income Statistics*, and 'Gross Fixed Capital Stock of Private Enterprises', mimeo, 1973; B.S., O.P.M., *Japan Statistical Yearbook*.

property income has been allocated to the corporate sector's capital share, thus artificially swelling its rate of return. The economy's rate of return on capital excludes the incomes of both the general government and of public corporations, since the latter are not separately available in Japanese statistics. Labour incomes, on the other hand, include the compensation paid to government employees. Thus if anything, the share of capital is somewhat under-estimated in relation to that of labour. However, in calculating returns to capital, rent was included in current revenue, but the housing stock was excluded from the capital stock because of lack of data. Hence it would be dangerous to try to compare the absolute shares or the rates of return on capital shown here with those obtained by other studies on Japan, let alone with the results of work on other countries. But it is unlikely that these various problems could seriously distort the shares' trends through time.

The broad conclusions which can be drawn from Table 8.3 confirm the preliminary impressions provided by Table 8.2. The share of capital in total income, in current or constant prices (and either net or gross of depreciation) has risen rapidly and consistently throughout the period, and so has the rate of return on capital. This seems to contrast with Japan's pre-war and other countries' post-war trends. Ohkawa and Rosovsky, using somewhat different imputation methods, show that labour's share rose slowly between 1908 and 1938 and stood at a much higher level throughout those years than it has done since the war.[19] Scattered international evidence, which has to be used with great caution, would on the whole suggest that the post-war share of labour in national income has slowly risen, or remained constant, in other developed market economies. Hence explanations for Japan's pattern are unlikely to be found in analogous experiences elsewhere.

As suggested by Solow,[20] structural shifts may have played a role, in view of the economy's rapid transformation and the different factor shares recorded in various sectors. Thus, taking a nine-industry division of the corporate sector, assuming that in 1970–2 the weight of each branch in national income was the same as in 1953–5, and applying to these weights actual factor shares, would have resulted in capital receiving a somewhat lower proportion of total corporate income ($27\frac{1}{2}$ per cent rather than the $30\frac{1}{2}$ per cent recorded), but still substantially more than its 1953–5 share of 22 per cent. For the economy as a whole, given the imputation methods used above, it is obvious that the gradual decline of the unincorporated sector, in which the share of capital is well below average, would, *ceteris paribus*, have increased the share of capital in total income. A similar simplified calculation, holding constant the share of unincorporated enterprises in national income, would have held the economy's capital share at $20\frac{1}{2}$ per cent in 1970–2, rather than the 25 per cent recorded, but still well in excess of the $12\frac{1}{2}$ per cent share in 1953–5. In both cases, structural shifts are significant, but in neither case can they account for more than about one-third of the change.*

One must, therefore, look for other explanations. Japan's increasing international competitiveness may have played some role. But, however profitable exports may have been, the rough stability of their share in (current price) output over the period suggests that other more important factors must have been at work. Kalecki's monopoly theory, in which the share of labour is inversely related to the degree of monopoly, could be invoked. But though the extent of business concentration in Japan has increased through time, it is unlikely that such explanations can take one very far. As already argued, Japan remains far more competitive than most Western economies which have experienced very different distribution trends.

An alternative approach would turn to neo-classical theory.[21] In the neo-classical framework, assuming for the moment neutral technological progress, changes in factor shares are a function of the elasticity of substitution between capital and labour and of the factors' supply elasticities. Figure 9 shows that the supply of capital rose much faster than that of labour throughout the period. This would be compatible with a rising share of capital in income only if the elasticity of substitution was above one. International evidence suggests that this is unlikely to be the case and Japanese estimates also point to an elasticity below one.†

Explanations for the paradox are, however, forthcoming if only for part of the period under consideration. It was argued in Chapter 5 that actual changes in labour supply concealed the underlying labour supply elasticity to the modern sector for a number of years. If indeed labour supply was 'infinite', and the elasticity of capital supply relatively low, then additional amounts of capital could only have been forthcoming provided the return to capital rose relative to that of labour. This is indeed what seems to have happened, but only until the early 1960s, as shown

---

* A combined calculation, which might have shown a more significant contribution, was not possible in the absence of capital and labour imputations by sectors in the non-corporate economy.

† For the years 1953–60 R. Sato found a 0·4 elasticity ('Technical Progress and the Aggregate Production Function of Japan(1930–1960)', *Riron Keizai Gaku* (*The Economic Studies Quarterly*), March 1968, p. 22). Shinohara in a recent investigation, published in Japanese in *Keizai Bunseki* (*Economic Analysis*), July 1974, obtains below one elasticities in practically all manufacturing sectors for 1960–71 time series. His cross-section evidence, however, suggests values very close to one.

by the ratio of factor returns in Fig. 9. After that date, the trend of relative factor returns reversed itself, and it is at, or around, this very time that many have placed the turning-point from the stage of 'unlimited' to that of fixed or semi-limited labour supplies. A more inelastic supply of labour relative to that of capital, combined with a below-unit elasticity of substitution, should have increased the return to labour in total income.

Since an above-unit elasticity of substitution in the last decade would seem unlikely, the only offsetting factor to this tendency could have come from biased innovations. Labour-saving technological progress (in a Hicksian sense) could have increased the return on capital relative to the return on labour, *assuming* infinitely elastic factor supplies. It is not unlikely that technological progress was labour-saving in the post-war Japanese economy,[22] but it is clear that, since the early 1960s, the supply elasticity of labour was far from infinite. Indeed, the acceleration in the economy's capital–labour ratio* indicates that capital's supply elasticity grew throughout the period, relative to that of labour. In these conditions, it is unlikely that the bias of technological progress could have offset the other forces at work.

In summary, even if some of the facts seem to fit the figures, others go in the opposite direction. Neo-classical theory, in order to be able to give a full explanation, would have to depend not only on the presence of perfectly competitive conditions but also on a particular constellation of factor supply elasticities which may have prevailed in the earlier years of the period under consideration, but seems unlikely to have existed more recently.

An alternative approach, developed by Kaldor, may throw more light on Japanese developments through these years.[23] In Kaldor's model, given some particular marginal propensities to save out of wages and profits, '. . . the share of profits in income depends solely on the ratio of investment to output'.[24] Purely statistical evidence for this proposition is forthcoming from the close development of the two shares through time. In value, the trend growth of the former was 0·73 per cent per annum, and that of the latter 0·70 per cent. And stretching the figures somewhat, a reasonable fit can be obtained for Kaldor's equation. The latter is $P/Y = (1/s_p - s_w)(I/Y) - (s_w/s_p - s_w)$, where P/Y

* The introduction of an acceleration term (t^2) in time trends (linear or exponential) fitted to the economy's capital–labour ratio significantly improves the equations' results.

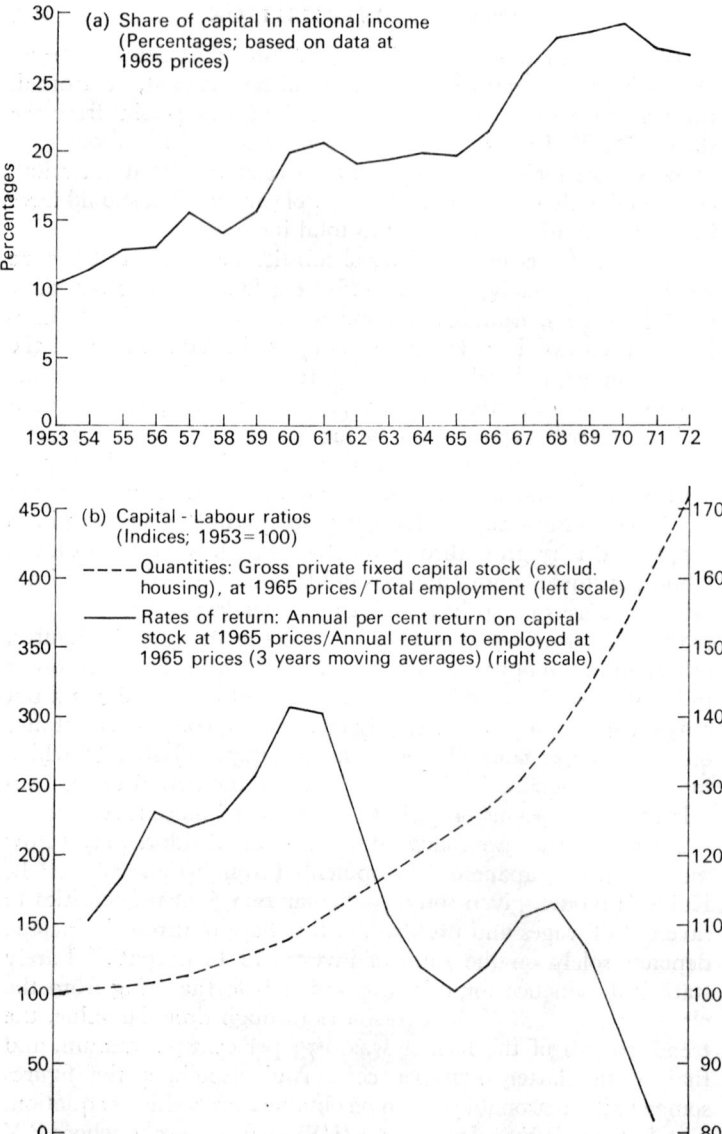

FIG. 9. *Selected capital and labour indicators*

Note: For derivation, see text.

Sources: See Annex table.

and I/Y are the shares of profits and investment in national income and s_p and s_w the marginal propensities to save out of profits and wages respectively.* Over the 1953–72 period, these marginal propensities work out at 0·70 and 0·21. Given a share of investment (including stockbuilding and the foreign balance) of 0·30 per cent of national income, the calculated share of profits in income is of the order of 0·18–0·19 per cent as against the 0·23 per cent actually recorded. Since some household savings are in fact savings out of returns on capital, it could be argued that the 'true' value of s_p should be higher and that of s_w lower. This would result in a calculated share of profits in income closer to the real one.

More economic evidence could come from the Keynesian hypothesis, implicit in the model, that investment is not affected by the values of the saving propensities but is an independent variable which determines the level of demand. This hypothesis would seem broadly to fit Japan's post-war experience. Not too much should be made of such parallels, however, since differences can also be found. The main point is that the exceptional increase in the share of capital in national income, as well as the rising rate of return on capital, could well be linked to the increasing share of investment in output, and not just because forces seem to exist which, in the longer run, tend to bring these two values into rough equality with each other in market economies. After all, investment was the main force which raised labour productivity and allowed it to grow more or less consistently faster than returns to labour. It is frequently argued that a very rapid rate of accumulation (i.e. a constantly increasing 'organic' composition of capital) tends to depress the rate of profit. This may well hold true in many instances but not in Japan's case over this period. The rate of return could rise partly because accumulation continuously embodied new techniques, and partly because the workers' bargaining position remained weak.[25]

Some implications

The foregoing has shown that in both aspects of income distribution touched upon here, Japan's post-war record is

---

* Profits and wage income are here defined as the returns to capital and labour. Savings out of capital income include corporate and government savings as well as a proxy for savings out of unincorporated capital income (i.e. the net investment of non-corporate enterprises). Savings out of wages are given by household savings, excluding the net investment of the non-corporate sector.

different, and perhaps significantly different, from that of most other developed economies, as well as from the country's own pre-war experience. This is not solely because Japanese data seem to refute the various laws of constancy propounded by Pareto or Bowley on the immutability of personal-income distribution or of labour's share in national income.* By now, these laws do not seem to hold anywhere else either. The contrast lies instead in a triple set of differences.

First, Japan's income distribution seems as equal, if not more, equal than elsewhere at the personal level but much more unequal at the functional level. Secondly, looking at trends, both the relative equality and the inequality were reinforced through time, in apparent contrast to developments elsewhere. Finally, the most striking, and perhaps paradoxical, difference lies in the simultaneous presence of relatively high degrees of equality and inequality depending on which indicator one considers. It would normally be expected that in a market economy a high return to capital in national income would lead to a relatively high share of income from assets in personal income, which in turn would tend to increase the skewness of personal-income distribution. Reasons for the Japanese paradox have already been given, of which the most important seem to be the equalizing effects which post-war reforms and high household saving propensities had on the concentration of private wealth, and the very high investment propensities of Japanese firms which led to the continuous ploughing back of profits.

So far, this analysis has devoted only scanty attention to the impact of growth on distribution and none at all to the influence of distribution on growth. The interactions between these variables have neither yet been sufficiently clarified in theory, nor has enough empirical evidence been assembled, for it to be possible to draw any definite conclusions. But it seems clear not only that distribution is affected by growth—in the direction of greater equality, in the longer run at least—but also that distribution must itself have some influence on economic development. In Japan's case, the relative similarity to Western European distributional patterns in the 1950s and the large gap

---

* An estimate of the Pareto coefficient for the upper tail of the 1965 total income distribution gives a value of 2·4, well above (i.e. implying more equality) than the 1·5 to 1·7 values to be expected from the presumed cross-country constancy on which Pareto's 'law' had been based.

at present suggest that income distribution trends were more a result of economic growth than vice versa. But arguments can also be developed to suggest at least a mechanism of interactions in which an initial departure from equality/inequality reinforces itself through feedback effects. This can perhaps be seen, if dimly, in the closing of wage and regional income differentials and is clearly evident if functional distribution is examined. Here, a rise in the rate of return on capital and in its share in income, by improving expectations and increasing the amount of funds available for investment, may well generate further investment and growing returns.

By themselves, such arguments should already be sufficient to suggest that income distribution was important for growth. It can be argued that the relatively equal personal-income distribution made a further—if not directly economic—contribution. Relatively equal and homogeneous standards of living must have strengthened the cohesion and stability of Japanese society, must have made the more or less equally shared privations of the 1950s and imbalances of the 1960s more bearable, and must have reinforced that seemingly unanimous consensus which was probably one of the essential preconditions of the country's growth.

Seen in another way, Japan's particular income distribution pattern seems to have combined the 'best of both worlds'. It was favourable to welfare, relative to other countries, since some of the more flagrant injustices in personal distribution were probably mitigated, and it was favourable to growth since it ensured a large and growing share of income for capital accumulation purposes, and a high and growing rate of return on investment. It is true that personal incomes might have been enhanced (in the short run at least) by a smaller return to capital, but this might well have jeopardized the longer-run growth of the economy. And it is equally, if not more, true that relative equality of personal-income distribution, fine distinctions on the impossibility of intrapersonal welfare comparisons notwithstanding, may sometimes matter more to an individual's sense of well-being than a somewhat larger income combined with much greater disparities.

Japan seems to have avoided, at least in part, the dilemma of reconciling equity and efficiency which faces so many of today's developing countries. Since growth needs investment and investment needs savings, the traditional argument goes, large income inequalities must be accepted—given that saving propensities are much higher in higher income brackets. This may be true but not inevitable, as Japan's experience would seem to prove, provided that the bulk of corporate profits is saved and that households' marginal propensities to save are high at all income levels.

Indeed, Japan's experience is not quite unique. Oddly enough, one may find similarities in the development patterns of Japan and of Eastern European countries. Both types of societies succeeded in compressing the share of consumption in output and raising that of investment, and both achieved relative equality in personal income and consumption patterns. But the similarities may stop here. In both cases governments wanted capital accumulation and did their best to increase the share of investment in income, but only Eastern European governments made conscious efforts to achieve some form of personal equality; and the policy instruments used, as well as the appropriation of the surplus created, were very different. But some parallels exist notably the emphasis on reinvestment rather than on (ostentatious) consumption of the surplus. Indeed, Japan was more successful in this policy, if the definition of success is restricted to quantifiable economic results. Japan recorded higher investment ratios and growth rates than Eastern Europe, while at the same time showing a degree of personal inequality not very much greater than those achieved by some socialist countries.

If it is accepted that income distribution trends were an important ingredient of fast growth, their future development would also seem crucial. Forecasts in this field are far from easy, but a tentative judgement would be that past trends stand a good chance of being interrupted, and perhaps reversed, in future. At the personal-income level, evidence of some reversal can already be found in recent years' figures,* presumably under the impact of more rapid inflation. Consumer price rises and, even more, soaring house-construction and land costs seem to have increased Japanese inequalities in both nominal and real terms, as evidenced by the numerous references to this problem in the FY 1974 Economic White Paper. It may not be justifiable to extrapolate trends of only a few recent years to the longer run, and they may

* After hitting a minimum of 0·27 in 1969, the Gini coefficient for total incomes has gone back to nearly 0·30 in 1973.

indeed reverse themselves, but such a forecast would depend crucially on a drastic slowdown in the rate of inflation and a change in the conditions governing land prices and the housing market. Neither of these two events can be taken for granted, in spite of pious wishes of government officials.

Future trends in factor-income distribution are equally uncertain. 1973 and 1974 have witnessed a record level of profits, but over the longer run some reversal might well take place. In terms of market forces, it would seem that growing labour scarcities, relative to capital, should put increasing pressures on the share of profits in income, which could be resisted only by an increasing degree of monopoly. In terms of the Kaldorian model mentioned earlier, much would seem to depend, in the first instance, on the development of the investment share. The latter may continue to rise in view of the progressively more capital-intensive structure of output likely in the future. But increasing capital–output ratios, if they lead to a slower growth of productivity and to declines in unit returns on capital, could have unfavourable effects on the propensity to invest and, hence, on the share of profits in income. These speculations are coloured by many uncertainties, but should income distribution tendencies turn out to be less favourable to equity and efficiency in the future than they have been in the past, they might—in conjunction with other forces already mentioned in passing in earlier chapters and taken up again in the next—bring about changes in Japan's economy greater than many observers have expected.

NOTES

1. N. Kaldor, 'Alternative Theories of Distribution', *Review of Economic Studies*, No. 61, 1955–6, p. 84.

2. Komiya, 'Supply of Personal Savings', pp. 160–4; Mizoguchi, *Personal Savings and Consumption*, pp. 68–9.

3. Komiya, *op. cit.*, p. 164.

4. S. Kuznets, 'Quantitative Aspects of the Economic Growth of Nations: VIII—Distribution of Income by Size', *EDCC*, January 1963, pp. 2–3.

5. E.P.A., *ESJ (1971–1972)*, p. 138.

6. I. B. Kravis, 'International Differences in the Distribution of Income', *RES*, November 1960, p. 408.

7. Data for Japan are for end-1972 and come from E.P.A., *White Paper on National Life, 1974* (in Japanese), p. 114. The Norwegian data are for 1970 and were taken from Statistik Sentralbyrå, *Statistikk over Lavinntekts-Grupper, 1970*, p. 113. As may be expected, the figures are not strictly comparable.

8. Lockwood, *Economic Development of Japan*, pp. 425–7.

9. E.P.A., *ESJ (1968–1969)*, p. 133.

10. Lockwood, *Economic Development of Japan*, pp. 271–80.

11. S. Kuznets, 'Quantitative Aspects of the Economic Growth of Nations: IV—Distribution of National Income by Factor Shares', *EDCC*, April 1959, p. 9; Bronfenbrenner, *Income Distribution Theory*, p. 90.

12. K. Ohkawa, 'Changes in National Income Distribution by Factor Shares in Japan', in J. Marchal and B. Ducros (eds.), *The Distribution of National Income*, London 1968, p. 183.

13. For an application to the United States, see I. B. Kravis, 'Relative Income Shares in Fact and Theory', *American Economic Review*, December 1959; items of the terminology as well as some of the approach used in the present chapter come from this source.

14. Ohkawa, *Differential Structure*, p. 46.

15. Ohkawa and Rosovsky, *Japanese Economic Growth*, pp. 253–71.

16. Kuznets, 'Quantitative Aspects: Distribution of National Income', p. 27.

17. *Ibid.*, p. 28.

18. This alternative approach was first suggested to the author, while at the O.E.C.D., by Masashi Katō.

19. Ohkawa and Rosovsky, *Japanese Economic Growth*, pp. 316–17.

20. R. M. Solow, 'A Skeptical Note on the Constancy of Relative Shares', *American Economic Review*, September 1958.

21. A modified version of the neo-classical approach, incorporating elements of dualistic theories as well, was already tried by N. Tsujimura for the 1950s ('The Employment Structure and Labour Shares'), in Komiya (ed.), *Postwar Economic Growth*.

22. T. Watanabe, 'Industrialization, Technological Progress and Dual Structure', in Klein and Ohkawa (eds.), *Economic Growth*, pp. 118–20.

23. Kaldor, 'Alternative Theories of Distribution'.

24. *Ibid.*, p. 95.

25. For some of these arguments see, for instance, Joan Robinson, 'The Production Function and the Theory of Capital', *Review of Economic Studies*, No. 55, 1953–4, p. 103.

---

employee compensation in the national accounts. The latter percentage was therefore used to boost the cash earnings of small firms' employees. In 1970 this percentage was 6·3; for the period as a whole it works out at 5·6 per cent.

2. Average of annual rates of return.

3. Compensation of employees divided by total number of employees.

4. Excluding public corporation and general government income; including household property income.

Sources: E.P.A., *National Income Statistics* for lines 1 and 13 as well as for the ratio of social security contributions to employee compensation (used in line 5), employee compensation (used in line 11), and the gross private fixed investment deflator (used in lines 8 and 14). B.S., O.P.M., *Japan Statistical Yearbook* and *Monthly Statistics of Japan* for line 2 and for the total number of employees (used in line 11). B.S., O.P.M., *Japan Statistical Yearbook* and M.o.L., *Labour Force Statistics* for lines 3 and 4. Data for the years 1953–6 not being available, use was made of figures for annual cash earnings in manufacturing establishments with 4 to 29 workers, as published in M.I.T.I., *Census of Manufactures*, which are almost identical to the figures here used for the 1957–60 years. E.P.A., 'Gross Fixed Capital Stock of Private Enterprises', mimeo, 1973, for lines 9 and 15.

Annex Table

Imputation of capital and labour returns in the non-corporate sector

	1970	1953–1972 ANNUAL AVERAGE
A. IMPUTATION		
1. Total income of non-corporate sector, net (bill. yen)	11,477	5,848
2. Self-employed and unpaid family workers (thousands)	17,820	..
3. Annual earnings in firms with 1 to 4 employees (th. yen)	439	..
4. Annual earnings in firms with 5 to 29 employees (th. yen)	672	..
5. Average of (3) and (4), including social security contributions[1] (th. yen)	591	295
6. Labour income in non-corporate sector = (2) × (5) (bill. yen)	10,530	5,644
7. Capital income in non-corporate sector, net = (1) − (6) (bill. yen)	950	204
8. Same, deflated by gross private fixed investment deflator (bill. yen at 1965 prices)	805	175
9. Gross private capital stock in non-corporate sector outstanding at end-year (bill. yen at 1965 prices)	19,458	..
10. Rate of return on capital in non-corporate sector (percentage)	4·1	1·5
B. RELATION WITH CORPORATE SECTOR		
11. Labour income per employee in corporate sector[3] (th. yen)	942	493
12. Ratio between non-corporate and corporate sectors = (5)/(11)	62·7	59·8[2]
13. Capital income in corporate sector, net (bill. yen)[4]	14,502	5,824
14. Same, deflated by gross private fixed investment deflator (bill. yen at 1965 prices)	12,290	5,382
15. Gross private capital stock in corporate sector, outstanding at end-year (bill. yen at 1965 prices)	64,827	..
16. Rate of return on capital in corporate sector (percentage)	19·0	16·2
17. Ratio between non-corporate and corporate sectors = (10)/(16)	21·6	9·3

1. An estimate for social security contributions by employers was added to the average of wages in the two sets of firms. In recent years, for which figures are available, it was found that the cost of compulsory welfare obligations in different sized firms represented a uniformly similar percentage of total cash earnings and was also close to the share of social security contributions to

(continued on page 186)

CONCLUDING REMARKS

Two things are usually expected from any book on Japan's economic development—a straightforward explanation of how it was done, preferably in the form of a recipe for other countries, and a quantified projection on whether it will continue, different, if possible, from what the forecasting consensus expects at the time of writing. These two ingredients may help sales, but they do not necessarily make for sensible economic analysis. Hence the following few pages, though they will bring together some of the arguments developed so far on the causes of Japanese growth and will also venture some comments on the future, will not come up with a few simple answers which will 'unveil' the reasons for the country's past record or provide a novel or shattering conclusion on prospects for the coming years.

The past

A tentative assessment of Japan's performance was made in Chapter 3. The present section will reconsider some of the economic arguments advanced in Chapters 4 to 8, to call attention to a number of significant aspects of Japan's growth process. But no attempt will be made to enumerate all the various elements which have contributed to Japan's rapid growth. Others have done this concisely and convincingly.[1] The following paragraphs will try to draw together some trains of thought either developed or hinted at, in earlier pages.

One such train of thought, pursued more in the tables than in the text of the preceding chapters, leads to the question how far the conditions and policies surrounding Japan's experience were unique. Conclusions on this are unlikely to be very clear cut. In some instances, Japan faced exceptional circumstances or followed exceptional policies; in others it did not. Three of the countries with which Japan can most profitably be compared (France, Germany, and Italy) shared some or all of Japan's initial advantages—e.g. flexible labour supplies, a very favourable (in fact even more favourable) international environment, the possibility of rebuilding an industrial structure using the most advanced techniques. Yet other conditions were very dissimilar. The most crucial difference was perhaps in the field of economic policies. Japan's government exercised a much greater degree of both intervention and protection than did any of its Western European counterparts; and this brings Japan closer to the experience of another set of countries—the centrally planned economies. Parallels can be found between Eastern European and Japanese development patterns—a high degree of state intervention, priority for heavy industry, similarities in income distribution structures. But Japan nevertheless remained much more open to competitive forces, both at home and abroad, than any of the socialist countries. This blend of some elements common to the experience of the centrally planned economies and of others common to some market economies may provide an insight, insufficiently explored in these pages, into the country's success.

At another level, of course, the whole of Japanese experience could be considered unique because of the country's very special social structure. As argued by Kuznets: 'The interplay between the social, political, and economic aspects in the process of Japan's economic growth was crucial . . . In a sense . . . the underlying determinants of Japan's economic growth were not the borrowed technology or dual structure, or foreign trade—all of which were mechanisms, necessary but far from sufficient. What made them sufficient was the underlying capacity of Japan's social and political system to respond to the challenges that the crises constituted; and to respond in such a way that technology would be borrowed, exports expanded, or modern components added to a strong traditional yet efficient component in the economy.'[2] Employment practices, public policies, the social consensus are all elements which contributed to this capacity to respond. And their combination resulted in the investment, income distribution, and foreign trade trends which look unique to the foreign observer.

This study has concentrated mainly on some of these trends. Investment is clearly among the more crucial, and equally crucial are the elements which stimulated it. Chapter 4 looked at many of the forces which helped Japan to achieve the highest share of investment in GNP in the world, and suggested that, for economic and perhaps also non-economic reasons, competition for market shares was probably a decisive element in business investment decisions. Chapter 8, on the other hand, presented evidence showing a close link between the over-all shares of investment and of profits in national income. In that chapter, the discussion concentrated on the effects of the former on the latter, but the arguments can also be reversed. Rising investment could easily be a function of rising profits, just as rising profits were a function of rising investment.

Enterprises invested not only because they wanted to preserve (or increase) their market shares, even if at the expense of short-run losses, but also, and perhaps more importantly, because they expected that the rate of profit would be maintained or would increase. And this expectation was based on a past record of continuously increasing profits. In other words, the sales- or growth-maximization approach advanced earlier can be integrated into a more macro-economic framework. It held at the level of individual firms since their day-to-day investment decisions seem to have been strongly influenced by market-share considerations. But it may not be sufficient to explain over-all, longer-run investment behaviour, since competition for shares would not have been pursued indefinitely had the macro-economic preconditions for high and rising profits not been there. It would seem, therefore, that investment was not carried out for purely profit-maximization reasons, nor for purely growth-maximization reasons, but rather in response to both motivations, with the latter influencing short-run plans and the former determining longer-run expansion. And in the few periods in which capital was in excess supply and profit rates fell, public intervention came to the rescue.

But public intervention was not limited to running successful counter-cyclical cartels or demand-management policies; it was probably a further decisive factor in Japan's economic growth. The government's role was paramount in shaping the direction of the country's development, in encouraging capital accumulation, in transferring resources to the corporate sector, and in shaping that popular consensus which, as remarked already, ensured a social cohesion and stability perhaps unparalleled elsewhere. No doubt, the government was not neutral (no government ever is). Its action reflected faithfully the priorities and preferences of the business community. But given this outlook, shared to some extent by most governments in capitalist countries, it seems to have acted more efficiently and more pervasively than its Western counterparts.

On the supply side a number of elements facilitated the growth process, or at least ensured the absence of supply constraints. One of these was an abundant labour supply. Though labour recorded increasing returns per man, and returns increasing faster than returns to capital, its share of national income fell in relation to the share of capital. Similarly, consumers saw a reduction in the share of output allocated to them and households witnessed a large erosion of the real value of their savings. Some of these developments have led one critic to suggest that '. . . Japanese growth is basically a disequilibrium phenomenon, marred by "engineered" excess capacity, questionable social priorities, and exploitation of labour and consumers in the neo-classical as well as the Marxist sense of the term.'[3] This type of argument could even be applied to a second permissive factor, whose importance in only now being realized, i.e. the almost infinitely elastic supply of primary products which faced Japan. In other words, Japan's growth may have been based upon, or at least greatly facilitated by, a double 'exploitation'—that of the country's working class and that of the world's poorer regions.

But this is not an argument to be applied only to Japan. In a sense, all economies, capitalist and socialist alike, grow through some form of domestic 'exploitation', or there would be no investible surplus; and in the post-war period here considered all industrialized economies have benefited from favourable terms of trade. But the 'exploitation' mechanism was perhaps more in evidence in Japan than in the rest of the capitalist world because of a greater reliance on imported raw materials and a more malleable labour supply.

There is, however, a reverse side to the coin. Abroad the Japanese economy's expansion bestowed some benefits on the less developed world. Without it, it is at least unlikely that the terms of trade for primary products would have been any more favourable, while the purchasing power of developing countries would have been a good deal lower. At home, though labour was 'exploited', its income rose by unprecedented amounts. The *relative* impoverishment of Japanese workers and consumers went hand in hand with a very substantial *absolute* enrichment. The decision as to which matters more should not be difficult.

More to the point perhaps, when criticizing the country's past record, is the indictment of its growth pattern made in Chapter 3. The country's material enrichment was paid for by a substantial destruction of the living environment for a majority of the population, the creation of one frightful megalopolis, the daily invasion of advertising and gadgetry to a degree unparalleled elsewhere, or at least in Europe, and the lack of an adequate social infrastructure which could have replaced, in some ways, a rapidly disappearing traditional family system. The advantages of a 10 per cent growth rate may have outweighed all this over most of the period; but over the last few years, at least, the cost–benefit ratio must have risen substantially.

The future

Forecasting is a favourite, but somewhat dangerous, pastime of most economists; and forecasting Japanese economic developments has in the past presented more pitfalls than have projections for most other countries. Japanese experts have scored an impressive list of mistakes, usually in the direction of excessive pessimism, and foreign observers have not fared much better. Two examples may be worth quoting. The first, written in 1948, is by a member of MacArthur's occupation team:

In the light of an analysis of its resources, the Japan of the next three decades appears likely to have one of two aspects if its population continues to grow to 100 million or more. (1) It may have a standard of living equivalent to that of 1930–4 if foreign financial assistance is continued indefinitely. (2) It may be 'self-supporting', but with . . . a standard of living gradually approaching the bare subsistence level. Either of these alternatives seems more likely than that of a Japan which will have made itself self-supporting at a 1930–4 standard through foreign trade and improved resource utilisation.[4]

The second example, written in 1969, is by a self-professed 'futurologist': '. . . the Japanese have . . . discovered or developed an ability to grow, economically, with a rapidity that is unlikely to be surpassed in the period at issue—and that might well result late in the twentieth century or early in the twenty-first, in Japan's possessing the largest gross national product in the world.' And this thanks to a rate of growth '. . . better than 10 per cent a year in the last two decades, and likely to be maintained at around that rate for at least the next two or three decades.'[5]

The views expressed in these two works were, of course, strongly influenced by the conditions of the time. The first was written in a war-devastated Japan whose output was down to mid-1920s levels; the second at the height of the longest post-war boom and just as the balance of payments was turning into structural surplus. Inevitably, perhaps, the outlook for the future presented in the following few paragraphs is also affected by present conditions. At the time of writing (Autumn 1974), Japan is recording virtually the highest rate of inflation in the developed world (over 20 per cent), a fall in real GNP in the first half of 1974, from the preceding half-year, at a seasonally-adjusted annual rate of some 9 per cent, and balance of payments deficits on current and long-term capital account, for the same period and on the same basis, of $8½ billion and $5 billion respectively, while the longer-run problems of pollution and inadequate social welfare are as pressing as ever.

This may, of course, be only a particular cyclical and/or special phase, and it will be implicitly assumed in what follows that, in the longer run, price inflation will come down to more tolerable levels, growth will be resumed, and the balance of payments will return to some state of equilibrium. But the seriousness of the present situation should not be overlooked. Any failure to cope with it rapidly might well jeopardize the longer-run prospects sketched out below.

These longer-run prospects will not be quantified. Rather, a few lines of thought will be developed which could provide some basis for assessing other forecasts. First, it seems to be almost universally accepted that the past growth rates of the order of 10 per cent per annum are now beyond the reach of the economy.* Hence the real issue is not whether 'super growth' can continue, but whether the 6–7 per cent growth rates accepted by the forecasting consensus are feasible; in other words, whether Japanese growth could still substantially exceed that of other developed countries.

Answers to this question are usually framed in terms of potential labour supplies, longer-run productivity growth, capital coefficients, and other quantified variables; but a more qualitative approach will be followed here—reviewing some of the conditions which made past growth possible and the likelihood of their persistence in future. As argued at length in earlier chapters, it was home demand which led Japan's growth over the last twenty

* The last official plan (for FYs 1973–7) foresaw a deceleration of GNP growth to an annual rate of 9·4 per cent. Present M.I.T.I. and E.P.A. tentative projections for the 1975–85 period (soon to be incorporated into a new long-term plan) are of an annual GNP growth rate of the order of 6·5–7 per cent. The only major exception to these views comes from the J.E.R.C.'s projections which, even though published in early 1974, still foresaw a 9–9·5 per cent growth rate for the period 1970 (or 1973) to 1985.

years. The central element in this very rapid growth of demand was private investment which, in turn, relied on two crucial pre-conditions—a public policy of active encouragement and guidance which created longer-run favourable expectations, and the presence of ample supplies of labour, technological know-how, and savings which allowed high, and rising, returns on capital. Growth was, in addition, buttressed by a probably unique measure of social consensus and acceptance of given quantitative aims.

Some, but not all, of these favourable influences are likely to continue into the future. Initially at least, problems are unlikely to arise on the demand side. Private investment propensities still seem to be very high, partly because growth has been rapid until recently and partly because new needs and circumstances have opened opportunities in a number of fields—pollution control equipment, energy-saving activities, less raw-material-intensive products, to name only the most obvious ones. Similarly, government intervention, in the form of policies actively encouraging the business sector, is unlikely to diminish if such policies remain politically acceptable. But it is not certain whether two of the more indirect stimuli to investment—rising profits and popular acceptance of government policies—can any more be taken for granted. The first issue is directly linked with possible problems originating on the supply side; the second raises much more complicated sociological and political considerations and will only be briefly mentioned at the end.

Supply has been relatively neglected in discussions on Japan's economic growth. Yet future problems could well emerge on that side, even abstracting from the possibility that the supply of some key primary product may be restricted. As argued earlier, investment demand was as large and buoyant as it was because the rate of return on capital was rising. For this to continue, both labour and technological progress must continue in ample supply. It has often been suggested that the conditions governing the availability of both have radically changed in recent years. The unexploited stock of foreign techniques has been exhausted as Japan 'caught up' with Western technological levels, and the stock of labour has been fully used as Japan achieved 'real' full employment some-time in the 1960s. Hence future growth will be drastically curtailed, constrained by a slowly rising population of working age and by the, presumably slow, progress of technical advance in industrialized countries. But both these views seem to be extreme. Japan has shown for a number of years that it is perfectly capable of innovating in numerous fields without Western help; its successes in shipbuilding or electronics, to name only the most obvious products, would otherwise hardly have been possible. The unlikely prospect of severe labour shortages has been discussed in Chapter 5.

But whatever Japan's potential for autonomous technical progress, it is true that:

There is ... a fundamental difference between closing a gap (or eliminating a lag) and depending on the extension of a domestic or foreign technological frontier. In the former case, if other conditions are right, one can proceed at great speed. Gains can accrue in a relatively short time. In the latter case, one may face lengthy bottlenecks. The technological frontier is inevitably surrounded by uncertainties, hesitations, and false starts.[6]

And whatever the amount of disguised unemployment in some sectors, the supply elasticity of labour has decreased and its return per unit, relative to the return to capital, has risen. Combined, these two factors make for increasing costs and either a falling rate of return on capital or rising prices. The second would have predictable consequences on the rate of investment; the third could lead to a permanently more cautious government stance in order to safeguard the balance of payments equilibrium.

The outlook for savings, the third permissive factor which facilitated past growth, is perhaps less uncertain. There seems to be no reason to expect a massive cutback in savings in the future. On the contrary, inflation, unless it becomes explosive, seems likely, if anything, to continue to boost household savings. There might be a factor working the other way if Japan were to embark on a much more serious welfare policy than followed so far, since this would then diminish the need for savings earmarked to finance pensions, house purchases, higher education, or illness. In fact, such a policy might well face a very specific difficulty in so far as the high investment requirements of some forms of social expenditure might not be matched by an equivalent volume of savings if the policy was successful. But it does not seem that Japan is yet moving very rapidly in that direction.

However, while this may lessen immediate inflationary dangers, it creates other problems. Thus the famous social consensus on which the country has relied for so long shows some signs of cracking. A trend towards a less equal distribution of income, reinforced by the effects of inflation on savings and housing, as well as the lack of any real solution to the problems of social welfare and the permanent difficulties posed by pollution and environmental problems is increasingly putting into question the stability of the country's social structure.

Per se, none of these factors taken individually need have particularly dramatic effects. But their combination could lead to cumulative difficulties which could be reinforced by a deceleration in the country's longer-run growth. Several of these issues have already come to the fore at one time or another but have usually been defused precisely because the economy has been sufficiently dynamic to generate rapid increases in personal income. But circumstances may have changed. More frequent impositions of restrictive policies to counter inflation, or lower investment propensities consequent upon falling profits, may slow down the growth of output; and the sharp shift in the terms of trade in favour of the oil-producing countries implies that the future expansion of consumption will inevitably be constrained. A longer-run interruption, or sharp deceleration, in a hitherto nearly continuous process of rapidly rising *per capita* incomes would create an unprecedented situation. The elasticity of individual expectations must have been very high until now, and perhaps rising as growth perpetuated itself. If growth slackens over several years, and if the effects on incomes are combined with a continuous erosion of savings due to a much more rapid rate of inflation, this could generate previously unknown difficulties.

Solutions can, of course, be proposed. At the business level, an obvious one, used in all capitalist economies when the rate of profit is falling, is to strengthen the degree of concentration. A somewhat more monopolistic structure in the future is likely in any case, given that technological progress will increasingly be generated at home by individual firms which will try to keep innovations for themselves; but it could be reinforced in a depressed market by a prolongation or reinforcement of M.I.T.I.'s recession cartels.* The alternative to this kind of solution, which

---

* A further, and fortunately less likely, possibility open to the business world would be to switch priorities to the highly profitable field of armaments, in which the scope for expansion is probably vast. By rekindling nationalism this could also mitigate any effects of public dissatisfaction on other counts.

would in any case be only a short-run expedient designed to restore entrepreneurial confidence but not to solve the country's imbalances, would be a switch to a welfare-type expansion seriously trying to alter the country's growth path. But apart from the purely technical difficulties of such a radical shift, the political situation in present-day Japan is such as to make this solution improbable.

Finally, and most likely, there could be a continuation of yesterday's economic policies, imaginative so far as projects of a specific technical nature are concerned (e.g. a changing industrial structure, or a lower level of pollution), but otherwise short-sighted and aimed at plugging specific gaps. Growth will then probably continue, if more irregularly and much more slowly, and so will the imbalances of the past. Contradictions may accumulate but the system may not explode. Japan has been a remarkably stable society for centuries and it is not impossible that some *appearance* of a solution will be given to the problems of social welfare, re-direction of growth, and land utilization which will defuse what, in European surroundings, would have all the connotations of a highly unstable situation. But the task for Japan's establishment in this instance would seem to be a good deal more difficult than in previous situations in which it has successfully imposed on the country radical changes in policies and goals.

NOTES

1. Among the many enumerations of crucial factors in Japan's growth see, for instance, those of Allen, *Japan's Economic Expansion*, pp. 249–50; S. Okita, *Causes and Problems of Rapid Growth in Postwar Japan and their Implications for Newly Developing Countries*, Tokyo 1967, pp. 9–33 and Shinohara, 'Causes and Patterns', p. 351.

2. S. Kuznets, 'General Remarks', in Ohkawa and Hayami (eds.), *Economic Growth*, p. 650.

3. M. Bronfenbrenner, 'The Japanese Growth Path: Equilibrium or Disequilibrium?', *Keizai Kenkyū (The Economic Review)*, May 1970, p. 108.

4. E. A. Ackerman, quoted in S. Tsuru, *Essays in Economic Development*, Tokyo 1968, pp. 219–20.

5. Kahn, *The Emerging Japanese Superstate*, pp. 2–3.

6. Ohkawa and Rosovsky, *Japanese Economic Growth*, p. 238.

A SELECTED READING LIST

THE preceding text has been littered with footnotes and references. Hence no fully fledged bibliography will be provided here but only a few selected titles which, it is felt, are among the better things written on the economy. The list is almost entirely limited to works in English. No reference is made to the Japanese literature because the author could not read it and probably nobody who could would find much interest in the present book. References to works in French, German, or Italian are limited, largely because the European literature on Japan's economy is so scanty.

General works

Among general works, a recent one which stands out and which has been greatly relied upon in the present book is K. Ohkawa and H. Rosovsky, *Japanese Economic Growth*, Stanford University Press 1973. For the pre-war period, a classic is W. W. Lockwood, *Economic Development of Japan*, Princeton 1968. For the post-war period, interesting surveys are provided by G. C. Allen, *Japan's Economic Expansion*, London 1965; K. Bieda, *The Structure and Operation of the Japanese Economy*, Sydney 1970, and C. Sautter, *Japon—Le prix de la puissance*, Paris 1973. Essential reading matter are the E.P.A.s (or, until 1956, Economic Stabilization, Economic Counsel and Economic Planning Board's) annual *Economic Surveys of Japan*, which cover the whole period here examined. Since 1964, the O.E.C.D. has also been publishing an annual *Economic Survey of Japan*. Even more than the E.P.A.s, however, these booklets are very preoccupied with short-run developments as well as being subject to some censorship.

In addition, very interesting work has come from a number of economists working at Tokyo's Hitotsubashi University. This school has adapted a number of Western theoretical concepts to Japanese conditions and has combined original insight with a very good knowledge of the basic data since the authors have themselves constructed many of the longer-run statistical series on the economy. Among the works which have been translated, the following stand out: M. Shinohara, *Structural Changes in Japan's Economic Development*, Tokyo 1970, K. Ohkawa, *Differential Structure and Agriculture*, Tokyo 1972, and R. Minami, *The Turning Point in Economic Development: Japan's Experience*, Tokyo 1973.

Finally, three collections of essays contain some very valuable research on the post-war economy: W. W. Lockwood (ed.), *The State and Economic Enterprise in Japan*, Princeton 1965; R. Komiya (ed.), *Postwar Economic*

Growth in Japan, Berkeley and Los Angeles 1966, and L. R. Klein and K. Ohkawa (eds.), *Economic Growth—The Japanese Experience since the Meiji Era*, Homewood Ill. 1968. By the time this book is published, a new and probably impressive collection of papers should have been published in a major study on the economy launched by the Brookings Institution.

More specialized references

The collections of essays just mentioned contain some of the best specialized research on the economy, and notably the articles by M. Bronfenbrenner, H. Kanamori, R. Komiya, S. Kuznets, W. W. Lockwood, H. T. Patrick, R. Tachi, K. Tsujimura, T. Watanabe and K. Ohkawa and H. Rosovsky. In addition, a selective list is given below of articles and books which seemed particularly interesting.

BLUMENTHAL, T., *Savings in Postwar Japan*, Harvard University 1970.

JINUSHI, S., 'Social Security System in Transition', *DE*, December 1972.

KAWAGUCHI, H., ' "Overloan" and the Investment Behaviour of Firms', *DE*, December 1970.

MADDISON, A., *Economic Growth in Japan and the USSR*, London 1969.

MICHALSKI, W., *et al.*, *Perspektiven der wirtschaftlichen Entwicklung in Japan*, Stuttgart 1972.

MINAMI, R., 'Transformation of the Labor Market in Postwar Japan', *HJE*, June 1972.

MIYAZAWA, K., 'The Dual Structure of the Japanese Economy and its Growth Pattern', *DE*, June 1964.

MIYAZAKI, Y., 'Rapid Economic Growth in Postwar Japan', *DE*, June 1967.

MIZOGUCHI, T., *Personal Savings and Consumption in Postwar Japan*, Tokyo 1970.

ODAKA, K., 'The Structure of Japanese Labor Markets', *Riron Keizai Gaku (The Economic Studies Quarterly)*, June 1967.

O.E.C.D., *Monetary Policy in Japan*, Paris 1972.

PAINE, S. H., 'Wage Differentials in the Japanese Manufacturing Sector', *Oxford Economic Papers*, July 1971.

SHIMOMURA, O., 'Consumer Price Problems', *The Oriental Economist*, November–December 1963.

SHINOHARA, M., 'Causes and Patterns in the Postwar Growth', *DE*, December 1970.

TAIRA, K., *Economic Development and the Labour Market in Japan*, New York 1970.

WATANABE, T., 'Economic Aspects of Dualism in the Industrial Development of Japan', *EDCC*, April 1965.

YAMAMURA, K., *Economic Policy in Postwar Japan*, Berkeley and Los Angeles 1967.

YAMANAKA, T. (ed.), *Small Business in Japan's Economic Progress*, Tokyo 1971.

Finally, two books which the author considers required reading for anyone who wants to know about Japan in a less narrow framework than the one developed so far: Ruth Benedict, *The Chrysanthemum and the Sword* and Chie Nakane, *Japanese Society*.

INDEX